AFTER HUMAN

Liverpool Science Fiction Texts and Studies, 69

Liverpool Science Fiction Texts and Studies

Editors
David Seed, *University of Liverpool*
Sherryl Vint, *University of California Riverside*

Editorial Board
Stacey Abbott, *University of Roehampton*
Mark Bould, *University of the West of England*
Veronica Hollinger, *Trent University*
Roger Luckhurst, *Birkbeck College, University of London*
Andrew Milner, *Monash University*
Andy Sawyer, *University of Liverpool*

Recent titles in the series

52. J. P. Telotte and Gerald Duchovnay, *Science Fiction Double Feature: The Science Fiction Film as Cult Text*
53. Tom Shippey, *Hard Reading: Learning from Science Fiction*
54. Mike Ashley, *Science Fiction Rebels: The Story of the Science-Fiction Magazines from 1981 to 1990*
55. Chris Pak, *Terraforming: Ecopolitical Transformations and Environmentalism in Science Fiction*
56. Lars Schmeink, *Biopunk Dystopias: Genetic Engineering, Society, and Science Fiction*
57. Shawn Malley, *Excavating the Future: Archaeology and Geopolitics in Contemporary North American Science Fiction Film and Television*
58. Derek J. Thiess, *Sport and Monstrosity in Science Fiction*
59. Glyn Morgan and Charul Palmer-Patel, *Sideways in Time: Critical Essays on Alternate History Fiction*
60. Curtis D. Carbonell, *Dread Trident: Tabletop Role-Playing Games and the Modern Fantastic*
61. Upamanyu Pablo Mukherjee, *Final Frontiers: Science Fiction and Techno-Science in Non-Aligned India*
62. Gavin Miller, *Science Fiction and Psychology*
63. Andrew Milner and J.R. Burgmann, *Science Fiction and Climate Change: A Sociological Approach*
64. Regina Yung Lee and Una McCormack (eds), *Biology and Manners: Essays on the Worlds and Works of Lois McMaster Bujold*
65. Joseph Norman, *The Culture of "The Culture": Utopian Processes in Iain M. Banks's Space Opera Series*
66. Jeremy Withers, *Futuristic Cars and Space Bicycles: Contesting the Road in American Science Fiction*
67. Sabrina Mittermeier and Mareike Spychala, *Fighting for the Future: Essays on Star Trek: Discovery*
68. Richard Howard, *Space for Peace: Fragments of the Irish Troubles in the Science Fiction of Bob Shaw and James White*

AFTER HUMAN

A Critical History of the Human
in Science Fiction from
Shelley to Le Guin

THOMAS CONNOLLY

LIVERPOOL UNIVERSITY PRESS

First published 2021 by
Liverpool University Press
4 Cambridge Street
Liverpool
L69 7ZU

Copyright © 2021 Thomas Connolly

The right of Thomas Connolly to be identified as the author of
this book has been asserted by him in accordance with
the Copyright, Designs and Patents Act 1988.

All rights reserved. No part of this book may be reproduced, stored in a
retrieval system, or transmitted, in any form or by any means, electronic,
mechanical, photocopying, recording, or otherwise, without the prior
written permission of the publisher.

British Library Cataloguing-in-Publication data
A British Library CIP record is available

ISBN 978-1-80034-816-5 cased

Typeset by Carnegie Book Production, Lancaster
Printed and bound by CPI Group (UK) Ltd, Croydon CR0 4YY

Contents

Acknowledgements	vii
Introduction – 'Beyond the common range of men': H.G. Wells, the OncoMouse™, and the human in Anglo-American SF	1
H.G. Wells and the OncoMouse™	1
Posthumanism, nature, and technology	7
Posthumanism and science fiction	16
1 Worlds Lost and Gained: Evolution, primitivism, and the pre-human in Arthur Conan Doyle's *The Lost World* and Jack London's *The Iron Heel*	27
Two lineages of the human in nineteenth-century SF: Shelley's *Frankenstein* and Verne's *Voyages extraordinaires*	29
Three forms of humanity in Conan Doyle's *The Lost World*	37
Socialism, evolution, and the pre-human in London's *The Iron Heel*	50
2 Soma and Skylarks: Technocracy, agency, and the trans-human in Aldous Huxley's *Brave New World* and E.E. 'Doc' Smith's *Skylark* series	69
The First World War and technology in interwar SF	71
The 'life-worshipper' and the end of time in Huxley's *Brave New World*	78

Early pulp SF: *Skylark* and 'a universe ruled by the human mind'   93

3   Homo Gestalt: Atomics, empire, and the supra-human in Isaac Asimov's *Foundation* and Arthur C. Clarke's *The City and the Stars*   111

Atomics and empire in the 'Golden Age' and beyond   113

Benevolent biopolitics in Asimov's *Foundation*   121

Ontological humility and the body as metaphor in Clarke's *The City and the Stars*   134

4   Disaster and Redemption: Utopia, nature, and the post-human in J.G. Ballard's *The Crystal World* and Ursula K. Le Guin's *The Dispossessed*   149

Utopia and the rejection of 'Faust' in 1960s and 1970s SF   150

Alienation and human transcendence in Ballard's *The Crystal World*   159

Embedded identity and ontological parity in Le Guin's *The Dispossessed*   173

Conclusion – Bio/Techno/Homo: The future of the human in SF   191

Works Cited   203

Index   219

Acknowledgements

This book grew out of my Ph.D. research, which was undertaken in Maynooth University from 2012 to 2017. I would first like to acknowledge the support of my supervisor, Professor Emer Nolan. From her first act of supervision—a research essay in the final year of my undergraduate degree in 2011—Emer's advice, encouragement, and guidance have been instrumental in helping me to improve as a scholar. Emer's careful readings of my chapters were the decisive factor in transforming a collection of scattered insights into a coherent argument, while her thoughtful supervision has helped me profoundly in my efforts to become a more effective thinker and writer. Of all the influences on my growth as a scholar, it is Emer who has had by far the most enriching impact—in return, I can offer only my heartfelt thanks and appreciation.

My thanks also to the various individuals who devoted time to critiquing the thesis that became this book: Mark Bould at UWE Bristol, Michael Cronin and Conor McCarthy in the Department of English in Maynooth, Alison Farrell in the Maynooth University Writing Centre, and Katherine Bishop at Miyazaki International College. Their thoughtful comments and suggestions were invaluable in helping to shape and improve this work. My thanks also to my colleagues in the Department of English in Maynooth for their generous input and advice during my years of postgraduate study. My research was funded by a generous scholarship from the Maynooth University Graduate Studies Office, to whom I extend my thanks and appreciation.

I would also like to acknowledge the support and comradeship of the other Ph.D. students in the English Department of Maynooth University, as well as the other users of the postgraduate workspace in the Iontas Building, during my time there as a student: Conor Dowling, Francis Lomax, Matt Fogarty, Sarah O'Brien, Alan Carmody, Chris Beausang, Daniel Curran, Cait Harrigan, Jack Kavanagh, Páraic Kerrigan, Brenda O'Connell, and Kira Collins. Misery loves company, as they say, and the various academic, financial, and personal pressures of doing postgraduate research can at times make a person fairly miserable indeed. At such times, it is helpful to be able to look to a group of friends and peers and see that, if nothing else, they are at least as miserable as oneself and for much the same reasons. Without a sympathetic group of fellow travellers, the road to completion, I am sure, would have proven significantly rockier. So, my thanks to you folks.

Most importantly, I would like to thank my family and friends for their unfaltering support over the last few years: my partner Virginia, mother Betty and father Eugene, brothers Patrick and Anthony and sister Áine, and friends Stefan, Ian, Eoin, and Fiona. Each of these will know what their encouragement, patience, interest, and endless cups of tea over the last few years have meant. Humble as a dedication in a book of this kind is, it is to them, with love, that the dedication goes.

Introduction
'Beyond the common range of men': H.G. Wells, the OncoMouse™, and the human in Anglo-American SF

H.G. Wells and the OncoMouse™

> With infinite complacency men went to and fro over this globe about their little affairs, serene in their assurance of their empire over matter. It is possible that the infusoria under the microscope do the same (Wells, *The War of the Worlds*).

In the early 1980s, researchers at Harvard Medical School produced a new kind of animal in their laboratories: the 'oncomouse'. Named from the Greek word *onco*, meaning 'mass' or 'tumour', oncomice, or 'Harvard mice', were designed to be particularly prone to the development of cancerous tumours, thereby reducing the time spent prompting tumour growth in lab mice. In 1988, Harvard University took the controversial step of issuing patents on their 'invention', the first three of which were licensed to Dupont. This move—the copyright of a living animal—was unprecedented at the time, but was subsequently repeated, not without controversy, in other parts of the world.[1]

The patent transformed the oncomouse, already a uniquely unnatural being, into the OncoMouse™, a privately owned and legally protected commodity. The alteration of animal bodies in the service of human needs is not a new concept—yet the case of the OncoMouse™ is, I argue, of particular significance. The OncoMouse™ was not simply bred but *produced*: an artificial species formed, *ex nihilo*, and on a genetic level, in a remarkably brief time. Like its genomic counterparts, including Dolly the Sheep, the GloFish, the 'spider goat', and featherless chickens, the OncoMouse™ registers a startling turning point in the exercise of human dominion over the natural world. Yet I begin with the OncoMouse™ not

---

[1] Much of this information on the oncomouse was derived from Hanahan (2007) and the World Intellectual Property Organization (2006).

only because of its dubious honour in being one of the first mass-market GM animals, but also because of the attention it has attracted in the field of posthumanism. Here, it has been interpreted in two distinct and opposing ways: as key to overturning the asymmetrical binary of human–non-human power relations intrinsic to classical humanist thought *and* as an urgent reminder of the need to recuperate some 'essential' human ontology in the face of radical new technological possibilities. As I will discuss in more detail later in this introduction, these opposing stances also represent two of the key positions adopted in depictions of the human in SF literature.

Representing the former position, Donna Haraway has argued that, '[symbolically] and materially, the OncoMouse™ is where the categories of nature and culture implode for members of technoscientific cultures. ... [It is] paradigmatic of nature enterprised up' (2004: 273–5). For Haraway, the OncoMouse™ is a being 'whose scene of evolution is the laboratory' (273), and which thereby transgresses the abstract boundaries of nature and culture in useful ways for those seeking to challenge such divisions. She thus approaches the creature with cautious optimism: it offers not merely a warning against growing human manipulation of non-human nature but also a potentially useful way of transcending the restrictive dualisms that have historically dominated western thought. The OncoMouse™ is a liminal being whose ultimate effect is 'the pollution of natural kinds' (Haraway, 1997: 79–80)—of 'natural' and distinct categories such as 'culture' and 'nature', or 'human' and 'animal'. Rosi Braidotti echoes Haraway's enthusiasm in this regard: the OncoMouse™ is 'the never dead that pollutes the natural order simply by being manufactured and not born' (2013: 75). It thus offers a material instance of posthuman possibility, albeit one that must be understood in the context of exploitative capitalist relations.

In opposition to this nuanced take on the OncoMouse™ as a transgressive revolt against classical humanist discourse, social theorist Frederic Vandenberghe views it as one 'of the most monstrous creatures ... fabricated and patented ... for the sake of profit' (2014: 293). It is, he argues, part of a horrifying drive in contemporary capitalism that seeks to 'invade ... life itself to modify and commodify it' (293). For Vandenberghe, posthumanism itself represents an active menace to human life, threatening to subsume humanity within a rubric of genetic and technological systems that will eventually evacuate the 'human' of any semblance of spirituality or sacredness. In the face of such 'monstrous' posthuman possibilities, Vandenberghe stresses the need to recapture some inviolable sense of human nature—what Francis Fukuyama terms 'Factor X', an ambiguous quality, 'universally possessed' by humans, that comprises 'the human essence, the most basic meaning of what it is to be human' (Fukuyama, 2002: 150). Vandenberghe's proposed means to achieve this are avowedly humanist—he calls for the development of a new 'gen-ethics' that 'sets normative limits to the human freedom to technologically alter human nature and change it beyond recognition' (302).

These radically opposed interpretations of the OncoMouse™ underline its status as a transgressive being: unquestionably a living non-human animal and so part of what is traditionally considered 'nature', the OncoMouse™ is also a direct product of, and inseparable from, human culture. Even Vandenberghe's insistence on the need to recoup a viable sense of 'human nature' in the wake of the OncoMouse™—to reaffirm the 'ontological hygiene', as Elaine L. Graham has termed it, of human nature (2002: 13)—points to the socially constructed natures of both 'human' and 'non-human'. Yet Vandenberghe is surely also correct to insist that such a creation can easily be turned against its creator, since not only non-human animal but also human genomes are now susceptible to technological and economic exploitation and manipulation. For this reason, the creation of the OncoMouse™ represents a crucial moment in thinking about not only 'nature' but also 'humanity'—to borrow Braidotti and Haraway's term, in the wake of the OncoMouse™ and its descendants, human nature itself has become irreversibly 'polluted'.

What is the connection between the OncoMouse™ and *The War of the Worlds* (1898), H.G. Wells's classic novel about the destruction of England by Martians? As I will show, both can be understood as key sites for investigating the nature of the 'human'. In diverse ways, Wells's novel and the OncoMouse™ reveal how our ideas about what it is to be—or not to be—'human' are informed by a complex web of historical beliefs, ideas, and attitudes. Over the course of this introduction, I will examine this proposition in more detail. For now, however, I want to begin with two crucial points in understanding the significance of the human in the SF tradition: firstly, *all* SF is posthuman, or, more accurately, all SF is engaged with recognisably posthumanist concerns; and secondly, and notwithstanding the first point, the classical figure of western humanism is, within SF texts, more difficult to escape than may be assumed.

Let us begin with a glance at Wells's *The War of the Worlds*. Wells's early scientific romances, beginning with *The Time Machine* in 1895, are widely regarded as a decisive innovation in the evolution of SF. Of these, perhaps the best known is *The War of the Worlds*, which depicts the sudden arrival of a Martian invasion force into the quiet English countryside and the havoc that is wreaked as, armed with superior technology, the

Martians proceed to harvest humans for food. *The War of the Worlds* is most often read as a reverse colonial narrative that brings the ill effects of empire to bear on the centre of nineteenth-century imperialism. David Seed, for example, refers to *The War of the Worlds* as 'the supreme example of invasion fiction', arguing that Wells's novel 'skilfully reverses the normal opposition within imperial fiction between civilization and otherness. Now civilization, specifically British imperial civilization, is under attack' (2010: 233, 234).

However, the novel also offers a commentary on certain ideas regarding human nature in nineteenth-century thought. As Michael R. Page argues, the novel clearly evinces an anti-progressive sentiment that strives to alter 'the general mood of late Victorian thought ... which complacently imagined man (particularly Western man) at the top of the evolutionary ladder' (2012: 175). In accounting for the ruthless treatment of the English population by the Martians, Wells invokes the inter-species 'destruction' which European civilisation 'wrought' on 'the vanished dodo and bison' as evidence of the violence inherent in the evolutionary process (1993a: 6–7). Accordingly, in the novel, humanity itself becomes just another species vulnerable to enslavement or elimination, 'pushed back' across the 'dividing-line' that separates it from 'the rest of earth-life' (Kemp, 1982: 22). The collapse of English society and the brief succession of a technologically superior race—one for whom humans signify little more than a conveniently abundant food source—thus overturns the orthodox partition between culture and nature, with humanity now firmly on the side of the latter.

The narrator's speculations regarding the Martian attack reflect Wells's own pessimistic view of humanity's evolutionary significance: humans, he writes, must be for the Martians 'at least as alien and lowly as are the lemurs and monkeys to us' (1993a: 6). Moreover, given their own barbaric treatment of the weak and defenceless—the 'dodo and bison', but also the human victims of British imperialism, particularly the Tasmanians—the British victims of the Martians are poorly placed to offer a moral critique of their usurpers. Wells's earlier novel, *The Island of Doctor Moreau* (1896), emphasises this point to an even greater extent: focussing on the eponymous scientist in his bloody attempts to transform animals into human beings, this novel stresses the extent to which, beneath the veneer of civilisation, humanity remains essentially bestial. The long-standing asymmetries dividing western humanity from the rest of the biological world—what Haraway calls the 'comfortable old hierarchical dominations' that characterise western thought (2004: 20)—thus appear in Wells's novel as tenuous partitions at best, holding good only so long as humanity retains its place as top species in the biological order.

There are, then, certain key parallels between Wells's novel and the OncoMouse™. Both belong squarely to the realm of SF: Wells's novel as a foundational text in the literary genre, and the OncoMouse™ as an example of science fiction become science fact, a previously fantastical idea that has become actualised in the contemporary world. Both, too, present a soritean challenge to established understandings of the human and non-human, posing in diverse ways the question of where the dividing line between these realms should be drawn and eroding any easy or absolute distinctions between the natural and the artificial. And both, finally, invite us in a startling manner to consider where the human ends and the non-human begins when, on the one hand, the traditionally distinct realms of 'human' and 'nature' become difficult or impossible to separate and, on the other, even the codes governing the biological can readily be penetrated, manipulated, and transformed through technological means.

These similarities, however, also mask an important distinction. Wells's novel offers a glimpse of a dystopian posthuman future—yet this vision is speedily withdrawn and 'corrected' as English society re-establishes itself in the wake of the invasion. The posthumanist energy of *The War of the Worlds* is thus limited by Wells's investment in *'bios'*: 'the portion of life—both organic and discursive—that has traditionally been reserved for *anthropos*' (Braidotti, 2013: 60). Even as Wells launches his savage critique of the great nineteenth-century humanist enterprises—the hypocrisy of European imperialism, the dangers of blind scientific advancement, and the brutal realities of capitalist industrialism—and in this sense gestures towards a *post*humanist outlook, the human in his works remains always ready to return, in *The War of the Worlds* and other romances, to its position at the centre of life and discourse.

By contrast, the living organism created in the Harvard laboratory represents a different kind of posthuman future that cannot so easily be undone. Indeed, the very existence of the OncoMouse™ testifies to the impossibility of such a return: the erasure of 'human' and 'non-human' as unambiguous categories, far from leading (as many posthumanist thinkers suggest) to a more profound understanding of and sympathy with the natural world, may instead lead to its intensified colonisation as nature is subject to the all-encompassing will of a *homo technic* that no longer sees anything—natural or otherwise—as outside its sphere of influence and control. It is clearly insufficient to adopt, as Vandenberghe does, a reactionary position on the human, insisting on a return to some 'essential' yet clearly constructed human 'condition'—yet it is equally clear that a posthumanist framework cannot be embraced uncritically as a straightforward antidote to the failings of humanism without further investigating what such a framework entails.

To return to my two key assertions regarding SF and posthumanism, Wells's novel, through its deliberate destabilisation of the categories of 'human' and 'nature', adopts a recognisably posthumanist standpoint—yet one also preoccupied with re-establishing specifically *human* forms of life. The OncoMouse™, meanwhile, for all the radical posthumanist energy with which Haraway invests this subversive creature, also symbolises the point at which western colonisation of nature reached the very level of DNA itself. In both cases, for all the subversive energy that comes from distorting the boundaries between 'human' and 'non-human', such an act can all too easily lead to a renewed and intensified humanism.

The pressing question informing our responses to both Wells's novel and the OncoMouse™ is: what does it mean to be considered 'human' or 'non-human'? This study will examine the 'human' as it has become a matter of intense thematic concern in works of Anglo-American SF from the nineteenth century to the 1970s. As will be seen, the human that emerges from these works is, like the OncoMouse™, a liminal being: it is not quite the universal, transcendent, or rational 'Man' of the classical humanist tradition—yet neither is it fully the 'cyborg', the 'autopoietic' system, or the 'embodied, embedded' symbiotic subject of posthumanist thought. Rather, the human in these works emerges most clearly as a discursive site on which a range of anxieties and beliefs concerning subjectivity, embodiment, agency, and individuality comes into play. The human of the SF tradition is a fluid category, capable of transforming, like the shapeshifting natives of the red planet in Ray Bradbury's *The Martian Chronicles* (1950), to reflect the assumptions, beliefs, fears, and ambitions of a diverse range of authors and contexts.

This study will thus focus on several specific and related questions: What role has technology played in defining what it means to be—or not to be—human in these SF texts? How do these writers draw the relationship between humanity and the rest of non-human nature? Is the human construed as something separate or distinct from the technological systems and natural worlds that surround it? Or are these systems and worlds viewed as vital to understanding the human, in ways not commonly recognised or acknowledged? And, finally, how can we use these texts to re-examine our ethical position towards those things— other living beings, or the wider environment—that have suffered from ingrained and unexamined attitudes about the meaning and significance of 'human' and 'non-human'?

As the example of OncoMouse™ proves, these are not trivial considerations. Ideas about the nature and meaning of the human have formed the basis for everything from systems of morality to political and economic praxis, from habits of eating to industrial production, and from religious discourse to cultural and aesthetic production. These ideas have been crucial in determining our cultural and ethical orientation towards beings different from ourselves, and towards natural entities whose exploitation we have taken for granted. There is no need here to rehearse the familiar and diverse forms of human mistreatment of the natural world: instead I follow Derrida in simply noting that our relationship with the non-human world has, in recent years, undergone an 'unprecedented transformation' (2002: 392–3), almost entirely for the worse. At the same time, refugee crises in Europe and the Middle East and the resurfacing of undisguised racism within western political discourse demonstrate exactly where the limits of western humanist and ethical consideration have often been drawn. In order to account for both the mass conscription of the natural world 'in the service of a certain being and the so-called human well-being of man' (Derrida, 2002: 394) as well as the collapse of the global 'Family of Man' (to borrow Barthes' term) in a wave of racism and economic and cultural isolationism, it is necessary to more fully understand the ideas, beliefs, and notions that have historically surrounded the 'human'.

The rest of this introduction will be concerned with establishing the framework within which these questions will be explored. I will begin with a discussion of critical posthumanism, outlining the ways in which a variety of cultural theorists have thought about the human, before moving on to more comprehensive definitions of 'technology' and 'nature'. I will then go on to explain my understanding of SF as a posthumanist mode of literature. Finally, I will describe the model of posthumanism that will inform my readings of SF texts and outline the various human 'archetypes' that will be examined in the four chapters of this study.

Posthumanism, nature, and technology

In her iconic 'Manifesto', first published in 1984 (a prophetic year for SF readers), Donna Haraway names the cyborg as the characteristic being of the late twentieth century. The boundaries separating human, animal, and machine, Haraway argues, although never fully stable, have been entirely erased by the rapid technological advancement of this era. In their place, she calls instead for ontological freeplay in which the machine penetrates the organic body and the animal 'speaks' from a position of moral equivalence with humanity—the latter now forced to fully recognise its biological and technological embodiments. For Haraway, the cyborg—'a hybrid of machine and organism, a creature of social reality as well as a creature of fiction' (2004: 7)—encapsulates this state of being. Importantly, the cyborg is not a *synthesis* of the organic and the technological: synthesis implies unity, whereas the very point of Haraway's manifesto is to get away from unities, since these can so easily be changed into the urge 'to be autonomous, to be powerful, to be God' (2004: 35).

'A Manifesto for Cyborgs' encapsulates the kind of subversive energy that has marked a certain strain of cultural theory, centred on the figure of the human, in recent years. Critical posthumanism seeks to both interrogate and accelerate the collapse of the monolithic (that is, white, male, heterosexual, cis-gendered, and able-bodied) 'human' of European philosophical and cultural thought, and to explore the new possibilities for thinking about humanity, identity, technology, and nature that result from the 'end of Man'. At the centre of critical posthumanism is a challenge to the corrupting dualisms—human–non-human, culture–nature, mind–body, male–female, white–non-white, and so on—that have sustained western thought. The aim in critical posthumanist thought, as Judith Halberstam and Ira Livingston put it, is 'not to replace a stuck mindbody [sic] dualism with a heterogeneous monism, but to insist on the "someness" of every assemblage' (1995: 8)—that is, on the partiality of identities that are 'without clear boundary, frayed, insubstantial' (Haraway, 2004: 35), and which therefore cannot be resolved into either unity or duality. Haraway's cyborg is an example of such an identity: neither fully organic nor fully technological, its disparate elements remain in tension, neither resolving into the other. It thus offers 'a way out of the maze of dualisms in which we have explained our bodies and our tools to ourselves' (Haraway, 2004: 39).

Classical humanism, as Neil Badmington argues, appeals to reason as the universal 'basic human essence' inherent in all 'true' human subjects (2000: 4). Yet, if traditional humanism has promoted the human as a singular, coherent, and autonomous subject—the Cartesian and transcendent 'man who says "I"', as Derrida puts it, at the centre of narratives of history, theology, metaphysics, politics, language, nature, ethics, and so on (2002: 400)—then critical posthumanism is concerned with challenging these limitations by acknowledging the technological and biological roots of the human. It does this not by rejecting the human either as textual fiction or biological redundancy nor by stressing the inevitable transcendence of human biology by means of technology. Rather it seeks, as Stefan Herbrechter argues, to adopt a critical vantage point on the history and meaning of the 'human'—to 'think the "end of the human" without giving in to apocalyptic mysticism or to new forms of spirituality and transcendence' (2013: 3). By questioning traditional western narratives of human reason and universalism, critical posthumanism makes space for alternative kinds of subjectivities and embodiments not traditionally recognised as having ethical or political value.

Hence critical posthumanism 'comes both before and after humanism'—it emphasises 'the embodiment and embeddedness of the human being in not just its biological but also its technological world' (Wolfe, 2010: xv). The primary aim of much posthumanist thought has been to shift the emphasis, as Braidotti (borrowing from Agamben) puts it, from *'bios'*—the sphere of human life—to *'zoe'*, 'the dynamic, self-organizing structure of life itself' that includes both the human and non-human (2013: 60). The human is seen as part of and contingent on a natural–material world threatened by the anthropocentrism of classical humanism. Indeed, perhaps the most dramatic examples of Haraway's cyborg are the mass environmental ruptures dominating contemporary political discourse. As Bruno Latour argues, phenomena such as the 'ozone hole story, global warming or deforestation' are difficult to conceptualise according to any traditional binary schema: 'Where are we to put these hybrids? Are they human? Human because they are our work. Are they natural? Natural because they are not our doing. Are they local or global? Both' (1993: 50).

This 'materialist turn' has been increasingly explored in recent posthumanist discourse. Materialism as a philosophical position has a long history, cresting in the nineteenth century with the theories of both evolution and historical materialism. Hence Marx insisted that the 'nature of individuals ... depends on the material conditions determining their production' (Foster, 2000: 40). Yet critical posthumanism takes this well-worn materialist position and imbues it with renewed ethical import derived from contemporary political discourse, particularly feminism. Such theories oppose the 'linguistic paradigm' of poststructuralist thought as not taking proper account of 'the concrete yet complex materiality of bodies immersed in social relations of power' (Braidotti, 2012: 21). As Pramod K. Nayar argues, the human is understood as a material as much as intellectual entity, enmeshed in localised processes of 'becoming, but a becoming-with other life forms'—that is, as an embedded and systemic component of a mutually constitutive material environment (2014: 47). This notion of the human in organic symbiosis with its material locality precludes the possibility of a transcendent, 'universal' human subject. Braidotti's 'vital materialism', too, rejects idealist or transcendent notions of 'human exceptionalism'—that is, of human subjectivity as removed from or unaffected by the material world—in favour of an embedded subject that evolves in kinship with material forces and other life-forms (Braidotti, 2013: 86). Robert Pepperell perhaps expresses this position most straightforwardly: 'In the posthuman schema', he writes, 'it is a mistake to separate the thing that thinks and the thing that is thought about'—in other words, to separate mind from matter (2003: 33).

The terms 'nature' and 'natural world', then, refer to both biological life *and* the natural–material world. Correspondingly, the clash between materialism and transcendence in notions of the human subject is one of the major theoretical concerns of posthumanism. N. Katherine Hayles, in her examination of the history of cybernetics, criticises a trend in western thought which views information as 'in some sense more essential, more important, and more fundamental than materiality' (1999: 18). Hayles highlights the material basis of even the most abstract thoughts and informational patterns—as she notes, 'for information to exist, it must always be *instantiated* in a medium' (13, emphasis in original). In opposition to the Platonic 'teleology of disembodiment' that prioritises information as 'the Real' over and above the messy complexities of materialism (22), Hayles instead calls for an understanding of humanity as both natural organism and technological being, represented by the figure of Haraway's cyborg.

Critical posthumanism, then, is wary of any line of cultural or philosophical thought (such as 'transhumanism') that would promote 'thought', 'mind', or 'consciousness' as more fundamental to the human than the material body. Hayles, for example, stresses the important co-evolution of cybernetic *with* biological theory in the late twentieth century, and points to the theory of 'autopoiesis' as crossing the boundary between these two fields. An influential idea during the 'second wave' of cybernetics from the 1960s to the 1980s, autopoiesis ('self-making') was originally developed by Chilean neurophysiologists Humberto Maturana and Francisco Varela to account for the material organisation of organisms (see Hayles, 1999: 131–59). Autopoiesis characterises biological organisms as self-reproducing systems, closed off from the environment around them but responsive to stimuli, or 'perturbations', from that environment. Such stimuli 'trigger' the sense organs of the organisms, who then interpret the stimuli according to the organisational structures of their physical being. The result is that different organisms will respond to different environmental stimuli in diverse ways, according to the 'internal rules and requirements' of their biological apparatus and internal organisation. Thus, by responding in distinctive ways to the flow of stimuli coming from the environment, each organism will 'create' a distinct internal image of this environment that is both unique to itself—since it is shaped by the organism's subjective capacity to sense and respond to stimuli—and also constructed, as there is no 'reality' for the organism 'outside' of this image generated by its systemic components.

This radical notion—that biological beings can be regarded as self-making material systems, both constituted by and constitutive of their surrounding environment—has since become highly influential within cultural studies, particularly in posthumanism and the systems theory of Niklas Luhmann. With this theory, human consciousness is reintroduced directly into the natural (that is, biological and material) world, since our experience and understanding of that world are fundamentally dependent on our physical 'sensorium', that is, the biological apparatus with which we are equipped.

It is not solely through our biological senses, however, that we interact with the world: in addition, and of equal importance, is our technological apparatus. Humanity, as Wolfe remarks, is 'fundamentally a prosthetic creature that has coevolved with various forms of technicity and materiality, forms that are radically "not-human" and yet have made the human what it is' (2010: xxv). The co-evolution of humanity—*homo faber*, in Tom Shippey's terminology (2016: 42)—with its technological 'prostheses' thus forms an important part of the posthumanist narrative. A common-sense approach might situate technology in opposition to nature: technology as that which is artificial, made-with-intent, purposely organised, or machinic; and nature as that which is non-intentional and arbitrary, bucolic or rural, organic, non-human, or (to be tautological) simply 'naturally' occurring. This is the way that Ian McNeill, for example, understands these terms in *An Encyclopaedia of the History of Technology* (1990), remarking that 'we live in a world in which everything that exists can be classified as either a work of nature or a work of man [sic]' (2002: 1). Even if this rigid separation of 'artificial' and 'natural' artefacts is a western cultural fantasy, nevertheless, as Kate Soper suggests, this fantasy underpins our usual modes of interacting with the world (1995: 267).

Yet disrupting this neat dichotomy is the OncoMouse™, a potent demonstration of Haraway's cyborg in practice. The OncoMouse™ is a direct product of the scientific and technological appropriations of nature that have been the hallmarks of western civilisation since the scientific revolution. Yet it is also unquestionably a living non-human animal, a mouse (without the trademark) whose biological nature is fundamental to its role in the social system that surrounds and created it. It is therefore also an irreducible element of what is traditionally called 'nature'. As discussed, however, neither of the two orthodox views of the OncoMouse™ examined so far—as a Frankensteinian threat to the sanctity of human life, *or* as a locus of subversive resistance to the very techno-industries that created it—is entirely satisfactory. What is needed is a more nuanced approach to the relationship between technology and nature that can mediate the relationship between these realms without allowing one to subsume or negate the other.

Such an understanding may be found in the later works of Heidegger, whose impact on philosophy and cultural theory can be felt throughout posthumanist thought: it is evident, for example, in the works of Derrida, several of which have proven highly influential in the field of posthumanism. Indeed, the very concept of 'poiesis' is central to Heidegger's understanding of technology—Heidegger, according to John Mingers, 'all but produced' the term 'autopoiesis' (1995: 109). The notion that individuals are shaped by the environments that they inhabit echoes Heidegger's own argument, in *Being and Time*, that the individual is conditioned by the 'fore-structures' of their historical and cultural 'horizons' such that true objectivity, free from subjective preconceptions, cannot be achieved. The 'past' of any individual, Heidegger argues, 'already goes ahead of it', so that 'the possibilities of its Being are disclosed and regulated' before the individual is even aware of them (2001: 41). The social environment of the individual, in other words, conditions and shapes their individual consciousness, rendering 'universal' human nature an impossibility.

In an influential 1954 essay, 'The Question Concerning Technology', Heidegger aims to uncover the 'truth' about technology and its impact on human relations to the material world. Making his way through a maze of Greek etymology and philosophical history, Heidegger eventually arrives at the concept of *'Gestell'*—a German word meaning 'skeleton' or 'framework'—and the notion of 'enframing' as the 'essence' of technology (1977: 19–20). Enframing, according to Heidegger, is 'neither only a human activity nor a mere means within such activity' but a 'rule ... which demands that nature be orderable as standing-reserve' (23). The western human relationship to nature, he argues, has increasingly viewed the natural world as an ordered surplus of resources for human use. He gives the example of the modern 'hydroelectric plant' over the Rhine river, which transforms the river into a source of human energy, 'something at our command' that must serve human needs, in contrast to the 'old wooden bridge' that made no demands on its natural surroundings (16). Modern science, Heidegger argues, insists that 'nature reports itself in some way or other that is identifiable through calculation and that it remains orderable as a system of information', whether the laws of mathematics, biological genera, the periodic table, and so on (23). Since 'science's way of representing pursues and entraps nature as a calculable coherence of forces', it thus 'prepares the way first not simply for technology but for the essence of modern technology' (21–2), which 'challenges' nature, in an 'unreasonable' way, to become subservient to the human desire to store up energy and resources (14).

Enframing, then, can be understood literally: it is a way of 'framing' the world in human terms to make it capable of being exploited, with modern technology emerging as the material means to achieve this. Heidegger's notion of technology as enframing thus anticipates (and, indeed, informed) Maturana and Varela's understanding of the relationship between organisms and environments. Both autopoiesis and enframing have in common the notion that the individual's experience of the world is constructed—the 'reality' with which we interact is shaped by both our psychological 'forestructures' and our biological senses. This is particularly significant given the claims of scientific discourse to objectivity and impartiality—that is, to reflect reality *as it really is*. Such a claim masks the constructed nature of knowledge and fails to consider both the ideological trappings of such knowledge and the extent to which sociocultural preconceptions shape scientific understanding and investigation. The social nature of scientific knowledge has been well-noted—yet Heidegger's emphasis on the shared roots of both scientific *and* technological phenomena in enframing is helpful in extending 'technology' beyond its usual limited meaning of machine, tool, or apparatus. The 'essence' of technology, for Heidegger, is more akin to a shaping principle that informs the technological or scientific systems of western human societies, dictated by 'man's ordering attitude and behaviour' (1977: 21).

Heidegger's analysis forms part of a philosophical tradition that has approached technology as a principle or system (or, more accurately, as a principle that gives rise to a system) rather than as a collection of material artefacts. One of the roots of this tradition lies with Nietzsche, who offered a powerful critique of the obsessive compulsion within modern science not '"to know" but to schematize—to impose upon chaos as much regularity and form as our practical needs require' (1968: n. 515). For Nietzsche, the knowing subject is not a concrete entity but 'a fiction', while Being, having 'nothing to do with metaphysical truths', is a mere consequence of 'the will to logical truth' which 'can be carried through only after a fundamental *falsification* of all events is assumed' (1968: n. 512, emphasis in original). In other words, it is only by imposing human order on the 'chaos' of nature that knowledge is generated: as Nietzsche writes, 'It is the powerful who made the names of things into law, and among the powerful it is the greatest artists in abstraction who created the categories' (1968: n. 513). For Nietzsche, Becoming, not Being, is the true state of all things: the apparent existence of Being in the world is merely an expression of the 'will to power', which is 'founded upon the premise of a belief in enduring and regularly recurring things ... Logicizing, rationalizing, systematizing as expedients of life' (1968: n. 552). Nietzsche's influence, like Heidegger's, can be felt throughout posthumanism—in Braidotti's 'vital materialism', for example, which rejects universal Being and frames the phenomenological experience of the human subject as a process of 'becoming-with'.

Later, in the twentieth century, French philosopher Jacques Ellul defined the technological principle as 'technique', 'the consciousness of the mechanized world' (1964: 6). Technique, according to Ellul, is 'the translation into action of man's concern to master things by means of reason, to account for what is subconscious, make quantitative what is qualitative, make clear and precise the outlines of nature, take hold of chaos and put order to it' (43). It is a machinic impulse that subjects all it encounters to the technological principles of order, efficiency, and control, and thus resembles Heidegger's principle of enframing in a number of ways: it represents a threat to nature, which it 'destroys, eliminates, or subordinates' (79); it is driven by rationality, which it 'brings to bear on all that is spontaneous or irrational', even time and space (78); it is universal, since everything in western civilisation comes to be 'constructed *by* technique [and] *for* technique' (78–9); and finally it subsumes humanity itself, since 'the life of man is now technicized' (128).

A similar account of the western technological impulse is put forward by the influential American historian and philosopher Lewis Mumford in *Technics and Civilisation* (1934). For Mumford, the clock is the archetypal machine of western civilisation, the tool which first 'disassociated time from human events and helped to create the belief in an independent world of mathematically measurable sequences: the special world of science' (15). He then identifies monasteries as the 'first machines' wherein 'the erratic fluctuations and pulsations of all the worldly life' were tempered by 'the iron discipline of the rule', while even earlier, the Roman Empire 'helped to give human enterprise the regular collective beat and rhythm of the machine' (1963: 13–14). They did this not by means of apparatus, but through the systematic and rational organisation of social life. Mumford goes on to describe how 'the concepts of science, hitherto associated largely with the cosmic, the inorganic, the "mechanical", were now applied to every phase of human experience and every manifestation of life', as the machinic rhythms of technology came to dominate the social organisation of life in technologically advanced countries (217).

Ellul and Mumford thus argue alongside Heidegger for an understanding of technology as a principle of rationalisation and technicity that has guided—and continues to guide—the social, political, economic, and environmental formations of western humanity. This notion of rationality as one of the defining qualities of western civilisation has been widespread within wider cultural and political theory. Max Weber's 'iron cage' of capitalist modernity, for example, follows along similar lines: in *The Protestant Ethic* (1930), Weber describes the 'technical and economic conditions of machine production which today determine the lives of all the individuals who are born into this mechanism ... with irresistible force'—a system which, lacking all inherent value, risks one day becoming mere 'mechanized petrification' (2001: 123–4). Similarly, Adorno and Horkheimer in *Dialectic of Enlightenment* (1944) argue that '[technical] rationality today is the rationality of domination' that drives the standardisation and commodification of culture and art (2002: 95). Elsewhere, they describe the 'conscious task of science' within Enlightenment thought as 'the establishing of a unified, scientific order' and 'the subsumption under principles' of all the world, a unity which is then 'imprinted' on the external world 'as an objective quality' (2002: 63–4).

The same anxiety regarding oppressive rationalisation and technicisation can be detected in the work of Hannah Arendt, who, in a passage from *The Human Condition* (1958), states that mathematics after Descartes 'succeeded in reducing and translating all that man is not into patterns which are identical with human, mental structures' (1998: 266). At the same time, the very function of the labouring human in contemporary techno-capitalist societies, she argues, is simply to 'care for the upkeep of the various gigantic bureaucratic machines whose processes consume their services and devour their products as quickly and mercilessly as the biological life process itself' (93). And, finally, Foucault's concept of 'biopower' describes the submersion of the individual within a rationalist socio-scientific system that operates on the level of the human species as a totality (2003: 239–64). Indeed, the concept of 'power/knowledge' that informs much of Foucault's thought can be viewed as an invasive system of knowledge acquisition which steadily assumes social authority within western society, such that 'discipline' and 'biopower' become characterised more than anything else by the erection of vast and impersonal systems of knowledge.

If intellectual rationality has been the defining quality of the human being within classical humanism since the time of Descartes, then, technological rationalisation has emerged, within this strand of philosophical thinking, as its nightmare inverse: rationality taken to such an extreme that it threatens to devour both human society and the natural world on which it is founded. Crucially, each of these thinkers emphasises the extent to which such processes of technological rationalisation threaten not only human society but also the natural world, everywhere scarred by human technological exploration.

To briefly summarise, then: the traditional western model of the human that has emphasised the mind over and above the physical and natural world (including, crucially, the body) is lacking. To expand this restrictive understanding of subjectivity, it is necessary to look at humanity's imbrication within both nature and technology. By 'nature', I mean the natural–material world, as well as the biological beings that inhabit such a world. By 'technology', I mean the principle of technological rationalisation and scientific systematisation as well as physical instances of technological apparatus. This principle leads the natural world to be represented as either an indifferent object of study or a ready supply of resources for human use. It is thus a hermeneutical principle that determines the ways in which humans shape, and are in turn shaped by, their material environments.

The importance of these issues cannot be overstated. If the OncoMouse™ represents anything other than the unfortunate beings manipulated to advance cancer research, it is the extent to which the non-human can be vacated of all inherent value or meaning and made to serve exclusively human purposes. What is needed is a means by which we may stem this rational appropriation of the natural world, and the human world along with it—one that allows for 'essential reflection on technology and decisive confrontation with it' (Heidegger, 1977: 35). Such reflection and confrontation, Heidegger argues, 'must happen in a realm that is, on the one hand, akin to the essence of technology and, on the other, fundamentally different from it' (35). The way to achieve this is through art. Like technology, art 'reveals' the world—it is a form of poiesis that can shed light on the processes of enframing in ways which positively influence our principles and actions. I will now look more closely at one specific art form—SF—as a site whereupon the intersections of technological rationalisation, the natural world, and the human may be powerfully articulated and critiqued.

Posthumanism and science fiction

SF has a rich history of debate concerning the significance of the human and the meaning of technological change and ecological upheaval. This extends from the 'Beast Folk' of Wells's *The Island of Doctor Moreau* (1896) to the 'cosmic consciousness' of Olaf Stapledon's *Star Maker* (1937), the robots of Asimov's *I, Robot* (1950) to the androids of Philip K. Dick's *Do Androids Dream of Electric Sheep?* (1968), and the ambisexual Gethenians of *The Left Hand of Darkness* (1969) to the virtual cyberspace of William Gibson's *Neuromancer* (1984).

Before I begin to investigate the form of the human in SF, however, it is necessary to offer some preliminary comments on the nature of the genre. I will not here add to the extensive corpus of discussions of 'what SF is'. Rather, I follow the example of Jack Fennell who, in his study of Irish SF, settles on a definition of 'Irishness' as something 'instinctive and emotive rather than logical' (quoted in Reid, 2016: 155). In a similar vein, Paul Kincaid, drawing on Wittgenstein, describes SF not as a specific set of characteristics but as a 'web of resemblances ... braided together in an endless variety of combinations', such that 'the more familiar we are with the genre, the more readily we can accept their variety, the more subtly we might interpret their combinations' (2008: 20). Thus, SF for Kincaid, as with Irishness for Fennell, becomes something felt, rather than strictly defined. This is the understanding of the genre that I will be using here.

I will focus on one specific family resemblance in my examination of the human in SF: the genre's habitual preoccupation with technology. Tom Shippey argues for an understanding of SF as 'fabril literature', that is, literature centred on 'the *faber*, the maker: often the blacksmith, the metal-beater, but also the Moreau, the manipulator of biology and even of society' (2016: 42). From the electric nodes of Shelley's *Frankenstein* (1818), the Nautilus of Verne's *Twenty Thousand Leagues Under the Sea* (1870), and the tripod Martians of Wells's *The War of the Worlds* to the 'scientifiction' of Gernsback, the super-weapons of the 'Golden Age', and the singularities and AIs of cyberpunk and beyond, technology is one of the defining tropes of SF. Furthermore, any representation of human technology also requires some account of humanity's relationship with the natural–material world. This, too, can be seen throughout the history of SF: in *Frankenstein*, where the Creature comes to represent the moral consequences of human interference with natural law; in Wells's romances, where evolutionary theory forces a revision of the human relationship with the natural world; in the pulps and the works of the 'Golden Age', where nature often features as a barrier to be overcome or a resource to be exploited in humanity's technological evolution; and in cyberpunk, where virtuality and cybernetics raise a new set of problematics concerning the experience of embodiment and disembodiment.

Hence, SF offers the ideal genre in which to examine the figure of the human and its construction in relation to technological and natural systems. This has been particularly the case with late twentieth-century SF works: at the same time that the OncoMouse™ was being 'born' in a Harvard research lab, SF was experiencing its own posthumanist moment with the emergence of cyberpunk, a subgenre highly preoccupied with questions of human–machine interface, corporeal transcendence, cybernetics, and virtuality. Bruce Sterling, in his well-known preface to *Mirrorshades* (1986), outlines a list of thematic concerns in which the terms 'cyberpunk' and 'posthumanism' could be interchangeable:

> Certain central themes spring up repeatedly in cyberpunk. The theme of body invasion: prosthetic limbs, implanted circuitry, cosmetic surgery, genetic alteration. The even more powerful theme of mind invasion: brain–computer interfaces, artificial intelligence, neurochemistry—techniques radically redefining the nature of humanity, the nature of the self (1986: xiii).

Such themes are prevalent throughout late twentieth-century SF, leading many thinkers to draw on SF literature from this period in their examinations of posthumanism. Haraway, for example, in her 'Cyborg Manifesto', refers to the novels of Joanna Russ and Octavia Butler; Wolfe analyses a novel by Michael Crichton in one of his essays; and Hayles uses the works of Philip K. Dick and Greg Bear to illustrate various points in her history of cybernetics.

Within SF studies itself, the affinities between late twentieth-century SF and posthumanism have been well noted. Veronica Hollinger's entry on 'Posthumanism and Cyborg Theory' in *The Routledge Companion to Science Fiction* (2009), for example, supports its discussion of posthumanism using examples drawn from late twentieth-century cyberpunk and postmodernist works by writers such as William Gibson, Greg Egan, Marge Piercy, Octavia Butler, and Bruce Sterling. In her discussion, Hollinger invokes the ubiquitous spectre of the OncoMouse™, which 'occupies the space where imagination and materiality intersect, the space of SF in the posthuman era' (2009: 277). Sherryl Vint, too, examines SF from the late twentieth and early twenty-first centuries in her critical study of subjectivity and embodiment, *Bodies of Tomorrow* (2007). Like Hayles, Vint is critical of the tendency to view subjectivity as disconnected from the experience of embodiment. 'The ability to construct the body as passé', she argues, 'is a position only available to those privileged to think of their (white, male, straight, non-working-class) bodies as the norm'—she thus argues for a 'return to a notion of embodied subjectivity' (2007: 8). And Thomas Foster, in *The Souls of Cyberfolk* (2005), argues that cyberpunk elaborates on a set of existing concerns regarding embodiment and subjectivity that are evident in SF as far back as Wells (2005: 6–7). Cyberpunk, he suggests, is not the 'vanguard' of posthumanism in American popular culture but rather 'an attempt to intervene in and diversify what posthumanism can mean', a debate with its roots in the history of SF literature (xiii). Foster examines cyberpunk and its various literary descendants as locus points at which questions of embodiment, subjectivity, gender, and particularly race can be powerfully articulated, with this latter category revealing one of the fault-lines of a posthumanist tradition that often 'ignore[s] and seem[s] to eliminate the problem of the colour line' (xxiii).

Although cyberpunk and postmodern SF have drawn the bulk of posthumanist critical attention, numerous critics have also examined classical SF texts from a posthumanist perspective. Elaine L. Graham, for example, uses older works of SF to explore 'how understandings of what it means to be human are contested and negotiated' (2002: 61). Such 'monstrous' beings as Shelley's famous Creature, Graham argues, 'destabilize evolutionary, technological and biological hierarchies that serve to privilege the rational male subject' (60). In doing so, they 'bear witness to the power of the marginal, the Other, to demarcate the known and the unknown, the acceptable and deviant', thereby functioning as 'keepers of the boundaries between human and Other' (60). Like Haraway's cyborg, such transgressive creatures pollute the neat ontological categories of traditional thought. Bruce Clarke takes this argument even further: given that humans are inextricably bound up in social systems that precede and encompass them, Clarke argues, human ontology is always-already 'polluted' by its imbrication in such external, pre-existing systems (2008: 17). As a result, '"the human" is both living and nonliving': a biological autopoietic system bound up in non-human and non-living systems. For Clarke, SF narrative focalisation offers a way of imagining subjective positions ordinarily unavailable to the human. By imagining the subjectivities of beings outside ordinary human cognitive experience—Clarke uses the example of Wells's Martians in *The War of the Worlds*—SF allegorises the actual operations of human subjectivity in which subjective experience captures merely one of a number of possible 'realities'.

These examples illustrate the rich overlap that exists between SF and posthumanism. My study forms part of this critical lineage of posthumanist studies of SF texts—albeit one that, like Graham's study, attempts to balance the dominant critical focus on late twentieth-century works. Whereas Graham focuses specifically on images of inhuman monstrosity in SF literature, I argue that a work need not feature explicitly 'inhuman' beings—such as aliens, robots, cyborgs, and monsters—to engage with posthumanist problematics. The central assertion of critical posthumanism is that humanity must be understood in material terms—not mind over matter, but mind *as* matter. Since all SF is concerned with humanity's imbrication within technological and natural systems, even the most avowedly humanist text raises posthumanist concerns. The 'post-' in 'posthumanism' does not imply that it comes 'after' humanism, but rather emphasises the constant presence of the posthuman *within* the human—the extent to which even the most avowedly humanist accounts of history, technology, biology, and so on cannot but admit the constructed nature of human experiences of the world. If we are 'after' humanism, it is only because we increasingly recognise that the 'human' of this humanist tradition never actually existed—as Halberstam and Livingston remark, in this respect we 'were never human' (1995: 8). By examining the intersections between nature, technology, and the human in SF, I will explore the ramifications of this—fundamentally posthuman—fact. In doing so, I will show that SF, in whatever era it has been written, is always engaged with posthumanist concerns.

Yet if the posthuman has always acted to subvert the traditional figure of the human, then it makes sense that this conventional human figure also remains lurking within the posthuman, ready to resurface at any moment. This dynamic can be seen at work in SF. Milburn remarks that, 'at the root of the posthuman condition (whether biological, technological, or cultural), there lies science fiction' (Latham, 2014: 527). Such a remark is accurate up to a point—SF has indeed depicted a range of posthuman beings and subjectivities—yet it is also disingenuous. So often, at the furthest reaches of an SF tale, what is encountered there is in fact a relatively conventional 'human' figure—humbled perhaps (as in Wells's romances), biologically unfamiliar, or even disembodied, but still inscribed in the familiar terms of classical humanism. In this way, SF may imagine a whole variety of posthuman beings and conditions, but often in superficial ways that merely reinscribe the ethical and ontological supremacy of the human itself. Badmington puts this point succinctly in his study of aliens and humanism in Hollywood cinema: the attempts of writers and directors to imagine the alien Other, he argues, are often merely tokenistic, with the result that 'the extraterrestrial', in these works, 'is always overwhelmingly terrestrial' (2004: 37). SF thus offers a *potential* mode of exploring a range of posthumanist concerns, but this exploration is often ambiguous or problematic—SF betrays an equivocal sense of desire for *and* fear of the dissimulation of the human.

We can more clearly understand this quality of SF by distinguishing between 'transformative' and 'assimilative' narratives of the human: whereas the former are open to encountering the truly non-human, the latter attempt to assimilate radically Other encounters or beings into pre-existing—and human-centred—cognitive frameworks, thereby neutralising their subversive or transformative potential. The speculative framework of SF, its ability to allegorise cultural narratives of difference and identity, means that SF works are continuously confronted with this choice between transformation and assimilation—between questioning the fundamental grounds on which the 'human' has been founded and neutralising the radically non-human in the service of preserving those grounds. Most works, as I will show, lie somewhere in between these two poles, exhibiting a tension between assimilative human and transformative posthuman modes of being as these are narrativised within the text.

Given this tension between humanist and posthumanist narratives of the human, we can more usefully regard posthumanism not as a specific state of being but as a hermeneutical principle analogous to Ernst Bloch's utopian 'function'. According to Bloch, utopia need not necessarily take the shape of a formal socio-political community but can be conceived more broadly as 'anticipation', defined as the human impulse to look forward and envision some alternative to present reality, however obscure or veiled. Such 'utopian functions', Bloch argues, are 'first represented in ideas', which 'extend, in an anticipating way, existing material into the future possibilities of being different and better' (144). Hence Bloch argues that any kind of human endeavour—the 'appeal of dressing up, ... the *world of fairytale*, brightened distance in *travel*, the *dance*, the dream-factory of *film*, the example of *theatre*', the more familiar *'planned or outlined utopias'*, or indeed any instance of future-oriented imagining carried out by human minds (1995: 13)—can be read as either implying or denying the possibility for a more positive future. For Bloch, as Carl Freedman argues, 'all genuine art—virtually by definition—finds its true significance in utopian construing' (2000: 77). Freedman stresses the value of Bloch's utopian hermeneutic for analysing SF, placing Blochean utopianism alongside 'Bakhtinian stylistics and Lukácsian genre analysis' as a key component of SF's 'critical-theoretical project' (78).

A similar construction can be employed for posthumanism: rather than collecting an entire work or body of works under the heading of 'posthumanist' or 'humanist', it is more constructive to conceive of posthumanism as a hermeneutical principle aimed at assessing the ideas, values, and notions that surround the human or non-human in these works. Using such a model, any SF text may thus be read as a complex admixture of humanist and posthumanist 'functions'. The human figure of SF thus becomes analogous to Moylan's 'critical utopia' (discussed in more detail in Chapter Four): just as the critical utopia occupies a liminal space between the originary world of the author and an idealised 'perfect' society, so the human in SF occupies a liminal space between humanist and posthumanist models of subjectivity and embodiment. Such an understanding also allows for more fluid understandings of the terms 'human', 'posthuman', and 'non-human'. In *The Cambridge Companion to Literature and the Posthuman* (2017), for example, Clarke and Rossini provide a 'Chronology' of the 'Posthuman', placing several SF authors within a timeline of posthumanist explorations of the subject (2017: xxv–xxix). Such a framework, however, risks promoting a homogenous figure—the 'Posthuman'—as a straightforward contrast to the 'Human', and thereby diminishing the diversity and complexity of human representations in literary works.

With this recognition, our discussion of posthumanism has returned finally to the two points with which I began: all SF is engaged in posthumanist concerns, but the attachment to the traditional human is more robust or enduring than it may at first appear. Or—as I may now express it in more explicitly critical terms—SF works are neither straightforwardly humanist nor posthumanist but can be more fruitfully read as heterogeneous mixtures of conflicting humanist and posthumanist functions.

The remainder of this study is divided into four chapters, each of which addresses a different era from the Anglo-American tradition of SF from the nineteenth century up to the 1970s. Each chapter will discuss two major SF works in relation to a specific human 'archetype' that, I will argue, embodies key humanist and posthumanist concerns from the period in question. These archetypes are a corollary of Damien Broderick's 'narrative archetypes' that together comprise the SF 'megatext'. Broderick (2005: 57–63), drawing on Gary K. Wolfe, outlines a number of SF 'icons'—'the spaceship, the robot and the monster' being three key examples—whose depiction in diverse SF works has generated a set of 'narrative vectors' and reader expectations. Broderick argues that such icons lack a truly fixed consensual significance, being instead characterised (in an image reminiscent of Kincaid's definition of SF above) by a set of 'family resemblances' (59). The human archetypes can be similarly interpreted: each is characterised by a set of 'family resemblances' that nevertheless remain stable in diverse narrative contexts. Like Broderick, I do not argue that these paradigmatic human archetypes hold true only in the specific periods in which I situate them here—on the contrary, a glance through any given period of SF will reveal a complex and contradictory range of ideas, values, and anxieties concerning humanity and human nature. My chronology here represents just one possible history of the human in SF—but one that, I believe, reflects some of the dominant trends of each given period.

For practical reasons, I have limited my consideration to Anglo-American authors. In doing so, I acknowledge the loss of key SF traditions which would undoubtedly prove fruitful in such a discussion. In the last number of decades, developments in the genre, including the advent of Afrofuturism and the emergence of various national SF literatures—including Indian, Chinese, and Latin American SF—have greatly expanded the scope and diversity of SF, deploying familiar SF tropes in new contexts and generating diverse responses to global technoscientific regimes. My particular focus on British and American SF authors stems from a recognition that these authors have in general been among the most widely disseminated throughout the twentieth century, and that these two countries have also shared a common language that has allowed for a continuous interplay of ideas, stories, and influences.

Chapter One, 'Worlds Lost and Gained', examines the figure of the 'pre-human' in Arthur Conan Doyle's *The Lost World* and Jack London's *The Iron Heel*. The pre-human is represented as a debased form of humanity—a 'degenerate' human who fails to exhibit the moral and intellectual qualities required to qualify for 'full' personhood. In *The Lost World*, this pre-human takes the form of the 'ape-men', a race of violent humanoids encountered by a group of imperial adventurers during a trip to the Amazon jungle. In *The Iron Heel*, by contrast, the pre-human can be seen in the 'People of the Abyss', London's term for the oppressed workers of industrial capitalism. In each case, the pre-human is treated as an evolutionary aberration: a regressive throwback to an earlier form of humanity that emphasises the contrasting moral and intellectual rectitude of the novel's protagonists. I will also discuss Conan Doyle's and London's use of evolution as a way of recasting their preferred social form—for Conan Doyle, his own European imperialist civilisation, for London, a future socialist utopia—as the outcome of evolutionary dynamics and, therefore, the most 'natural' human social form. Before exploring these works, however, I will first begin with a brief examination of two major writers from nineteenth-century SF: Mary Shelley and Jules Verne. Shelley and Verne, I argue, serve as paradigmatic figures for two distinct lines of nineteenth-century humanist thought: the first characterised by scientific scepticism and a wary attitude towards technological development, the second by a triumphalist humanism in which technology serves as a means to further human progress. These two lines of humanist thought, I will argue, remained central to SF until at least the mid-century period.

Chapter Two, 'Soma and Skylarks', moves on to examine the figure of the 'trans-human' in two key works from the interwar period, Aldous Huxley's *Brave New World* and E.E. 'Doc' Smith's *Skylark* series. I will begin with an examination of the SF of this period more widely, focussing particularly on the impacts of the First World War on SF representations of humanity and its relationship to technology. The two lines of thought traced out in nineteenth-century SF persist into the early decades of the twentieth century, taking the form of 'technophobic' and 'technophilic' strains of SF. These contrasting attitudes towards technology decisively shape how the trans-human is accommodated within my two major works. Both Huxley's and Smith's works depict the figure of the trans-human—a figure defined and determined by technological systems—but to vastly different ends. Huxley's famous dystopian work depicts the subversion of traditional human nature by external technological systems. For Huxley, these systems—Fordism, the 'culture industry', the mass media—deprive western humanity of the capacity to think and act for itself and result in a population of mechanised beings lacking true agency or creativity. Against this sterile existence, Huxley instead advocates 'life-worshipping', a recognition of both the 'animal' and 'spiritual' aspects of the human. By contrast, Smith depicts an expansion of the human intellect to encompass the whole galaxy within a technological network. *Skylark* is typical of the pulp SF that emerged in the United States in the interwar years: triumphantly imperialist and humanist, and deeply concerned with extending the capacities of the human mind beyond their traditional limits. In both *Brave New World* and *Skylark*, we can detect a form of the trans-human—but where Huxley turns away from this technological being to recapture a more traditional form of human, Smith instead pushes his human figures ever further beyond their material limits, towards a technological embrace of the entire galaxy itself.

Chapter Three, 'Homo Gestalt', moves on to the mid-century period, examining the figure of the 'supra-human' in Isaac Asimov's *Foundation* and Arthur C. Clarke's *The City and the Stars*. The technophilic and technophobic strains of SF identified in the works of the interwar period are also evident here: the former in the works of the 'Golden Age', which exhibit a technocratic attitude inherited from earlier pulp SF, and the latter in the more pensive works that emerged in the post-war period. In particular, the growth of bureaucratic regimes in the mid-century period, coupled with the tremendous impacts of Second World War, brought individual agency and mass society into conflict—as a result, it is no longer the fate of the individual, but that of the mass that is the primary concern of these SF works. In Asimov's *Foundation*, the population of the galaxy becomes subject to mass biopolitical control by anonymous scientific institutions. These institutions function as paternalistic guardians, ensuring the continuity and safety of human civilisation—but at the cost of human agency. Clarke's *The City and the Stars*, conversely, advocates a holistic union of technocracy and pastoralism, and ends with a totalising vision of the human species as part of a transcendent 'cosmic consciousness'. Both offer a vision of the 'supra-human'—a mass of individuals forming a composite social body that acts as a metaphor for the relationship between the individual and mass society.

Finally, Chapter Four, 'Disaster and Redemption', examines the SF of the 1960s and 1970s and the figure of the 'post-human'. The post-war decades were a period of radical social change, marked by accelerated rates of technological innovation, the growth of mass bureaucratic structures, the atomisation of the individual, and pervasive mass media. In addition, the massive upsurge in post-war capitalist production also contributed to environmental concerns that propelled the relationship between western humanity and the natural world into public consciousness. These concerns fed into the SF produced during this period. Ballard's *The Crystal World*, the final volume in his 'disaster trilogy', responds to the altered conditions of post-war society by retreating into 'inner space' and the psychological landscapes of the human mind. Such inner-directed narratives, however, come at the cost of meaningful engagement with the external world: Ballard's novel sacrifices the natural world to a vision of human individual transcendence. Le Guin's *The Dispossessed*, conversely, engages directly with humanity's relationship to the natural–material world. Le Guin's fiction explicitly repudiates the universalism, imperialism, and rationalism of earlier SF narratives, emphasising instead the relativity of such terms as 'human' and 'non-human'. *The Dispossessed* depicts an organic, ethical society in which the human and non-human exist in a state of ontological parity. Each work thus offers a vision of the post-human, but whereas for Ballard this 'post' is meant literally—in his work, humanity confronts its literal (albeit utopian) extinction—in Le Guin this 'post' gestures 'beyond' the humanist limitations of other SF works.

Throughout this critical history of the human in SF, I will both affirm and challenge the view of SF as a genre of what Elana Gomel calls an '"as if" ontology' (2014: 3)—that is, as a genre of radical ontological possibilities. Earlier in this introduction, I outlined the pressing need to better understand the ideas, values, and attributes that surround the figure of the human, and to better account for—and challenge—the increasingly fragmented and destructive western modes of interaction with the natural world and with those humans perceived as being different from 'us'. I repeat these assertions here: to understand where we are going, we need first to examine where we have come from. The speculative mode of SF establishes it as a vital site of inquiry into the legacy of humanist thought.

Chapter 1

Worlds Lost and Gained: Evolution, primitivism, and the pre-human in Arthur Conan Doyle's *The Lost World* and Jack London's *The Iron Heel*

> Progress ... is not an accident, but a necessity. Instead of civilization being artificial, it is part of nature; all of a piece with the development of the embryo or the unfolding of a flower. The modifications mankind have undergone, and are still undergoing, result from a law underlying the whole of organic creation; and provided the human race continues, and the constitution of things remains the same, those modifications must end in completeness. As surely as a tree becomes bulky when it stands alone, and slender if one of a group ... —so surely must the human faculties be moulded into complete fitness for the social state; so surely must evil and immorality disappear; so surely must man become perfect (Spencer, 1913: 32).

In this passage, Herbert Spencer summarises some key ideas that will inform this discussion of the human in early twentieth-century SF. Spencer was an enthusiastic exponent of evolutionary thought, and here offers an evolutionary model of social development—a vision of civilisation moving organically, by way of 'modifications', towards a state of culminative 'completeness'. What such completeness might look like was, of course, a matter of much debate. In this chapter, I will examine two opposing views of the 'perfect' civilisation from the early twentieth century—one imperialist, the other utopian–socialist—as well as the nature of the 'mankind' that would inhabit it. In doing so, I will discuss some of the ways that European imperialism and capitalist modernisation impacted on contemporary ideas surrounding the human.

The *fin-de-siècle* period was a time of dynamic social, political, cultural, and economic change. The rapid pace of this change, and its rising human cost, were increasingly apparent in every area of life: the industrial revolution rewrought the economic and political landscapes of the western world; evolutionary theory upturned traditional ideas regarding humanity's relationship with the natural world; the intensification of European, and later US, imperialism brought 'developed' and 'primitive' peoples into closer and more violent contact than ever before; and the acceleration of scientific and technological development utterly transformed the nature of humans' interactions with the world around them. Central to these dynamic processes, as David Harvey notes, was the notion of 'creative destruction': the recognition that to progress towards the new enlightened world, one must destroy the old irrational one (1992: 15–18). Such destruction runs the risk, however, of exposing the impulses of violence and irrationalism that Enlightenment thought had attempted to negate.

Each of these diverse phenomena contributed to contemporary ideas concerning the human in the late nineteenth and early twentieth centuries. I will examine two key SF works from the early twentieth century, Arthur Conan Doyle's *The Lost World* (1912) and Jack London's *The Iron Heel* (1907). Both of these novels emphasise the presence of repressed 'animal' characteristics within the rational human—a set of qualities gathered by Bradley Deane under the heading 'primitive masculinity', defined as a propensity towards 'raw strength, courage, instinctive violence, bodily size, and homosocial commitment to other men' (2008: 206). As will be seen, these characteristics become articulated in both texts as 'primitive' qualities that re-emerge in response to the volatile conditions of both European imperialism and capitalist industrialisation. My discussion of these works will focus on the figure of the 'pre-human', defined as a regressive human figure whose ostensible barbarity and primitivism function within each text as a foil to the moral correctness and intellectual sophistication of the 'fully' human protagonists. The presence of the pre-human in these works registers the extent to which their narrative and thematic structures are informed by evolutionary thought. The end to which such thought is directed, however, differs markedly in each work: *The Lost World*, and indeed much lost-world fiction, deploys evolution to underpin a hierarchy of human evolutionary development, with imperial Europe at its summit; while *The Iron Heel*, conversely, employs it in the service of London's convictions regarding the inevitability of a future socialist utopia. In either case, the 'perfect' civilisation is achieved only at the cost of denying moral consideration to certain kinds of humans.

Before examining these two novels, I will first attempt to trace the ways in which these texts emerge from and respond to the earlier tradition of speculative fiction, particularly the works of two earlier authors: Mary Shelley and Jules Verne. After a brief discussion of

Shelley's *Frankenstein* (1818), which will be read as an 'urtext' that prefigures many of the posthumanist concerns of SF, I will argue that the influence of Verne and Shelley can be traced in different ways within the works of later authors. In this way, I will identify two distinct lineages of the 'human' that can be traced in SF up until the mid-twentieth century.

Two lineages of the human in nineteenth-century SF: Shelley's *Frankenstein* and Verne's *Voyages extraordinaires*

'This manuscript will doubtless afford you the greatest pleasure', writes Marlow Saville to his sister in *Frankenstein*, referring to his pages documenting the strange story of Victor and his long-suffering Creature, 'but to me, who know him, and who hear it from his own lips, with what interest and sympathy I shall read it in some future day!' (Shelley, 1987: 20).

Mary Shelley's classic novel is framed as a series of letters written by a young English adventurer who, during an expedition to the North Pole, encounters Frankenstein in pursuit of his Creature across the Arctic wastes and records the story told by this unexpected shipmate. This framing narrative serves two distinct purposes. On the one hand, it presents a vivid and dramatic narrative to the reader by allowing Frankenstein to record his own tragic descent into obsession and ruin. In this way, it emphasises the seeming proximity of the bizarre events: the novel's atmosphere of unease and eeriness relies partly on the fact that, like Stoker's Dracula, Frankenstein's uncanny Creature transgresses, and thereby threatens, the very space of European civility and culture. Hence, although the clashes between Frankenstein and his Creature are staged primarily at the remote reaches of civilisation—the North Pole, a glacier in Switzerland, even a rainy coastal town in Ireland—nevertheless the Creature's hostile presence also extends to the heart of the European justice system, to the courts in which Justine, wrongly accused of his brutal deeds, is sentenced to death. On the other hand, however, this epistolary form also shields the reader from the story, reassuring them that, though grotesque and horrifying, the recorded events are by now merely historical. By the time word of them reaches civilisation, the bizarre occurrences have already concluded, with the key players dead and the secret of creating life forever lost.

In this way, the structure of *Frankenstein* reflects one of the key early modes of shaping SF—as a tale already ended, or occurring in a remote location, or both—while also anticipating the future preoccupation, given its first sustained expression in Wells's romances, with the technological upheaval of contemporary society. Shelley's importance in setting the stage for later SF is, of course, widely acknowledged: her classic account of radical scientific possibilities in *Frankenstein* anticipates those of two influential figures of late nineteenth-century SF, Verne and Wells. More significantly for this study, however, Shelley's text also anticipates the major SF anxiety concerning the limits and capacities of the scientific imagination. This concern is explicitly elucidated by Shelley herself, who writes in the 1818 preface to the novel that the 'event on which this fiction is founded has been supposed ... as not of impossible occurrence' (1987: 1). In contrast to the fantastic voyages of her predecessors Swift, Voltaire, and Cyrano, Shelley is not 'merely weaving a series of supernatural terrors' (1) but dealing instead with the real world and some very real possibilities within it.

For Darko Suvin, Shelley's novel offers a response to the uprooting of traditional political authority resulting from the French Revolution: Frankenstein's horror at his creation reflects the horror of the instigators of the Revolution towards the violent and ugly outcomes of their revolutionary zeal (1979: 133–4). Yet it was not merely in politics that old systems of belief were being overturned in eighteenth- and nineteenth-century European thought. Just as the revolutionaries stripped away what Edmund Burke called the 'decent drapery' of tradition from figures of political authority, so Enlightenment science was slowly demystifying the natural world in a hitherto unprecedented way. The new epistemologies and empirical methods that emerged from the scientific revolution in the seventeenth century led philosophers to anticipate the ultimate liberation of humankind from the vagaries of nature—they sought, as Francis Bacon writes in *The New Atlantis* (1627), not only 'the knowledge of causes, and secret motions of things', but also 'the enlarging of the bounds of human empire, to the effecting of all things possible' (2008: par. 54). No longer, it seemed, would nature impede the progress of humanity—instead, the natural world would fall into step as a realm to be examined and catalogued, or a resource to be utilised in the realisation of an earthly technological utopia.

In this regard, Frankenstein's dismissal of 'the wild fancies [of] Paracelsus and Albertus Magnus', with their treatises on 'the search for the philosopher's stone and the elixir of life' (Shelley, 1987: 31, 30), suggests also a dismissal of outmoded forms of irrational, superstitious, or metaphysical knowledge and an embrace of the positivist worldview slowly taking shape within European thought. Yet, at the same time, Shelley's novel also recoils from the 'sacred duties of humanity' (as she terms them) to dissect and comprehend the natural world as propagated by the thinkers of the Enlightenment (253). *Frankenstein* betrays an uneasiness with the methodical and rationalist mindset championed by Bacon, Kant, and Newton, which, as Shelley writes, 'might dissect, anatomise, and give names', but to which, 'not to speak of a final cause, causes in their secondary and tertiary grades were unknown' (31). These higher causes include moral and ethical imperatives—categories ignored by Frankenstein to his ultimate doom and which, the novel suggests, are neglected at the risk of one's physical and spiritual well-being. Even as Frankenstein disrupts natural law to uncover the secret to creating life, there is an abiding sense throughout the novel that, to use the old cliché, there are things humanity was never meant, or equipped, to know.

Shelley's own stance towards scientific knowledge is thus ambiguous. On the one hand, the tragedy of Frankenstein's life springs from the unnatural Creature that he fashions and particularly the violation of natural law that the Creature embodies. This maligned being not only slays the family of his creator but also strips Frankenstein of his intellectual idealism, leaving him only a burning desire to destroy the 'wretch whom with such infinite pains [he] had endeavoured to form' (1987: 51). Frankenstein affronts the laws of nature by moulding a living being with his own hands and pays a fitting price as this unnatural and 'demoniacal corpse' turns on his creator (52). Such anxieties surrounding the uncanny 'inhuman' being pervade nineteenth-century speculative fiction, from the automaton of E.T.A. Hoffman's 'The Sandman' (1816) and the 'living livid corpse' of Polidori's 'The Vampyre' (1819) to the petrified corpse of Poe's 'The Facts in the Case of M. Valdemar' (1845) and the invisible humanoid 'Thing' of Fitz-James O'Brien's 'What Was It? A Mystery' (1859). Such beings, in part like 'us', but also representing our 'monstrous' mirror image, threaten to obscure the boundaries of the human—'Distorted, uncouth, and horrible', as O'Brien writes of the invisible creature of his tale, 'but still a man' (2012: 97).

On the other hand, however, it is also clear that the Creature need not have turned out as dreadful as he eventually becomes. The rage that drives him is not that of the blundering monster familiar from James Whale's cinematic adaptations of the 1930s. On the contrary, the Creature of the novel is an eloquent and sensitive being whose initial nature, shaped by his clandestine study of a loving rural family and of classic works of literature, emanates goodwill towards all humanity. It is the malice of those humans who fail to see past the Creature's grotesque appearance that drives his misanthropy—the real significance of the Creature is thus paradoxically to demonstrate the *in*humanity of ostensibly enlightened thought, which so alienated humanity from the rest of nature as to blind it to the moral value of anything not recognisably 'human'. As Elaine L. Graham argues, 'the text invites the reader to question the ontological hygiene that might forbid Victor's creature even an adoptive humanity' (2002: 83). The mistreatment of the physically repulsive Creature suggests the symbolic blindness of the 'all-seeing' human, whose 'fatal prejudice' so 'clouds their eyes' that, 'where they ought to see a feeling and kind friend, they behold only a detestable monster' (Shelley, 1987: 140).

The Creature, Anne K. Mellor notes, may thus be viewed as 'the sign of the unknown', the Other denied subjectivity whose 'outer appearance' is considered 'a valid index to his inner nature' (2006: 20). Frankenstein's Creature is undeniably a 'monstrous' being, if that term signifies an aberration from the natural order: simultaneously technological and biological, the Creature seems more posthuman than human, both unnatural *and* a product of the 'natural' laws of vitality. Yet, measured by the standards of ethics or fellowship, the Creature begins his tragic life as the most 'human' being of all. Like Shelley herself, the Creature is even vegetarian—in opposition to his human counterparts, he does 'not destroy the lamb and the kid to glut [his] appetite' (Shelley, 1987: 155). Both author and Creature reject such 'unnatural habits of life', as the other famous Shelley, in his essay 'A Vindication of Natural Diet' (1813), describes the eating of animal flesh (1993: 75). The real purpose of the Creature, it seems, is to act as a mirror in which the rest of humanity may see reflected the true measure of their orthodox humanist values.

This latter essay is couched partially in evolutionary terms as Shelley (the poet) attempts to situate the 'origin of man' within 'that of the universe of which he is part' (1993: 75). Indeed, the various permutations of nineteenth-century evolutionary thought—from Erasmus Darwin's (grandfather of Charles) proto-evolutionary *Zoonomia, or The Laws of Organic Life* (1794–1796), through Jean-Baptiste Lamarck's theory of 'transmutation', outlined in his 1809 work, *Philosophie Zoologique*, to the more famous outlines of 'natural selection' described by Darwin in the mid-nineteenth century—constituted a serious assault on conventional thought regarding the natural world and humanity's dominion over it. Humanity, it seemed, was no longer the foremost product of a benevolent deity—instead, evolutionary theory reconstituted human existence as merely another random outcome of a natural process. It is a lesson that Shelley took to heart in her fiction: *Frankenstein*, as Brian Aldiss has argued, is indebted to an evolutionary worldview, since the 'concept of *Frankenstein* rests on the quasi-evolutionary idea that God is remote or absent from creation: man is therefore free to create his own sub-life' (1975: 29). In her later novel, *The Last Man* (1826), Shelley further condemns the 'arrogance' of humanity that 'we call ourselves lords of the creation, wielders of the elements, masters of life and death' at the same time as 'the visible mechanism of our being is subject to the slightest accident' and humanity may become 'the victim of the destructive powers of exterior [non-human] agents' (Shelley, 2004: 184). Cautioning that humanity should be mindful of its position within the broader scheme of nature, *The Last Man* resituates life on earth within an expansive universal ontology, invoking an image of a 'beauteous and imperishable universe' filled with 'other spirits, other minds, other perceptive beings' (172), and heralding a cosmical mode later developed more fully in the works of Olaf Stapledon, Camille Flammarion, and others. This image is simultaneously tragic and celebratory, and may even be said to constitute a truly posthumanist moment—a shift from *bios* to *zoe*, as it is revealed that the extinction of humanity is not, after all, the extinction of all life, beauty, and meaning.

The fruitful interplay between evolutionary theory and SF is thus evident from the very outset of the genre, originating in a shared emphasis on materialism. SF, as Adam Roberts argues, is the literature of materialism: the mode of cognitive extrapolation characteristic of SF 'requires material, physical rationalisation, rather than a supernatural or arbitrary one' (2000: 5). 'This grounding of SF in the material rather than the supernatural', Roberts continues, thus 'becomes one of its key features'—SF is 'a particular coding of the very materiality of science's practices' and thus distinct from other non-realist genres such as fantasy and folk tales (19). It is due in part to this commitment to materialism that SF has lent itself so well to the examination and exploration of ecological, environmentalist, and posthumanist problematics, all of which recognise humanity's fundamental rootedness in the material–physical world. As I have argued, Shelley's preface asserts that hers was no mere 'supernatural terror', but a quasi-realistic extension of material possibilities as then understood. Wells expounds a similar materialist position in his preface to the 1933 republication of his 'fantasies', insisting that whenever a writer employs an 'impossible hypothesis', they must extract from the reader 'an unwary concession to some plausible assumption', which may be obtained by means of 'an ingenious use of scientific', rather than mystical, 'patter' (1977: par. 3). By rooting deviations from conventional reality within the material world of science, rather than the transcendent world of mysticism, religion, myth, fairy tale, and so on, the author can ground the story in a socially realistic, rather than fantastical, setting.

Moreover, it is possible to connect the plethora of inhuman 'Others' that populated nineteenth-century fiction to the contemporary emergence of scientific positivism. Istvan Csicsery-Ronay Jr. (2008) links 'modern forms of the grotesque'—the undead, vampires, monsters, and other inhuman beings that populated nineteenth-century fiction—to the rise of scientific materialism in Europe. As he argues, since 'techno-science is the guardian of the rational categorization of matter, the grotesque attacks the very rationality that made its apprehension possible' (Csicsery-Ronay Jr., 2008: 7). In other words, the aberrant nature of the grotesque—its rejection of 'the abstract divisions and intellectual puritanism' of scientific thought (2008: 183–4)—subverted and thereby threatened the rationalist basis of scientific materialism itself. In this view, Shelley's Creature is not only a product of scientific materialism but also a repudiation of the abstract categorisation on which such thought rested: neither fully human nor inhuman, the Creature cannot be easily accommodated within the cognitive frameworks and rationalist 'systems of intermeshing laws' (2008: 184) of European scientific thought.

Evolutionary theory, too, posits materialism as a necessary precondition for the rationalisation of biological phenomena, rejecting transcendental or idealist causes, and so lends itself to easy incorporation within the ideological frameworks of SF texts. It is no coincidence that, at the historical moment in which evolutionary thought was gaining traction within western scientific thought, the works of Shelley, Poe, and Hawthorne were defining an agnostic narrative mode preoccupied with exploring the material and psychological boundaries of human experience. The emergence of evolutionary thought also accounts for the shift within speculative literature from spatial themes—which envisaged alternate societies existing in 'an as yet unknown island', 'a valley behind the mountain ranges', or 'an extrapolated planetary island in the ocean of ether' (Suvin, 1979: 116)—to temporal concerns, which imagined *when*, rather than *where*, alternate social structures might exist. This 'well-known shift', as Jameson puts it, 'from the accounts of exotic travellers to the experiences of visitors to the future' was also motivated by a growing awareness within eighteenth-century Europe of the potential for science and technology to radicalise society (Jameson, 2005: 2). Thus, if a writer wished to generate a vision of radical social difference, they had only to imagine their own society after a sufficient lapse of time.

This account of a shift from spatial to temporal concerns in SF at first appears inadequate to address the travelogues of the 'Great Frenchman', Jules Verne, whose *Voyages extraordinaires* include a host of journeys to speculative locales and landscapes. Yet Suvin suggests that time can be 'read' in Verne's works by means of traversing space. This quality is evident, for example, in one of Verne's best-known works, *Around the World in Eighty Days* (1872): as Phineas Fogg makes his long journey eastwards around the globe, he keeps meticulous note not of the distance clocked up but of the time elapsed. Indeed, the primary concern of the long-suffering Passepartout, who accompanies Fogg as his servant, is the perpetual need to recover time lost in the various misadventures of their journey—'the loss of time', Verne writes, 'nearly drove Passepartout out of his senses' (1994b: 97). Movement through space, by contrast, presents little challenge to the travellers: most of Fogg's journey is undertaken in relative luxury by means of global European railway and shipping networks, whose 'Trains, like time and tide, stop for no one' (152). His travels take him through a series of homogenous and interchangeable spaces—the 'hospitals, wharves [and] macadamized streets'—that give even so distant a place as Hong Kong 'the appearance of a town in Kent or Surrey' (115). As Mark Bould argues, like Nemo's Nautilus in *Twenty Thousand Leagues Under the Sea* (1870), 'all materiality' in *Around the World in Eighty Days* is reduced 'to a space of undifferentiated flow' (Bould and Miéville, 2009: 10), nullifying the tangible experience of material space.

The passage of time in *Eighty Days* is, like the journey itself, not progressive but cyclical: the typical Vernian text depicts a journey through space-as-time that eventually returns the protagonist to his original starting point—more knowledgeable perhaps, but with himself and the society around him unchanged. This structure is evident throughout the early *Voyages*: in *Journey to the Centre of the Earth* (1864), for instance, in which the German Professor Lidenbrock and his nephew Axel descend into an extinct volcanic crater in Iceland only to be regurgitated by an active volcano somewhere in Italy. The two thus describe a circular rather than progressive narrative—from descent to ascent, death to life, and wintry bleakness to balmy warmth. These works, as Marc Angenot notes, offer 'narratives of circulation', with the entire globe laid bare to the enterprising subjects of bourgeois Europe (quoted in Bould and Miéville, 2009: 5).

The need to witness or chronicle real progress—that is, fundamental change, development, or discovery—in Verne's *Voyages* had been vastly diminished by the technical and social accomplishments of nineteenth-century Europe. Scientific knowledge, which for Shelley denotes a threat to traditional authority, for Verne instead represents a form of power, specifically a mastery over nature which, as Pierre Macherey notes, comprises 'the *subject* of all Verne's work ... Verne's *elementary* obsession' (1978: 166). Hence Verne's exclusively middle-class protagonists project a sense of technical and scientific assurance that enables them to view everything in nature as in some way knowable, obtainable, traversable, or edible. Indeed, the desire to name nature—to encode the natural world within rational and ordered schemas—is one of the motivating principles of the *Voyages extraordinaires*: Verne sought to 'survey ... the whole world ... My object has been to depict the earth, and not the earth alone, but the universe' (Sherard, 1894, sec. 4).

The failure of Lidenbrock and Axel in *Journey* to actually *reach* the centre of the earth, then, is beside the point. On their descent into the Icelandic crater, Lidenbrock and Axel pass through a specifically European account of geological history: they encounter 'rocks of the transitional period, the Silurian Period', and the 'whole history of the coal period ... which preceded the Secondary Period' (1994a: 117, 122). As the days pass, their journey eventually takes the form of a literal chronicle of progress, culminating in humanity, as they trace the very history of the earth on the walls of their tunnel:

> Creation had obviously made considerable progress since the previous day. Instead of the more rudimentary trilobites, I noticed remains of a more advanced order of creatures, including ganoid fishes and some of those saurians in which palaeontologists have detected the earliest reptile forms. ... It was becoming obvious that we were climbing the ladder of animal life on which man occupies the highest rung (120–1).

Axel's implied mastery of scientific discourse enables him not only to name nature but to impose meaning on historical time: in the context of European scientific thought, natural history takes the form not of infinite progression into the future but of ascension with a definite endpoint, the 'highest rung' of which is occupied by bourgeois humanity. Geological time itself, then, is recast in the service of a narrative of European teleology.

The material reality of nature in the *Voyages* is thus subordinated to human systems of thought—his explorers' journey into the apparent 'unknown' is more properly understood as a journey into an always-already-familiar set of scientific precepts. While the encounter with the *truly* unknown—the humanoid creatures found to inhabit the centre of the world in *Journey*, for instance, or the underwater city in *Twenty Thousand Leagues*—requires the adaptation of certain scientific ideas, the emphasis remains the same: whether defined by rational or empirical epistemologies, the prioritisation of the human intellect over the natural–material world remains a key feature of these works. The human in Verne's *Voyages* is thus descended directly from the figures of Enlightenment humanism, whose motto is supplied by Kant: '*Sapere aude!* [Dare to know!]' (1979: 250).

It is thus possible to trace the emergence of two distinct lineages of the human in nineteenth-century SF. The first originates with Shelley's *Frankenstein* and *The Last Man*, which question the tenets of scientific rationalism and the legitimacy of a human-centred view of the universe. The second emerges from the *Voyages* of Verne, which emphasise Enlightenment reason as justification of European chauvinism and imperialism. Of the two, it is the former that offers the greater potential for the emergence of posthumanist functions. The poignant image of human extinction that closes Shelley's *The Last Man* clearly registers a set of preoccupations much different from those evoked by Verne's vision of humanity as the 'highest rung' of evolution. In the rest of this chapter, I will begin the task of tracing out these two lineages of the human in twentieth-century SF, beginning first with Conan Doyle's *The Lost World*.

Three forms of humanity in Conan Doyle's *The Lost World*

Conan Doyle is in many ways a spiritual successor to Verne, incorporating the same blend of imaginative science and adventure into unknown lands that characterises Verne's *Voyages*. This influence of the Frenchman—whom Conan Doyle had eagerly read in his youth (2008: 53–4)—and the literary model that he handed down is crucial to understanding the temporal and spatial structures of *The Lost World* and its corresponding notion of human nature. Conan Doyle's novel is a key example, like Verne's *Journey*, of the 'lost world' or 'lost race' genre of speculative fiction, which came to prominence in European literature from the mid-nineteenth century onwards. Lost-world fiction was an important subgenre for early SF, providing a key testing ground for ideas and motifs that would later become central to the genre.

As Everett F. Bailer notes, however, although *The Lost World* can be considered 'one of the patterning works of science fiction' (1996: 358), it has not received much critical attention, particularly when compared to the voluminous scholarly output on Conan Doyle's most famous literary creation, Sherlock Holmes. This may be due partially to what Randy Hayman has described as the 'hideous political incorrectness of the work—its racism, sexism, and imperialism' (2005: 516). The novel, as with much popular fiction produced in Europe at the turn of the twentieth century, incorporates a comprehensive range of crude racial stereotypes. 'Among the book's dramatis personae', Michael Dirda remarks, 'one finds easily spooked native bearers, traitorous half-breeds, and even a gigantic negro named Zambo, ever loyal to his "Massa"' (2011: 36), all of which contribute to an unattractive air of imperial arrogance typical of much of Conan Doyle's fiction. Despite these dated colonial characterisations and the dearth of critical writing on the novel, however, Conan Doyle remains an important figure within a line of speculative authors—including Poe, Verne, Edward Bulwer-Lytton, Samuel Butler, H. Rider Haggard, Wells, Charlotte Perkins Gilman, Edgar Rice Burroughs, and A. Merritt, to name only the most familiar examples—whose works of lost-world fiction explore nineteenth- and early twentieth-century ideas of humanity, nature, and technology in far-reaching and complex ways.

The Lost World centres on the character of Professor Challenger, a brilliant yet bullish English scientist who appears in several of Conan Doyle's speculative works. Alongside three companions—the gentleman adventurer John Roxton, irritable Professor Summerlee, and Anglo-Irish journalist Edward Malone, whose journals and letters to his editor form the bulk of the novel—Challenger embarks on a journey from London to the rainforests of Brazil in search of a hidden plateau rumoured to be home to a range of biological and geological marvels. After a series of trials and setbacks, the four adventurers eventually succeed in locating and scaling the plateau, where they encounter a collection of archaic creatures, including carnivorous bipeds, pterodactyls, and iguanodons. They also quickly find themselves swept up into an ongoing war between a race of 'ape-men' and a tribe of native 'Indians', who are battling for control of the plateau. The Englishmen aid the losing Indians in their fight for survival, massacring the ape-men before escaping from the plateau by means of a secret tunnel leading to the base of the structure. Arriving back in London to great acclaim, Malone and Roxton make immediate plans to return, this time with their eyes fixed on the plateau's rich supply of diamonds.

As I will argue, *The Lost World* shows a clear preoccupation with evolutionary themes and the discourses of social Darwinism and eugenics proliferating within European thought in the latter half of the nineteenth century. Such discourses, as R.J. Halliday (1971) has argued, provided an intellectual means for rearticulating the genocidal results of imperial practices as the 'natural' outcomes of racial competition, expressions of hereditary qualities of evolutionary 'fitness' and 'unfitness' in relation to different human 'types'. Indeed, in a later Challenger story, *The Poison Belt* (1913), Conan Doyle provides a positive cartographic hierarchy of world races. As the extra-terrestrial poison gas 'daturon' spreads across the globe, 'the less developed races', he writes, are 'the first to respond to its influence' (2001: 187). While 'India and Persia ... Africa, and the Australian aborigines' succumb instantly, the 'Northern races', conversely, demonstrate 'greater resisting power' (187).

Yet the principle of Darwinism also introduces problems of its own to a European cultural model founded on a clear division of humanity from nature: by revising human history in biological terms, evolution resituated humanity within a broader framework of *natural*, as opposed to strictly *human*, history. This recontextualisation of human history has, I argue, an ambiguous impact on the imagined relationship between humanity and nature that informs Conan Doyle's novel, and indeed much nineteenth- and early twentieth-century lost-world fiction. Specifically, it generates a tension between, on the one hand, an ideological view of the rational human as the 'natural' endpoint of evolutionary history and, on the other, a desire to maintain moral and ontological distinctions between what is 'human' and what is not. These are distinctions that underpinned contemporary cultural production and imperialist practices.

This tension can be seen in *The Lost World* in the interactions between the three 'kinds' of humanity that populate the novel: the adventurers, the Indians, and the ape-men. Pramod K. Nayar argues that, 'armed with biological theories about the inferiority of the black races, European colonials relegated … Africans to the domain of the non-human and the animal' (2014: 42). I will make a slightly different argument about *The Lost World*. The Indians and ape-men of the novel are conceived not as *non*-human, but as *pre*-humans—that is, as ostensibly 'primitive' humans lacking the technological and intellectual sophistication of their 'superior' European counterparts and thus undeserving of equal moral consideration, whilst not being considered utterly alien to European humanity. The Indian natives of *The Lost World*, I argue, are conceived as 'good' pre-human figures—by acknowledging an evolutionary kinship between Europeans and Indian natives, the novel situates them inside the opposition of 'the self and the Other' identified by Patricia Kerslake as a central icon of imperial SF (2010: 8–24). The annihilation of the ape-men, conversely, is a symbolic purging of the 'bad' pre-human from human history—a purging that also mirrors Conan Doyle's distinction between the 'good' and 'bad' practices of European imperialism. In both cases, Conan Doyle deploys a familiar imperial trope of construing non-European populations as remnants of the European human past. In doing so, *The Lost World* attempts to account for bourgeois European civilisation as the product of a 'natural' process of evolutionary history, while also preserving a notion of human nature as morally 'higher' than the rest of nature.

I begin this analysis by examining the structure of the novel which, like Verne's *Voyages*, is indebted to an evolutionary framework. Indeed, the similarities between *The Lost World* and Verne's works are evident.

Like the *Voyages*, *The Lost World* is a narrative of circulation, taking the reader from the society of upper-class London to the rainforests of South America and back again. Like the *Voyages*, space in the novel becomes, to some extent, intangible: though the trek through the Amazon rainforest is long and fraught with difficulty, nevertheless the efficiency of a global shipping network and the willing aid of the obsequious Brazilian natives ensure that Malone's letters to London always arrive in time for publication. And like the *Voyages*, the traversal of space takes on temporal significance as the quartet travel not only to the opposite side of the world but also back in time through natural history.

This temporal structure, Kenneth Wilson argues, is in part a consequence of European imperial expansion, which by the time of Conan Doyle's novel had in effect entirely colonised the physical space of the non-European world and, apparently, left no room for narratives of infinite discovery. Conan Doyle's adventurers, Wilson remarks, are simply 'a generation too late' (1993: 30): as Malone's editor puts it, the 'big blank spaces on the map are all being filled in, and there's no room for romance anywhere' (Doyle, 2001: 8). Conan Doyle himself, echoing Conrad's Marlow, even laments that the 'romance writer' no longer knows where to turn 'when he wants to draw any vague and not too clearly defined region', given the transformation of the 'blank spaces' of the map into a set of rigidly defined colonial territories (vii).

The solution to this dwindling of imaginative space was to be found in the Darwinian past, which provided an inexhaustible imaginative resource for imperialist adventure and speculation. As Wilson remarks, by transposing temporal qualities onto space, the 'journey from metropolis to frontier' is thus changed into 'a journey into the distant past' (1993: 31). In this way, John Rieder argues, *The Lost World* 'makes explicit the paradigmatic basis of colonial expeditionary science ... by viewing the plateau primarily as a living record of "our" own past' (2008: 58). The journey of the adventurers forms an adventure not *in* time, but literally *into* time, which is read through space: from the modern urbanity of London to the Jurassic period of the plateau, time in *The Lost World*, as in Verne's *Voyages*, becomes a dimension of space.

This preoccupation with the Darwinian past is most clear in the novel's treatment of scientific discourse. The two quarrelling professors, Challenger and Summerlee, call to mind the learned protagonists of Verne's travelogues: much of the comic relief in the novel, for example, derives from the abstruse and ill-timed quarrels between Challenger and Summerlee as they debate some classificatory minutiae, 'as comprehensible' to Malone and Roxton—and presumably to the reader—'as Chinese to the layman' (Doyle, 2001: 74). This scientific angle, however, also reflects Conan Doyle's own preoccupations with natural history. *The Lost World* was inspired by Conan Doyle's interest in paleontological exploration: in the years leading up to 1912, for example, he had become involved in numerous unsuccessful excavations in the countryside of south-east England in search of dinosaur fossils. This preoccupation influences much of his fiction: 'The Terror of Blue John Gap' (1910), for example, centres on a convalescent doctor 'of a sober and scientific turn of mind' (Doyle, 2000: 99) who encounters a prehistoric 'old cave-bear' in the unlikely locality of South Kensington (113).

This interest in turn spurred the meticulous attention to detail paid by Conan Doyle to matters of scientific accuracy in his fiction. Indeed, biographer Andrew Lycett defends Conan Doyle from charges of involvement in the famous 'Piltdown Man' scandal of 1912 precisely on the basis that his own spirit of scientific integrity would not allow him to become involved in such an unscientific practice as forgery.[1] After publication of *The Lost World*, as Lycett notes, Conan Doyle was even contacted by 'the former head of the Natural History section of the British Museum', who congratulated him on the accuracy and plausibility of his story (Lycett, 2008: ch. 18). Given these efforts at scientific verisimilitude—as well as journalistic authenticity, as suggested by the staged photographs originally published alongside the story in the *Strand Magazine*, with a heavily bearded Conan Doyle in the role of Challenger[2]—*The Lost World* may thus be read as Conan Doyle's own imaginative contribution to paleontological history.

Yet scientific knowledge in *The Lost World* represents more than a body of abstruse facts to be debated by eccentric academics. Rather, it is a means to classify, categorise, and, most importantly, hierarchise the human and non-human worlds. Even before leaving London, Challenger exercises his scientific authority over the plateau by accounting for its very existence in terms of European geological discourse: it is, he declares, 'basaltic, and therefore plutonic', the result of 'a great, sudden volcanic upheaval' (Doyle, 2001: 29). Later, he christens the plateau 'Maple White Land' after its original British discoverer, thereby reimagining the plateau in terms more familiar to the British spatial

---

[1] The Piltdown Man was a set of hominid remains, found in Piltdown in Sussex in 1912, that were alleged to comprise the 'missing link' between humans and apes. The remains were revealed to be a hoax in 1953, with Conan Doyle among those suspected as a perpetrator of the forgery. For a discussion of the merits of this accusation, and of Conan Doyle's experiences in palaeontology and archaeology, see Lycett (2008: ch. 18).

[2] Amy R. Wong has made a similar argument concerning the journalistic pretensions of *The Lost World*—see Wong (2015).

imagination (84). The scientific tradition thus supplies a lens through which Conan Doyle's characters may view natural history within specifically European terms. Indeed, the ideological underpinnings of *The Lost World* are even more explicit than those of Verne's *Voyages*: natural history is literally altered as Conan Doyle's adventurers, rifles in hand, aid the Indians—'representatives of the human struggle against the beasts in evolutionary history' (Deane, 2008: 211)—in securing control over the plateau by exterminating the ape-men.

The ideological bent of the novel in this respect could hardly be clearer: as Wilson notes, 'if the text leaves no doubt that the world is a better place without the ape-men, neither does it leave any doubt that the Indians needed European help' (1993: 32). 'The adventurers', he goes on, 'thus represent both faces of the colonial project: the civilizing mission and the conquering force' (32). The role of the contemporary Englishmen in liberating the Indians—their symbolic ancestors—from the vagaries of nature is useful in understanding Conan Doyle's humanist attitudes. The adventurers are conceived not as intruders in a foreign land but as heroes, while the Indians are only too willing to accept imperial aid in order to better their own lives—an example of the 'imagined history of Western endowments and free hand-outs' common to imperialist fiction (Said, 1994: 24). Malone even describes the Indians as 'our devoted slaves ... they looked on us as supermen' (Doyle, 2001: 142). This depiction of grateful natives lying down before the British explorers allows Conan Doyle—an unabashed 'Imperialist' (Doyle, 2008: 579n)—to reimagine the role of the British empire within non-European space as a positive force for good while also naturalising the unequal power exchange between coloniser and colonised by sketching it in specifically evolutionary terms.

Of particular interest in this regard is the novel's complex attitude towards violence and barbarism. In one sense, *The Lost World* revels in the gory side of nature: the carnivorous dinosaurs and violent ape-men of the plateau, locked in a grisly struggle for existence, symbolise in diverse ways the bloody underbelly of the natural world. Significantly, however, these violent characteristics also extend to the human characters of the work. Conan Doyle's novel forms part of a trend in late nineteenth-century culture in which, as Deane notes, 'middle-class masculinity began to drift away from the domestic values that had anchored it for decades' (2008: 212). In their place, there emerged a more 'primitive masculinity' that valued physical strength, ruggedness, and adventure (213). Within such discourses:

> atavism becomes a sign of strength rather than of weakness or criminality; impulse and irrationality can be taken for passionate

> masculine authenticity; and regression—even the relapse into barbarism—offers an empowering fantasy rather than a paralyzing anxiety ... lost world novels generally depict modern men discovering that barbarians of any number of races may be as manly as themselves (or even more so), and that Victorians can only express their potential manhood by converging with the primitive (207).

Conan Doyle was a strong proponent of such physicality. An enthusiastic cricketer and hunter throughout his life, he prided himself on having, as he put it, 'perhaps the strongest influence over young men, especially young athletic men, of anyone in England (bar Kipling)' (Doyle, 2008: 434). It was partly this influence over the young manhood of Britain that influenced Conan Doyle's decision, at the age of forty, to enlist in the Boer War as part of the medical corps. His fiction in turn routinely focusses on themes of physical prowess and bloody endeavour. In the historical novels *The White Company* (1891) and *Sir Nigel* (1906), for example, Conan Doyle paints an openly nostalgic picture of patriotic violence and soldierly conquest in fourteenth-century England. Indeed, even Sherlock Holmes was not above the occasional fistfight, being 'an expert singlestick player, boxer, and swordsman' (Doyle, 2006: 21).

In *The Lost World*, this trait can be seen in the characters of Malone, a prepossessing Irish rugby player, and Roxton, a keen hunter and adventurer modelled on the Irish diplomat and revolutionary republican Roger Casement. Yet such primitive masculinity finds its most sustained expression in the character of Professor Challenger. In part inspired by one of Conan Doyle's own professors in Edinburgh University, Challenger is at once 'famous zoologist' and physical behemoth—equally capable of imparting 'mental' and 'physical shocks' to those who cross him, and equally at home in the laboratory or the jungle trail, classroom or rainforest (Doyle, 2001: 8, 30). Variously described as 'an Assyrian bull', a 'bull-dog', and even a 'bull-frog', the professor boasts a 'huge spread of shoulders and a chest like a barrel', 'two enormous hands covered with long black hair', and 'a bellowing, roaring, rumbling voice' (15). His actions, furthermore, accord with his animalistic appearance: Challenger's first meeting with Malone results in a physical scuffle between the two, while his response to the subsequent complaints of his wife regarding his boorish behaviour is to physically restrain her, picking her up and depositing her on a high stool (19).

The character of Challenger is thus inseparable from his sheer physical exuberance: as Malone puts it in a later story, Challenger is, at heart, 'a primitive caveman in a lounge suit' (Doyle, 2010: 424). Indeed, in *The Lost World*, Malone dwells on Challenger's resemblance to the king of the ape-men: their likeness, as he writes, is one of 'absurd parody', with the two differing physically only in the shape of their respective skulls (Doyle, 2001: 123). These latter descriptions frame Challenger as a human atavism—a relic whose physical characteristics and turbulent personality belong more properly to an earlier stage in natural history. Nor is he alone in possessing such primal qualities: in the climactic battle with the ape-men on the plateau, each of the adventurers discovers within himself the 'strange red depths' to be found 'in the soul of the most commonplace man' (124). During the battle, Malone describes the 'blood lust' that wells up inside the adventurers, who consequently find themselves 'cheering and yelling with pure ferocity and joy of slaughter' as they systematically exterminate the ape-men (124).

This atavistic regression of the warring adventurers, and the physical likeness between Challenger and the king of the ape-men, reflect a broader nineteenth-century anxiety, expressed in such works as Stevenson's *Strange Case of Dr. Jekyll and Mr. Hyde* (1886) and Stoker's *Dracula* (1897), regarding the alarming possibility that human rationality is merely a veneer concealing a suppressed 'animal' nature. Certainly, as Malone writes, 'It needed a robust faith in the end'—the liberation of the Indians—'to justify such tragic means': the wholesale slaughter or enslavement of the population of ape-men (Doyle, 2001: 137).

Yet the novel *does* find the means to justify this violence, in two distinct ways. Firstly, it is significant that the resurgence of atavistic tendencies within humanity unfolds not in the cultured space of London, but in the wilderness of South America. Indeed, whenever this impulse towards physical violence emerges within civilised society, as it frequently does where Challenger is concerned, it is severely censured. Within ostensibly *un*civilised space, however, violence becomes an appropriate moral response to a wide variety of events. As Lewis Mumford remarks, imperialism provided 'a great safety valve for the aboriginal human impulses' denied expression in the 'methodical urban routine' of the metropolis, whose populations turned instead to 'the raw, unexplored, and relatively uncultivated regions of America and Africa' to act out fantasies of primitivism (1963: 295). Reflecting this imperialist trend, *The Lost World* offers a normative cartography in which codes of behaviour governing characters' actions become contingent on their physical location.

This connection is best viewed in the character of Roxton. In contrast to the undisciplined outbursts of Challenger, Roxton's violent actions are governed by a set of strict protocols dictated by whatever space he happens to be in. While in Britain, only the controlled violence of such a sport as rugby—'the manliest game we have left' (Doyle, 2001: 43)—or hunting is permissible. In contrast, 'the great waste lands and the wide spaces' at the peripheries of empire offer suitable arenas in which Roxton, with 'a gun in [his] fist and somethin' to look for that's worth findin', may exercise a propensity for bloodshed denied him in the 'soft and dull and comfy' centres of civilisation (45). Hence Roxton, years before the expedition, had single-handedly slain a group of 'slave-drivers' in Peru in a war '[d]eclared ... waged ... and ended' by him alone (44). Such vigilante justice—punishable by law when attempted in Britain, as Jefferson Hope in *A Study in Scarlet* (1888) discovers to his detriment— is conversely applauded when conducted at the outskirts of empire. Roxton's initial interest in the expedition to the plateau stems from the promise of the 'huntin' of beasts that look like a lobster-supper dream' (45). South America here functions not merely as an 'uncivilised' space in which a writer may situate their fantastic fictions, but as a *de*-civilising space in which a repressed European impulse towards irrational violence may be both given free rein and reinvested with moral purpose. This is a schema often repeated in Conan Doyle's fiction—in the stories of Sherlock Holmes, for example, in which the most brutal or grotesque episodes are often relocated to the outskirts of empire or, in a number of works, to the gothic landscapes of the American West.

Secondly, and at the same time, the novel also makes clear that acts of violence are not to be undertaken for their own sake, but must instead be directed and shaped by a European moral framework—'that great wall of individual responsibility', as Haggard writes in *She* (1887), 'that marks off mankind from the beasts' (1994: 197). In this, Conan Doyle drew on a nineteenth-century tradition of humanist thought that saw morality as a direct outcome of the processes of evolution. As Maurice Mandelbaum argues, thinkers such as Spencer, T.H. Huxley, and Darwin stressed the 'natural' cultivation of morality among humans, a process 'which involved a transformation of men from a condition in which they were dominated by appetite and instinct, to a condition in which knowledge, taste, and a feeling of being at one with others, were the sources of their fullest enjoyment' (1974: 214). Darwin, for example, saw morality as the result of social instincts among the 'higher' animals, leading to a higher chance of survival and even overtaking carnal drives as the principle basis for action. This leads naturally to an understanding of morality as a biological instinct centred on 'the general good of the group' (Mandelbaum, 1974: 227).

This perception of morality as a 'higher' natural principle accounts for Conan Doyle's inconsistent response to violent acts within *The Lost World*. Although, as Malone writes, it was 'a staggering and fearsome thought' that the dinosaurs of the plateau should 'deliberately track and hunt down the predominant human', he recognises that these beings cannot be blamed for their transgressions: they are, after all, 'practically brainless' (2001: 110, 112). In contrast, the ape-men are violent without reason, routinely flinging their captured Indian prisoners from the edge of the plateau onto a forest of sharp bamboos for the sake of cruel sport. The adventurers refuse to tolerate such violence, just as Conan Doyle himself refused to tolerate 'unrestrained' violence when employed by Europeans in the furtherance of imperial aims. In the years preceding the publication of *The Lost World*, Conan Doyle had waged an energetic campaign against the genocidal practices of the Congo Free State. Like Conrad, Conan Doyle was a frequent and vocal critic of the actions of King Leopold II in Africa and published a widely circulated pamphlet on the topic in 1909 entitled *The Crime of the Congo*. In contrast to the perceived civilising mission of the British empire, under which 'great nations' may flourish 'under the same flag with the same language and destinies' (Doyle, 2012: 310), the genocide and slavery presided over by Leopold constituted the 'greatest crime ever committed in the history of the world' (Doyle, 2008: 562). And what is worse, Conan Doyle goes on, is that 'all this has been tolerated in an age of progress' (Doyle, 2018b: ch. 8).

Hence, although *The Lost World*, as he wrote to Roger Casement in 1911, was 'frankly Jules Verney and fantastic so that no sober cause could be the better for it' (quoted in Wynne, 2002: 109), it is nevertheless difficult not to read the novel as attempting to redeem a certain notion of European imperialism. The 'chief thing' to be considered by any empire, Conan Doyle remarks, is its 'moral responsibility' to native populations—thus *The Lost World* ennobles its British protagonists while rebuking the ape-men for their amoral behaviour towards the Indians. In this light, the slaughter of the ape-men comprises not the technological genocide of a weaker people by a stronger but an evolutionary cleansing of a 'bad' imperialist civilisation that failed to develop the 'correct' moral sentiments. Like Haggard's Ayesha, 'unshackled by a moral sense of right and wrong', the ape-men thus find their amorality visited back on them in a disturbing and violent manner (Haggard, 1994: 197). The massacre of the ape-men is thus conceived as a fundamentally *moral* act—motivated not simply by their violence but also and more significantly by its apparent lack of any ethical or natural purpose. As Roxton states, by 'clear[ing] out the whole infernal gang' of the ape-men, the Englishmen were simply leaving the plateau 'a bit cleaner than [they] found it' (Doyle, 2001: 130).

In contrast to the amorality of the ape-men, the immediate affinity established between the explorers and the Indians—their physical resemblance as well as their improbable ability to 'converse' through gestures and facial expressions—suggests a kinship between these two groups. As Deane notes, 'the notion of a forgotten shared identity' between colonisers and colonised means 'that differences between peoples can be regarded as circumstantial rather than ontological' (2008: 216). This is a common trope of lost-world fiction from the Amahagger of Haggard's *She* to the Martians of Burroughs' *A Princess of Mars* (1912) and the *ladala* of A. Merritt's *The Moon Pool* (1919). At heart, such novels seem to suggest, we are all—'primitive' and 'civilised' alike—the same human species with the same desires and fears.

The Indians' aversion to useless violence, furthermore, suggests that the moral impulse guiding the adventurers and influencing their violent actions is rooted in evolutionary biology. In fact, it appears that the only difference separating the adventurers from the primitive Indians is the fledgling condition of the latter's technology: they do not lack the will to defeat the ape-men but merely the means, which arrive in the form of sturdy European rifles. The destruction of the ape-men can even be understood, in this light, as an extreme example of modernist creative destruction at work: in order for the Indians to 'escape' from the natural world of the plateau, the old irrational order of nature must be destroyed and they themselves advanced to the top of the natural hierarchy as a result. The Indians are thus figured as merely needing, in Said's term, 'a European presence' to jumpstart their evolutionary development (1994: 202). The trope of shared identity, then, reinforces the notion of the pre-human as sharing an ontological kinship, if not a level of technical or social sophistication, with the 'true' human, such that their behaviour becomes subject to moral regulation.

The temporal 'distance' between the adventurers and pre-human Indians and ape-men also informs the 'ideal' model of human society underpinning the novel. As with Verne's *Voyages*, the form of Conan Doyle's novel, and of much lost-world fiction, is that of a departure from and return to 'bourgeois normality' (Suvin, 1979: 151)—consequently, there can be no extraordinary revelations during the course of the journey that would radically disrupt that normality. The cyclical structures of imperial lost-world narratives are underpinned by the assumed permanency of European civilisation—the immunity of Doyle's London, in the case of *The Lost World*, to any substantial historical change. Yet Conan Doyle's novel *does* acknowledge temporal change of a different order, that is, geological, biological, astronomical, and other kinds of 'natural time' not directly experienced by the individual. Consider, for example, Challenger's description of the plateau, which characterises the space in specifically temporal terms:

> An area, as large perhaps as Sussex, has been lifted up *en bloc* with all its living contents, and cut off by perpendicular precipices of a hardness which defies erosion ... What is the result? Why, the ordinary laws of Nature are suspended. The various checks which influence the struggle for existence in the world at large are all neutralized or altered. Creatures survive which would otherwise disappear ... They have been artificially conserved by those strange accidental conditions (29).

The language used in this extract is explicitly Darwinian: the phrase 'checks which influence the struggle for existence' could have been lifted verbatim from the pages of *On the Origin of Species* (1859). The plateau, like the subterranean world of Verne's *Journey*, serves as a metonymic snapshot of a past still caught up in Darwinian time into which arrive the three variations of human: the ape-men who arrived in 'past ages', the native Indians, 'more recent immigrants from below', and finally the explorers themselves (Doyle, 2001: 129).

In other words, such works of lost-world fiction are premised on the assumption that the inevitable endpoint of all evolutionary history is the society—whether it be London, or Paris, or Hamburg (the home city of Verne's travellers in *Journey*), or any other imperial capital—from which its adventurers initially depart. Challenger himself makes this temporal framework explicit:

> 'We have been privileged,' he cried, strutting about like a gamecock, 'to be present at one of the typical decisive battles of history—the battles which have decided the fate of the world. What, my friends, is the conquest of one nation by another? It is meaningless. Each produces the same result. But those fierce fights, when in the dawn of the ages the cave-dwellers held their own against the tiger folk, or the elephants first found that they had a master, those were the real conquests—the victories that count. By this strange turn of fate we have seen and helped to decide even such a conquest. Now on this plateau the future must forever be man (Doyle, 2001: 136).

Those 'meaningless' wars between developed imperial nations are, according to Challenger, redundant in evolutionary terms—the real developments in the course of human progress are, for those nations, now relegated to the past. This temporal structure in *The Lost World* is imbued with particular significance given its own historical context: written on the eve of a war that was to shatter all notions of social or cultural stability (and Conan Doyle was well aware that such a war was a possibility),[3] the idea of social immunity to sudden ruptures must indeed have been a comforting one.

The adoption of circular narratives within the lost-world fiction of Verne and Conan Doyle, then, offers a means of resolving the tension between evolutionary and teleological frameworks of European historical development. I can perhaps follow the example of Brian Aldiss in terming such novels 'jolly journeys',[4] insofar as the conflicting temporal frameworks of centre and periphery—the opposition between a state of cultural 'Being' in the capitals of Europe and of primitive Darwinian 'Becoming' at the peripheries of empire—are reworked into a 'safe' circular framework that both acknowledges and neutralises the dynamics of Darwinian time. Given this temporal schema, it is apparent that any radical discoveries encountered during the fantastic sojourns of lost-world fiction must be treated as always-already enfolded within, and therefore neutralised by, the evolutionary terminus of advanced European civilisation.

The several 'types' of human on the plateau also form part of an ascending scale of human evolution—distinct stages in an evolutionary timeline that culminates in the rational European human. Beginning with the ape-men, atavistic relics of an amoral and thus redundant stage of evolution, it moves through the evolving Indians up to the dominant British adventurers. The Indians thus occupy a liminal position: both human and not human, they share the moral sympathies of their European counterparts, or as Challenger puts it, 'the instincts of the natural man', while lacking the technological or social sophistication that would gain them 'true' human status (Doyle, 2001: 132). The connection formed between the Indians and the Europeans is marked by a conflicting attitude towards the non-European that recognises their human potential while denying them full human rank—in evolutionary terms, the natives may one day be fully human, but *not yet*. The Indians, it might be said, are Europeans-in-waiting, or humans in natives' clothing—caught between civilisation and savagery and resembling

---

[3] See, for example, his short story 'Danger' (1914), one of the many 'future war' stories to appear in the years prior to the First World War, which, as I.F. Clarke notes, was 'propaganda in aid of the Channel Tunnel project' and 'won the interest of all Europe and the scorn of most naval experts'. See I.F. Clarke (1970: 103–5).

[4] I refer here to Aldiss's description of the post-apocalyptic works of John Wyndham as 'cosy catastrophes', referencing the fact that Wyndham's protagonists often find themselves in a position of remarkable physical and psychological well-being in the post-apocalyptic world. See Aldiss (1975: 335–6).

Kipling's 'Native States' in 'The Man Who Would Be King' (1888): 'touching the Railway and the Telegraph on one side, and, on the other, the days of Harun-al-Raschid' (Kipling, 1999: 303).

Darwinian evolution, then, serves two purposes in Conan Doyle's novel. On the one hand, it provides intellectual ballast for conceiving European civilisation and 'rational man' as the natural endpoints of history. On the other, it also provides a means by which to elevate a set of moral qualities as essentially—because 'naturally'—human, thereby providing normative justification for the domination and destruction of 'bad' humans. In this way, the novel inverts the moral structure of Shelley's *Frankenstein*: whereas the outwardly inhuman Creature is repudiated by those who fail to recognise his moral qualities, the outwardly 'human' ape-men are punished precisely for lacking those same qualities. In either case, the idea of the human is linked with a certain understanding of moral feeling, present in the Creature and absent in the ape-men, that is assumed to raise humanity above the level of the surrounding natural world.

Socialism, evolution, and the pre-human in London's *The Iron Heel*

Like Conan Doyle, Jack London has not yet gained much recognition as a writer of SF. Despite this, he produced a wide range of fiction—four longer works, and at least a dozen short stories—that falls under the umbrella of SF, fantasy, or speculative utopian writing. *The Iron Heel*, London's 1907 work of utopian socialism, represents both a continuation of and a break away from the nineteenth-century utopian tradition. Such works were a popular literary subject in the Anglophone world around the turn of the century: writers such as Wells, William Morris, W.H. Hudson, Charlotte Perkins Gilman, and others contributed to a well-established utopian tradition in *fin-de-siècle* literature, while one of the most popular and influential American novels of the period, Edward Bellamy's *Looking Backward* (1888), was a utopian work.

Both London's *The Iron Heel* and Bellamy's *Looking Backward* are concerned with the dehumanising conditions of turn-of-the-century industrial capitalism, and particularly the replacement of exploitative capitalist relations with socialist co-operation. The means by which the socialist society is achieved, however, differ markedly between each novel. The foundations of Bellamy's global utopia are steeped in the blood of neither labourer nor capitalist—rather, Bellamy's utopia quite simply *happens*, 'the result of a process of industrial evolution which could not have terminated otherwise' (Bellamy, 1986: 29). In this utopian future, the heads of industry were content to simply relinquish control of their trusts and corporations to the proletariat when it seemed that 'Public opinion was fully ripe for it, and the whole mass of the people was behind it' (33).

On the contrary, as Gorman Beauchamp notes, London 'was convinced that power is never relinquished from above, but must be wrested from below: not moral suasion nor lessons in economics, but superior force would alone suffice to overthrow the capitalist system and institute the era of socialist brotherhood' (1976: 311). In this, London followed Marx, who criticised the 'utopian socialism' of Fourier, Saint-Simon, Owens, and others who 'see in poverty nothing but poverty, without seeing in it the revolutionary, subversive side' (Marx, 1967: 99). *The Iron Heel*, as Beauchamp argues, should thus be understood as 'London's answer to the blithely optimistic belief of Bellamy that the plutocrat will roll over and play proletariat in the service of brotherhood' (1976: 312). Both writers offer a vision of a more hopeful human future—but where Bellamy attempts to give this hope a solid politico-economic shape, London instead offers a bleak warning about the bloodshed and sacrifices that will be required to get there.

London's firm political beliefs inform the humanist concerns of *The Iron Heel*. The novel depicts the formation, in the early twentieth-century US, of a tyrannical 'Oligarchy' comprised of capitalists, industry chiefs, and religious leaders, who impose their brutal autocratic will on the oppressed proletariat. While most of these 'wage slaves' accept their subjugated position, reverting to bestial status as the 'People of the Abyss', a small group of socialist revolutionaries secretly band together to form an underground movement committed to overthrowing the 'Iron Heel' (as the oligarchy comes to be called). Most of the novel takes the form of a manuscript written in the early twentieth century by capitalist-turned-revolutionary Avis Everhard, telling the story of her husband Ernest, one of the leaders of the revolutionary movement in its early days. This manuscript is then discovered and published in the twenty-seventh century, by which time the Iron Heel, after three hundred years of despotic rule, has finally been overthrown and society reformed into a socialist utopia. In addition to Avis's text, the novel also features an introduction and footnotes provided by a twenty-seventh-century historian, Anthony Meredith, who offers historical context for various events and characters in the manuscript. Meredith also hints at some of the features of the socialist society in which he lives—'the only utopia, surely', as Beauchamp remarks, 'ever to be couched exclusively in footnotes' (1976: 307).

Evolutionary dynamics, as I will argue, occupy a key position in *The Iron Heel*. Darwinian time functions in the novel to impel capitalism towards a socialist utopian ideal—what Nadia Khouri terms 'a state of biological equilibration' (1976: 180)—as society is determined by imperatives ostensibly derived from evolutionary theory. In embracing this notion of the 'inevitable' socialist utopia that will replace capitalist modernity, London deploys evolution in a comparable manner to Conan Doyle's *The Lost World*, using the dynamics of Darwinian time to naturalise a particular ideology concerning human civilisation. However, in contrast to the stable 'bourgeois normality' of Verne's and Conan Doyle's fiction, in which evolutionary forces affect only the 'primitive' spaces at the periphery of empire, the societies depicted in London's scientific romances, like those of Wells, are conceived as imperfect and susceptible to sudden and profound change. Hence, whereas Conan Doyle views European civilisation as the endpoint of evolutionary time, London instead reduces capitalist modernity to simply another stage in the evolution of human society and situates the culmination of history in a future socialist utopia.

But this notion of an evolutionary process edging the world towards socialism also shifts historical emphasis away from the human itself towards greater non-human processes. Indeed, the novel stresses the apparent redundancy of individual human action: the seeming historical inevitability of the revolutionary moment, as depicted by Avis, inspires a paradoxical sense of human fatalism in the face of unswerving evolutionary principles. Active human agency is thus sacrificed to a notion of social evolution as predestined towards a socialist utopian end. To recuperate some sense of individual human significance, London constructs an idealised version of the human captured in the figure of Ernest Everhard, while simultaneously characterising 'The People of the Abyss'—London's term for the working classes—as 'pre-human' foils to the perceived moral and physical rectitude of his protagonists. These pre-humans are, for London, the true victims of capitalist exploitations who, as will be seen, come to symbolise his anxieties regarding the tenuousness and fragility of nineteenth-century humanism.

I begin by examining the impact on London's fiction of evolutionary thought, stemming from his most significant literary predecessor, H.G. Wells. Wells had a substantial influence on the younger writer, and indeed the parallels between the lives of the two men are striking. Born ten years apart into working-class backgrounds, both were exposed at an early age to the degradation and tedium of late nineteenth-century industrialism—Wells in a draper's shop in Southsea, and London in a variety of industrial jobs in his native Oakland. In a bid to escape a life of menial labour, both succeeded, after some effort, in entering education, with Wells winning a scholarship to study biology under Thomas Huxley, and London entering, though never graduating from, the University of California, Berkeley. Both then turned to writing, eventually becoming two of the most influential writers of the period. And both, finally, were influenced from an early age by socialist and Darwinist ideas, using their fiction as a vehicle to challenge the injustices of capitalism and explore the possibility of a socialist future.

By the time of London's first professional publication in 1899, Wells was already well established in both Britain and the United States. London acknowledges the influence of the older writer on *The Iron Heel*: in his notes of 1906, he states that he will 'Perhaps write a novel, a la Wells, out of the idea of wage slaves, ruled by industrial oligarchs, finally ceasing to reproduce', a work that he tentatively titled 'CAPTAINS OF INDUSTRY' (quoted in Labor, 2013: ch. 19). London is likely referring to Wells's *When the Sleeper Wakes* (1899), which shares with London's novel a sense of dread concerning the dehumanising conditions of industrial capitalism. The form of Wells's romances, as Suvin remarks, usually consists of some ordinary 'outer framework' whose serenity is shaken by the sudden arrival of a 'destructive newness', which allows Wells to critique the inequalities and complacencies of *fin-de-siècle* British society (1979: 208). Hence Wells's speculative fiction contrasts sharply with the fantastic expeditions of Verne: his stories are rooted in the transformation of the familiar spaces—the small country villages, or middle-class households—of Britain itself. Even when his narratives do centre on expeditions to far-flung places, his protagonists rarely return to the everyday world unchanged. Edward Prendick in *The Island of Doctor Moreau* (1896), for instance, becomes a recluse from humanity following his experiences on the island of the 'Beast Folk', while neither the Traveller in *The Time Machine* (1895) nor Cavor in *The First Men in the Moon* (1901) succeeds in returning at all. The radical sociocultural upheaval and the fragility of the European psyche suggested by Wells's works are clearly at odds with the static social orders of Verne's *Voyages*. For Wells, as for Nietzsche, European society was characterised by a mistaken sense of invulnerability to historical change.

The projected impermanency of 'bourgeois normality' and its susceptibility to radical change were themes later picked up and portrayed with tremendous force in *The Iron Heel*. As with Wells, London viewed evolution not as a remote process affecting only the outskirts of civilisation, but as an active force determining the very shape of capitalist society and human history. His 1906 novel, *Before Adam*, for instance, depicts a twentieth-century man afflicted with 'race memories'—'vast and terrific vistas' revealing 'the progression of life, not upward from ape to man, but upward from the worm'. These race memories, according to the narrator, connect contemporary humanity to 'the raw beginnings of mankind', with 'Evolution [as] the key': each human, according to the narrator, carries within them 'a memory of [the] past-day experiences' of their direct ancestors, made accessible during the unconscious processes of sleep (2005a: 35). As Lawrence Berkove notes, 'Among the many intellectual influences on Jack London, none is so central and profound as that of Darwin' (2004: 243), except perhaps the social Darwinist ideas of Herbert Spencer and T.H. Huxley.

London's integration of evolutionary dynamics into *The Iron Heel* is joined to his concerns regarding the exploitative socio-economic formations of the late nineteenth-century United States. London can be placed alongside several early twentieth-century socialist writers, including Upton Sinclair, Theodore Dreiser, and Frank Norris, whose works directly address the brutal conditions of nascent industrial capitalism and 'finance capital'. His 1908 short story, 'A Curious Fragment', for example, takes the form of a recorded narrative from the twenty-sixth century, 'the fifth century of the terrible industrial oligarchy', in which a rebellious slave confronts a ruling 'capitalist' with the severed arm of his fellow worker. Another popular story, 'The Strength of the Strong' (1914), set in the early days of humanity, highlights both the hypocrisies of capitalism and the complicity of religion in underpinning the capitalist ethos. London even devoted several months in 1902 to living and working in the East End of London, culminating in 1903 with his publication of *The People of the Abyss* (a phrase he borrowed from Wells), a journalistic account of the misery and squalor of the capital's urban poor. Already in such works we can see an emerging anti-industrial humanist narrative: industrialisation, London remarks, with its extremes of urban poverty and brutal labour conditions, can amount only to 'an unnatural life for the human' in sharp contrast to 'the fresh virile life from the country' (London, 2013: 34).

In *The Iron Heel*, the rise of capitalist modernity is viewed as simply another phase in the continuing process of human evolution, and a particularly grim one at that:

> We must accept the capitalist stage in social evolution as about on par with the earlier monkey stage. The human had to pass through these stages in its rise from the mire and slime of low organic life. It was inevitable that much of the mire and slime should cling and be not easily shaken off (London, 2005b: 187).

As protagonist and working-class philosopher Ernest Everhard says to the capitalist barons whom he has vowed to overthrow, 'you have not studied social evolution at all. You are in the midst of a transition stage now of an economic evolution' (101). Darwinian evolution in *The Iron Heel*, as in *The Lost World*, is here deployed to support an understanding of a particular human social formation as the 'natural' endpoint of historical evolutionary time—however, now it is the 'developed' societies, rather than 'primitive' spaces, that remain imbricated within evolutionary dynamics, subject to sudden upheavals that may radically alter the social landscape.

Yet, for all its influence on his thought, London is inconsistent in his responses to evolutionary thought. In *The Iron Heel* and other works, London wavers between an understanding of evolution as, on the one hand, a natural force whose operations are entirely blind and impersonal and, on the other, a social force that can be directed towards the attainment of specific ideological ends. Capitalism in *The Iron Heel* is presented both as a natural stage in the evolution of humanity *and* as a human evil to be crushed. Its collapse, Everhard insists, is inevitable, and yet the bloody scenes of the 'Chicago Commune'—a failed 'first blow at the nervous system of the Oligarchy', undertaken by the revolutionaries at the climax of the narrative (London, 2005b: 219)—dramatise the violence required to challenge entrenched authorities. These depictions of the Commune were inspired by the frequent manufacturing strikes of the late nineteenth- and early twentieth-century US, of which London was a vocal supporter and frequent participant. The fierce encounter with established authority, and its recreation in London's fiction, offered a stark warning that any challenge to the orthodox socio-economic narrative, though necessary, will be bloody and, more than likely, a failure. Yet the narrative framework of London's novel—the 'meta-setting' located in the eventual socialist utopia—also leaves no doubt that those powers would eventually succumb to the will of the proletariat, 'whether it is in one year, ten, or a thousand' (79).

This tension between historical determinism and individual political agency is most clearly embodied in the character of Ernest Everhard, London's 'superman, a blond beast such as Nietzsche has described' (2005b: 17), and clearly an idealised image of London himself. In the admiring and hyperbolic prose of his wife Avis, Ernest is the revolution itself personified, a furious and energetic opponent of the conceits and hypocrisies of bourgeois capitalism. The characterisation of Everhard demonstrates the extent to which, however much he aspired to emulate the older writer in other regards, London diverged from Wells's beliefs concerning the proper path of socialist development.

Whereas Wells's attitudes towards such development were broadly Fabian in nature, focusing on the need for improved education and technological advancement,[5] London's were a potent mix of Marx and Nietzsche. For him, the transition to socialism would come about not through the education of the masses, but through bloody revolution led by charismatic overmen.

Notwithstanding his larger-than-life aspect, however, Everhard's eventual place in history, as future historian Anthony Meredith remarks, is 'not so exceptional' as Avis would have us believe: he is 'but one of many able leaders' of the revolutionary movement (2005b: 11, 27). This recasting of the charismatic hero of the novel as merely one historical figure among many allows London, as Khouri remarks, 'to reject in the footnotes the idea of a unique hero and advance that of many heroes' (1976: 177). At one point in the novel, Everhard participates in a confrontational debate with the 'Philomaths', a social club consisting of intellectuals and business and religious leaders. To these emblematic representatives of invested authority, Everhard appears not as an individual but as 'the spirit of regnant labour ... his hands that had appeared in their eyes were the hands of the fifteen hundred thousand revolutionists' (London, 2005b: 69, 72).

Jonathan Berliner argues that such ambiguous characterisation— London's vacillation between Everhard as larger-than-life Übermensch on the one hand, and collective symbol of impassive historical forces on the other—results from the merger of Darwinian and socialist thought within revolutionary literature of the time (Berliner, 2008: 61). In this formulation, socialism appears both as a social force to be proactively harnessed in the here-and-now *and* as a natural state to be attained through inexorable evolutionary principles. The process of socialist development is thus, Berliner argues, 'a dialectical one, with the social process supported by the natural one' (61). Socialism, in other words, was regarded in much early twentieth-century socialist literature as a natural state as much as a social one. Indeed, such an understanding

---

[5] Raymond Williams, for example, suggests that Wells's utopian imagination is underpinned by 'social engineering', 'rapidly developing technology', and a 'clean, orderly, efficient and planned (controlled) society' (2011: 105). *When the Sleeper Wakes* is unusual among Wells's works in this regard, ending with the oppressed citizens of London revolting against Ostrog, their dictatorial leader. Given, however, that Ostrog himself began as a revolutionary who overthrew the oligarchic 'White Council' then betrayed the working classes by refusing to end their exploitation, it is also possible to read the novel as a critique of revolution as an ineffective political tool vulnerable to the corrupting influence of charismatic leadership. See Williams (2011: 93–112).

informs Bellamy's *Looking Backward*: 'All that society had to do', observes a citizen of the future, reflecting on the nineteenth century, 'was to recognise and cooperate with ... evolution, when its tendency had become unmistakeable' (1986: 29). We find similar ideas running throughout London's socialist thought. As he writes in an essay from 1902, under the direction of 'Natural Selection' the proletariat will inexorably move from 'chattel slavery to serfdom, and from serfdom to ... "wage slavery"', onwards towards the day 'that all labor shall become conscious of itself and its class interests' (London, 1964: 433). Everhard, in this sense, is not so much an individual—since any true socialist, as London argues in 'How I Became a Socialist' (1903), will have had the 'individualism effectively hammered out of [them]'—as he is a representative of a social class operating under irresistible natural principles (London, 1964: 365).

The effect of such historical determinism is to undercut the ability of London's characters to act as true historical agents. The dramatic political energy of the Chicago Commune, for example, is severely weakened by the narrative logic of London's 'mathematically ... inevitable' revolution (London, 2005b: 114)—the failure of the revolutionaries to claim Chicago cannot truly be said to matter since the socialist revolution, we are assured, will in any case occur. *The Iron Heel* is caught between what Stephen Kern (borrowing from Eugene Minkowski) calls the 'active' and 'expectant' modes of futurological experience. Whereas in the 'active' mode, Kern remarks, 'the individual goes towards the future, driving into the surroundings in control of events, in the mode of expectation the future comes toward the individual, who contracts against an overpowering environment' (Kern, 2003: 89–90). Kern points to the Fordist factory as instigating a shift in the modes of time experienced by labourers and manufacturers: 'The assembly line and Taylorism ... relegated [the labourer] to an expectant mode, waiting for the future to come along the line, at the same time increasing the manufacturer's control' (92). These two modes, which for Kern comprise the characteristic ways of experiencing time during the *fin-de-siècle* period, are marked by active and passive orientations towards historical change: the active individual forges their own path through the future, while the expectant individual waits for the future to wash over them.

It is therefore significant that, only four years before the publication of *The Iron Heel*, Henry Ford had founded the Ford Motor Company in Michigan, a corporation later to become a key symbol (as I will examine in more detail in the next chapter) of the decreasing levels of agency available to individuals within the 'iron cage' of capitalist modernity—a 'machine age', as Mumford terms it, that 'limits the actions and movements of human beings to their bare mechanical elements' (1963: 41). London's personal experience of industrial labour conditions—he had seen 'the walls of the Social Pit rise around' him (London, 1964: 365)—led him to a strong critique of its practices. His fiction consistently imagines an escape or retreat from the 'special forms of brutality' characteristic of industrial capitalism: to the unfettered reaches of the Pacific in *The Sea Wolf* (1904), the Alaskan wilderness in *The Call of the Wild* (1903), the early days of pre-technological humanity in *Before Adam*, a post-apocalyptic future in *The Scarlet Plague* (1912), or a host of pre-modern historical eras in *The Star Rover* (1915). In such imaginative spaces, human action can again become qualitative: the conflicts between Wolf Larsen and Van Weyden in *The Sea Wolf*, 'Big-Tooth' and 'Red-Eye' in *Before Adam*, or Buck and Spitz in *The Call of the Wild* become allegorical enactments of human conflict with natural forces.

The Iron Heel specifically adopts as its setting the industrial landscapes of early twentieth-century America, a context from which the means of escape were much less clear. The lack of an obvious 'out' from modernity perhaps accounts for London's failure to narrate the actual moment of revolutionary change: *The Iron Heel* depicts the consolidation of autocratic capitalist authority and gestures towards a future socialist society, but does not indicate how the radical transition from the former to the latter is to be achieved. In the context of capitalist modernity, the desirable shape of effective human political agency—the resolution of the allegorical conflict between capitalists and revolutionaries—is simply not forthcoming. Rather, the moment of successful revolution takes the form, as Allesandro Portelli argues, of a missing link in the narrative:

> Too often, the essential [revolutionary] part of the story is placed in blanks, in gaps: this suggests that the impossibility of naming and describing the revolution is a recurrent motif in American literature. Revolution—the violent substitution of one order with another—is a 'black hole' in the national consciousness. ... The People of the Abyss, the death of the hero, the social revolution—all are untold. This structure implicitly tells us more about London's attitude toward revolution than all his explicit political statements (1982: 182–3).

London, in effect, kicks the can of revolutionary 'Becoming'—an unrepresentable moment linking two antithetical poles of dystopian and utopian 'Being'—into the future without attempting to elucidate its exact shape, and so the precise mode of enactment of the 'natural' utopian society of the twenty-seventh century remains elusive.

The failure of *The Iron Heel* to reveal how its utopia may be materially achieved suggests the novel's investment in what Jameson terms 'wish-fulfilment': a yielding to 'some naïvely satisfied and satisfying realization' that undercuts its potential as a guide to political praxis (2005: 83). 'Wish-fulfilments', Jameson notes, are 'by definition never real fulfilments of desire; and must presumably be marked by the hollowness of absence or failure at the heart of their most dearly fantasized visions' (2005: 83). The absence in *The Iron Heel* is that revolutionary step of 'Becoming' that escapes representation: even as London 'accumulate[s] the objections and the reality problems that stand in its way so as the more triumphantly and "realistically" to overcome them', he remains reticent on the nature of this moment of 'Becoming' (2005: 83). Despite his commitment 'to Marxist communism to an extent seldom equalled', as William J. Burling remarks (2009: 240), London's work fails perhaps the most important Marxian test: his Marxism is idealist rather than materialist, more a product of his ideological and metaphysical preoccupations than of engagement with the material realities of the turn-of-the-century US. This in turn weakens its subversive energy as a critique of the manifest degradation and dehumanisation inherent in the processes of industrial capitalism.

At the same time, the novel promotes a specific variant of historical materialism that shifts the locus of agency away from individual humans towards a form of historical determinism that stresses 'Humanity', rather than individual humans, as the true actor in history. This places London in sharp contrast to Wells, who conversely insisted on the need within any utopia to defend the sanctity and agency of the human individual. Wells characterised capitalist society as 'the world of the Crowd', made up of 'Thousands and thousands of swarming people'—for him, socialism offered the only means by which to 'exalt and ennoble the individual' (2016: 286) by ensuring that the individual is not subjugated to economic demands of production and consumption. In *A Modern Utopia* (1904), Wells insists on 'the individual difference as the significance of life' and lambasts the 'hardness and thinness' of 'Utopian speculations' that contain 'no individualities, but only generalised people' (2017: 209). Wells was thus aware, to a greater extent than London, of the conflict that may arise between the desires of the individual and the demands of society, and saw the ideal society as 'a universal becoming of individualities'—a collective mass of distinct individual personalities (215).

The narrative gap generated by London's failure to imagine the material shape of his revolution, conversely, can be read as corresponding to the absence of human agency itself, which in the context of an increasingly bureaucratic modernity had become ever more difficult to imagine. *The Iron Heel*, like Wells's utopian works, enacts the conflict between the individual and the social—but in contrast to Wells, in London's novel it is the latter that is given precedence in his evolutionary notion of utopian socialism. By prioritising socio-evolutionary determinism over meaningful human agency, *The Iron Heel* adopts what might be called an *anti*-humanist position—that is, a rejection of the classical humanist positioning of the individual human as the most relevant or significant political actor.

Turning now to the actual form of the human in the novel, however, this position is partially tempered by London's commitment to a model of the 'ideal' human, familiar from nineteenth-century humanism, as one which synthesised qualities of intellectual refinement and physical fortitude along the lines suggested by Deane's 'primitive masculinity'. As with Conan Doyle's work, London's novel evinces a variety of anxieties regarding the distinction between 'animal' and 'human'—even on a purely stylistic level, London's prose is littered with references to 'savage' nature, with every class open to comparison with some natural entity or other. Hence, the working class are first 'lambs sold into slavery and worked to death' (2005b: 37) before being transformed into the 'abysmal beast' (216); the 'Philomaths' are 'cave-[men], in evening dress, snarling and snapping over a bone' (64); the press are a 'parasitic growth' (92); the street mob in the climactic 'Chicago Commune' move with 'the blind squirm of the monster' (240); and the heads of industry are, among other things, 'arch-beasts' (87), purveyors of the 'frightful brutality and savagery' (36) of 'dog eat dog' capitalism (100).

Indeed, the principal conflict underpinning much of London's fiction is that between the refined intellect and the savage beast—between the rule of 'mind' and the rule of 'body'. As Portelli notes, London's work forms part of a naturalist tradition 'in which rationality, spirituality, and culture are opposed to the body, to the instincts, to the atavistic remains of man's animal nature' (1982: 187). One of the most famous literary creations of the twentieth century, Burroughs' *Tarzan of the Apes* (1914), was also the product of such an opposition. John Taliaferro argues that Tarzan is a mixture of 'Old World and New', equally comfortable in 'loincloth' and 'tailored suit' (in Burroughs, 2003: xv–xvi). Alongside his rippling body and lion-wrestling prowess, Tarzan possesses a 'clever little mind' and a 'divine power of reason' (Burroughs, 2003: 44)—qualities put to good use in his transformation, over the course of that first novel, from vine-swinging jungle being to the beau of French aristocratic society. Both Tarzan and Everhard are visions of the 'ideal man' of the early twentieth-century American imagination: a potent synthesis of rugged animal physicality and refined social and intellectual rationality, viewed by both London and Burroughs as the most compelling manifestation of the human.

Indeed, London himself was an embodiment of the 'primitive masculinity' that Deane, as outlined above, associated with much nineteenth-century lost-world fiction. By turns a working-class labourer, oyster pirate, deckhand on a sailing schooner, vagrant, prospector in the Alaskan Yukon, ranch owner, and captain of a round-the-world sailing vessel, London's own life encapsulated the frontier ideals of rugged individualism and romantic self-realisation described by Frederick Turner in his famous 1893 essay, 'The Significance of the Frontier in American History'. 'Virility in a man', London declared, 'first and always', while elsewhere he states that 'the man who is afraid to take the fish off the hook or the guts from the bird he expects to eat is no man at all' (quoted in Labor, 2013: ch. 11: 14). London's propensity for physical exploits and his lifelong urge, as he wrote in a letter in 1905, to get 'back to nature to be made well again' emerge in his fiction in the qualities of bodily strength and fortitude with which he routinely endows his—almost exclusively male—protagonists (London and Stoddard, 2000: 109).

At the same time, however, London was all too aware of the perils associated with an over-reliance on the body, having experienced first-hand the physical strains and degradations of industrial labour. As he wrote in 1903, London swore from an early age not to *'do another day's hard work with my body than I absolutely have to do'*, since that way lay 'the bottom of the Pit' (1964: 364). Progress, he saw, was dependent on a strong brain as well as a strong body, since 'reason is mightier than imagination' and 'the scientific man ... superior to the emotional man' (quoted in Labor, 2013: ch. 1). London's attitudes towards intellectual refinement were not wholly consistent: as he wrote to his father in 1900, he would quickly 'sicken' of 'the hammering away and the hammering away' after purely objective knowledge that he saw as characteristic of the academic life (Stoddard and London, 2000: 106). Nevertheless, following a brief spell in a New York prison in 1894 on a vagrancy charge, London worked hard to educate himself: as biographer Earle Labor writes, he 'realized that education would lead him out of the Pit', out of a life of physical and industrial drudgery and onto a more rewarding intellectual path (Labor, 2013: ch. 6).

London thus 'inverted the nineteenth-century middle class's aversion to the muscular body', and instead 'depicts brutishness as eminently clean and socially uplifting' (Berliner, 2008: 61–2). It is in *The Iron Heel*, and in the figure of Ernest Everhard, that London best succeeds in capturing this synthesis of mind and body. Everhard, with his 'bulging muscles' and 'bull throat' (London, 2005b: 17), encapsulates the distinctive form of physical masculinity later immortalised in Burroughs' Tarzan. At the same time, his socialism takes Marx's 'Eleventh Thesis' to heart, offering a materialist praxis in which metaphysical abstractions are useless until translated into qualitative empirical action. Everhard is 'simple, direct, afraid of nothing', his 'sledge-hammer manner of attack' adopted during his intellectual debates with authority figures shattering the idealisms of the aristocratic 'metaphysicians' of Christendom and the bourgeoisie alike (17, 19). Everhard thus emerges as an idealised Rousseauean type exemplifying both human rationality and animal physicality.

Such paragons also appear in many of London's other works. The notion of ideal balance between body and mind informs the clash between the brutal Wolf Larsen and 'soft' Van Weyden in *The Sea Wolf* (1904), and in the conversion of Van Weyden from pampered intellectual to capable sea-hand over the course of that novel. The difficulties of attaining this balance, meanwhile, can be glimpsed in the submerged 'racial memories' that haunt the protagonists of 'When the World Was Young' (1913) and *Before Adam*. In this latter text, the atavistic 'Red-Eye', a cruel and aggressive early hominid representative of an earlier stage in human evolution, falls victim to the more intellectually sophisticated 'Fire People'—a clear instance of the imperfect human variant succumbing to a more 'improved' successor. It can also be seen (albeit in modified form) in the reversion to wildness of the once-tame Buck in *The Call of the Wild* (1903), and in the contrasting domestication of the savage dog-wolf in *White Fang* (1906), both of which emphasise the need to temper the instincts of the body with those of the mind and vice versa.

The preoccupation with combining human refinement with natural power can be detected even in the space of nature itself in London's works. It is significant that, as the Oligarchs of *The Iron Heel* are constructing the sprawling wonder-cities of 'Ardis' and 'Asgard', the revolutionaries, with Everhard at their head, instead retire into nature— to an estate in the Sonoma Mountains where, like London, they may recharge both physically and spiritually. Nature for London is not simply to be equated with Tennyson's 'red in tooth and claw': as he writes in *The Scarlet Plague*, the idyllic rural landscape consists not of a 'sea of rank vegetation' resulting from 'pure' nature, but rather of a domesticated and 'splendidly tilled' agricultural landscape (London, 2005a: 159).[6] The

---

[6] In this, London is once again following the example of Wells, in whose

central distinction between the revolutionaries and Oligarchs thus takes the form of a spatial distinction between georgic rurality and industrial urbanity, while the novel symbolically registers the 'ideal' human as a synthesis of natural *and* human qualities from which the urbane capitalists—and the dehumanising processes of urban industrialism more generally—represent an aberrant break.

At the same time as they promote this 'ideal' form of human, however, London's works are also persistently troubled by ideas of evolutionary degeneracy—a fear that 'regressive' forms of humanity might threaten to overthrow the 'ideal' human and cast humanity back into a state of unregulated barbarism. In *The Scarlet Plague*, for example, a 1914 work set in a post-apocalyptic world in which a deadly virus has wiped out most of humanity, survivor Edwin describes to his grandchildren the catastrophic devolution of the working classes:

> In the midst of our civilisation, down in our slums and labor-ghettos, we had bred a race of barbarians, of savages; and now, in the time of our calamity, they turned on us like the wild beasts they were and destroyed us. And they destroyed themselves as well (2005a: 148).

In the wake of the pandemic depicted in this work, the whole of western humanity succumbs to a process of evolutionary degeneration to a more 'primitive' state: Edwin's grandsons, for example, are described as 'true savages', who wear necklaces of human teeth and speak only in 'monosyllables and short jerky sentences' (129). The anxiety here concerns human moral and intellectual regression and the subsequent reversal of historical progress: 'The human race', Edwin laments, 'is doomed to sink back farther and farther into the primitive night ere again it begins its bloody climb upward to civilisation' (129).

This anxiety is projected particularly on the working classes, who feature prominently in several of London's works as 'The People of the Abyss'. London's use of this term as a descriptor of the working classes changes significantly over time. In *The People of the Abyss*, published in 1903, for example, the tone adopted towards the English working poor wavers uneasily between sympathy and contempt for 'the miserable multitudes' of the East End. By the time of *The Iron Heel*, four years later, this contempt for the 'machine-serfs and labor-serfs' of industrial

---

scientific romances, as I have argued elsewhere, the countryside functions as a utopian liminal space between the unnatural conditions of the city and the 'violence' of pure nature. See Connolly (2017).

capitalism has crystallised into open hostility (2005b: 216). The People of the Abyss as depicted in *The Iron Heel* constitute 'the great helpless mass of the population' who, on being released from the slums of Chicago, abandon all moral or social binds whatsoever, turning instead to acts of senseless violence (216). They are subsequently described in some of the most disturbing language of the novel:

> men, women, and children, in rags and tatters, dim ferocious intelligences with all the godlike blotted from their features and all the fiendlike stamped in, apes, and tigers, anaemic consumptives and great hairy beasts of burden ... withered hags and death's heads bearded like patriarchs, festering youth and festering age, faces of fiends, crooked, twisted, misshapen monsters ... the refuse and the scum of life, a raging, screaming, screeching, demoniacal horde (232–3).

This passage and others describing the People of the Abyss are written in explicitly dehumanising language: the workers are 'herded' from place to place, mere 'beasts ... housed in wretched barracks where family life cannot exist, and where decency is displaced by dull bestiality' (216). Like the ape-men of Conan Doyle's *The Lost World*, the 'fiends' of the Chicago slums, who attack indiscriminately and lack any more moral direction, are assigned no moral value. They are not merely 'animals', but animals who were once human—they thus figure as an explicitly degenerate form of humanity, a devolved inhuman mass whose regression to an ostensibly pre-human intellectual and physical state is negatively contrasted with the moral and physical integrity of Everhard and the other revolutionaries.

In one sense, this characterisation of the proletariat can be correlated to London's wider views on race: London was, of course, a well-known exponent of the fears in the early twentieth-century US regarding the so-called 'Yellow Peril', evident in such stories as 'The Unparalleled Invasion', published in 1914, in which the population of China is characterised as a 'fearful tide ... a monstrous flood of life' (2005b: 309, 311). Yet London's treatment of the working classes appears particularly puzzling: the proletariat are, after all, the purported benefactors of his very explicit Marxist sympathies. The fear here is one of integration—of becoming a passive victim of a faceless and overpowering multitude. In *The People of the Abyss*, for example, the working classes are described as 'a vast and malodorous sea, lapping about me and threatening to well up and over me' (London, 2013: 8). In another passage, London describes the People of the Abyss as a 'noisome and rotten tide of humanity', an evolutionary aberration whose future, marked by 'the deadly inertia that precedes dissolution', is destined to be a degenerate one (2013: 22, 33). The emphasis on inertia here reveals the true motivation for London's resentments: the working classes are simply impotent, incapable of realising the potential of their lives in the way that London felt he had realised the potential of his own. Despite his socialist inclinations, London returned repeatedly to vibrantly realised *Übermensch* in his fiction, a propensity towards self-realisation that also prevented him from fully exonerating the working classes from at least part of the blame for their own destitution.

London's characterisation of 'ideal' and 'degenerate' human types thus arises from his opposing individualist and communist beliefs: the People of the Abyss are figured as redundant and passive victims of history, swept aside by the emergence of the 'ideal' physical and moral actors of the revolution—even as the actual form of this revolutionary action, as discussed above, can never be portrayed. Yet this pre-human figure also has the unintended effect of highlighting the contingency of its 'ideal' counterpart. The 'pre-' in 'pre-human' points to its nature as antecedent—it is what comes before the human—but its recurrent re-emergence in London's fiction also points to its presence *alongside* the human in London's thought. It is not merely what came before, but what is always there, threatening to emerge and engulf humanity's rational nature and return the human, as Edwin writes in *The Scarlet Plague*, to the 'primitive night'. London's works gesture—continuously and, I suggest, reluctantly—towards the contingency of the humanist narrative itself. Even as he constructs his ideal human, London is persistently troubled by its ephemerality, its very constructedness, threatened by those same qualities that his works attempt to negate: barbarism, primitiveness, brutality, amorality, and all the other qualities that the humanist tradition had expunged from the human. In its role as scapegoat sacrificed on the altar of the 'truly' human, the pre-human comes to function as the manifest trace of humanism's attempts to govern the form of the human itself.

Like Conan Doyle, then, London incorporated a multitude of human 'types' into his work. His deep commitment to the social communism of Marx clashed inevitably with his own tenets of Nietzschean-infused individualism and self-affirmation. The threat of the working multitudes can be read, in humanist terms, as the threat posed by the mass of the population to the individual human—the fear that the species may end up taking precedence over the individual human being. The division between the revolutionaries on one side, who combine physical potency with intellectual and moral fortitude and thus occupy a median position between animality and rationality, and the degenerate and amoral 'People of the Abyss' on the other, reproduces the imagined gulf, familiar from *The Lost World*, between 'idealised' and 'regressive' variants of the human.

Conclusion

I am now able to draw some crucial parallels between Conan Doyle's *The Lost World* and London's *The Iron Heel*. Both works recast the human subject in animalistic terms: Challenger and Everhard are representatives of what Deane terms 'primitive masculinity'—a merging of the rational qualities of the human with the violent strength of the animal. This violence is, however, in both cases distinguished from the amoral violence of 'bad' pre-humans—the ape-men and the 'People of the Abyss'—whose barbarity is without ostensible moral or social function and must therefore be repressed. The moral boundaries between the human and the animal are in this way modified without, crucially, being overturned: the inescapable violence of imperial expansion and the brutal processes of industrialisation are assimilated into a pre-existing moral framework as *necessary* forms of violence—'modifications', as Spencer might put it—undertaken in the service of 'completing' or sustaining the evolution of human civilisation.

It is useful here to draw a line between, on the one hand, the speculative works of Verne and Conan Doyle and, on the other, those of Wells and London. Whereas the former two authors conceive of Darwinian time as having already reached its *telos* in imperial and capitalist Europe, London and Wells conceive of industrial capitalist society as just another stage on the evolutionary path of socio-natural time. All these writers, however, shift the emphasis from the present of socially realist fiction to either the past or the future, and define their respective ideal societies—for the former, bourgeois imperial Europe, and for the latter, a future socialist utopia—in terms of evolutionary development. Each writer suggests that, whether viewed as the end of evolution, or as a species-in-the-making, humanity is always at the top of the ladder.

To return to the two lineages of the human outlined above, it is clear that the image of humanity that emerges from *The Lost World* corresponds with the chauvinist imperial humanism of Verne's *Voyages* rather than the more sceptical or circumspect position adopted by Shelley and, later, Wells. London's work, despite the influence of Wells, demonstrates a similar position, although his commitment to a radical form of historical determinism, as shown, also means that his larger-than-life human figures are mostly stripped of any meaningful political or social agency. Given this, it may be most accurate to say that *The Iron Heel* wavers between a Nietzschean interpretation of humanity as self-realising actors on the one hand and a notion of grand evolutionary determinism on the other. Broadly speaking, both *The Lost World* and *The Iron Heel* remain committed to a human-centred view of the world, or to what in the introduction I described as an assimilative mode of humanist narrative: their concerns are firmly centred on *bios*—on human life and human society—and the humans that populate their works are immediately recognisable from the humanist discourses of the nineteenth century.

In relation to both works, the most significant posthumanist motif to be found is, of course, the figure of the pre-human. The pre-human functions as the portrait in the attic, so to speak, of the humanist narrative of the *fin-de-siècle* period, symbolising all those human beings—the victims of colonial expansion, or of the dehumanising conditions of urban industrialisation—on whom were visited the sins of progress. As suggested above, however, this liminal position also imbues the pre-human with subversive potential: its very hybridity—what Halberstam and Livingstone call its 'someness', being neither fully human nor inhuman—undermines and transforms the hierarchical binaries of humanist thought. This threat is nullified in both works discussed here. Nevertheless, these qualities of liminality, hybridity, and 'someness' will prove essential in future SF works to developing more critical ideas regarding the human.

Chapter Two

Soma and Skylarks: Technocracy, agency, and the trans-human in Aldous Huxley's *Brave New World* and E.E. 'Doc' Smith's *Skylark* series

In a 1957 essay, Julian Huxley, brother to Aldous, outlined what he saw as twentieth-century humanity's 'inescapable destiny':

> The human species can, if it wishes, transcend itself—not just sporadically, an individual here in one way, an individual there in another way, but in its entirety, as humanity. We need a name for this new belief. Perhaps *transhumanism* will serve: man remaining man, but transcending himself, by realizing new possibilities of and for his human nature (1957: 17).

Huxley's notion of 'transhumanism' here is remarkably similar to later accounts of the phenomenon. In an essay published in *Extropy: the journal for transhumanist thought* in 1990, transhumanist philosopher Max More echoes Huxley's essay by defining the ultimate goal of humanity as 'expansionary transcendence': 'Life and intelligence ... must re-order, transform and transcend its limits in an unlimited progressive process. ... As extropians pursuing and promoting transcendent expansion we are the vanguard of evolution' (1990: 10). The 'trans-human' is a being at once human and more than human, penetrated and shaped by technological systems. For Huxley and More, the trans-human is a milestone on the road to humanity's utopian destiny. Yet utopia can all too easily revert to its opposite: far from serving as a neutral means for achieving ultimate human perfection, 'utopian' technology can also wrest agency from the humans it is supposed to serve.

The trans-human is the archetypal human figure for this chapter, which will focus on the SF of the interwar period. This was a crucial time for both SF, which crystallised as a genre in the pulp magazines from the mid-1920s onwards, and for the humanist project, which as Tony Davies notes exhibited a 'growing desperation ... in the decades either side of the First World War' as a result of the social and political upheavals of the early part of the century (1997: 41): the 'Great War', the rise of fascism and totalitarianism, the growth of the Fordist factory and mass consumerism, and so on. These events resulted in a surge of speculative fiction preoccupied with the human relationship with rapidly mutating technological and political systems.

I will be focussing particularly on two key works from this period: Aldous Huxley's *Brave New World* (1932) and E.E. 'Doc' Smith's *Skylark* series (1928–1934).[1] I will first examine Huxley's novel, perhaps the most famous technophobic work to emerge from the SF tradition. The discussion here will focus on questions of human agency in Huxley's novel: to what extent, he asks, is the 'human' in fact determined by technological systems? This is a key question in the scholarship surrounding *Brave New World*: the novel has often been read as a bleak summation of Huxley's pessimistic views on technological and scientific progress. Certainly, with its dark vision of humanity addicted to material and sensual pleasure, the novel expresses Huxley's very real fears regarding the perceived loss of individual agency engendered by capitalist modernity. Yet the temptation to therefore read the novel as an outright expression of anti-progressivism or bland liberal humanism must also be resisted—Huxley was committed to a dialectical understanding of human nature which gave equal weight to the intellectual *and* the sensual, a form of human individual he termed the 'life-worshipper'.

I will then move on to Smith's *Skylark* series, an important early work of interstellar SF. Like *Brave New World*, the *Skylark* series explores the relationship between the individual and mass society—yet whereas Huxley views technology as a root cause of the corruption of human nature, Smith conversely sees in technological advancement the means of transcending humanity's limitations. The human in Smith's series is best understood in a 'post-biological' sense: it refers not to biological species of *homo sapiens* but to a set of transcendent abstract qualities that may be shared by any number of (biologically) human or inhuman beings. Hence, although the beings depicted in Smith's works may be *biologically* alien, they remain recognisably 'human' in thought and action, leading Smith to idealise the mind as the site of 'true' human existence over and above the body.

---

[1] I use the term '*Skylark* series' to refer to the original trilogy of *Skylark* novels, comprising *The Skylark of Space*, *Skylark Three*, and *Skylark of Valeron*. Smith eventually added a fourth title to the series, *Skylark DuQuesne* (1966). Given its much later publication, this final work will not be considered in this chapter.

In both cases, we will encounter a version of the trans-human—but each writer's reaction to this technological being will be radically different. Before I turn to these texts, the chapter will begin with an examination of SF in the context of the First World War, the wider changes taking place in western society in the early part of the twentieth century, and the consequences of these for human individuals and society.

The First World War and technology in interwar SF

> He was a mighty beast, mightily muscled, and the urge that has made males fight since the dawn of life on earth filled him with bloodlust and the thirst to slay; but not one whit less did it fill me with the same primal passion. Two abysmal beasts sprang at each other's throats that day beneath the shadow of the earth's oldest cliffs—the man of now and the man-thing of the earliest, forgotten then (Burroughs, 2014: 75–6).

In this passage from Edgar Rice Burroughs' famous lost-world trilogy, *The Land That Time Forgot* (1918), American shipbuilder Bowen J. Tyler is locked in a deadly struggle with a 'hatchet-man', a prehistoric human whom he encounters on the lost island of Caprona near Antarctica. As they clash, Tyler recognises the similarities between himself and his atavistic foe: they are both 'beasts', driven to violence by the same biological urges—in this case, the attentions of Tyler's female companion, Lys. At the same time, the distinction between these two 'kinds' of humanity is inscribed in the familiar terms of evolutionary time and technology: whereas Tyler is a 'modern man' of the twentieth century, his enemy derives from the ancient past, 'the earliest, forgotten then'. Tyler accordingly bests his opponent, a 'clumsy, unskilled brute', by means of the knife dangling at his side (76)—a symbol of his greater technological prowess.

This brief passage would suggest that Burroughs' novel can be read in terms similar to Conan Doyle's *The Lost World*. As discussed in the previous chapter, the revelations of evolutionary science made clear that the classical dichotomy between human and non-human could no longer be unproblematically sustained—yet once established, the moral prioritisation of human over non-human remains nonetheless secure. Burroughs' novel, like Doyle's, stresses the human as a bodily as well as intellectual entity and suggests that the human propensity towards barbarism and violence may always re-emerge in certain less-than-'civilised' spaces.

Yet Burroughs' novel also contains subtle differences from its predecessor. Far from the 'jolly journeys' of Haggard and Conan Doyle, for example, in which the return of imperial explorers to European civilisation is safeguarded, the modern world from which Tyler departs and to which he returns is a space of violent conflict and uncertain future. At the time that the novel was written, the First World War had been under way in Europe for three years. That conflict establishes the context for Tyler's maritime adventures, which begin with an attack on his vessel by a German U-33 submarine. In contrast to the clearly demarcated regions of *The Lost World*, the 'civilised' west has, in *The Land That Time Forgot*, become a space of menace and unease: the initial villains of the work are not 'primitive' natives but German soldiers, while the possibility of safe return to 'civilisation' is precluded by the threat of Allied military attack on the German submarine. The distinction between 'primitive' and 'civilised' humans, too, is more ambiguous in Burroughs' work: the second instalment of the trilogy concludes with the American Tom Billings remaining on Caprona to continue his relationship with a native woman while the third sees two of the native women return to the United States. Such intermingling of opposing human 'kinds' threatens the traditional ascendancy of the western traveller over the inhabitants of the lost world.

The Land That Time Forgot, then, is less definite in its depiction of 'modern' and 'primitive' humans, in contrast to the rigid hierarchy of human types in *The Lost World*, a shift attributable to the backdrop against which Burroughs wrote his work. As Eric Hobsbawm argues, the period of the First World War 'marked the breakdown of the (western) civilisation of the nineteenth century', which proved unable to survive the shower of destruction rained down on its political and economic institutions, its moral and scientific certainties, and its teleological notions of historical narrative (2006: 6). In place of enlightenment, there now began what Hobsbawm terms the 'Age of Catastrophe', a distinct historical phase between the two world wars marked by the twinned forces of economic depression and political authoritarianism.

The 'Great War' may also be understood as a posthuman event, exposing the irrational impulses that lay beneath the professed civility of European society. 'This civilisation', Hobsbawm argues, had '[gloried] in the advance of science, knowledge and education, material and moral progress' (6). Following the years from 1914 to 1918, however, it was no longer possible to speak of the unquestioned triumph of European reason and progress. As Wells writes in *Men Like Gods*, published in 1923, a 'belief in progress was' by that time 'at least six years out of date', since the 'nationalists, financiers, priests and patriots had brought all ... hopes to nothing' (2016: 232). The pillars of nineteenth-century capitalist imperialism came under widespread attack in the period after 1914, with nationalist revolution in Ireland, communist revolution in Russia, and political agitation from both suffragist and—particularly in the US—civil rights groups. The assault on classical humanism was thus twofold: the war itself exposed the brutality and fragility that had lain concealed beneath the veneer of western, and particularly European, progress, while the various ideological movements that gained increased traction during this period—nationalist, communist, suffragist, civil rights, and so on—increasingly challenged the supremacy of the white, bourgeois, liberal male as the universal human subject. The events that followed 1914, then, and the tremendous political and technological changes of the period, challenged classical humanist ideas of rationalism and progress and opened the way for new explorations of the form and meaning of human nature and society. What were writers of SF to make of the new cultural conditions in which they now produced their works?

Some speculative writers attempted to replace or refine traditional metanarratives of social progress. It was at this time, for example, that Olaf Stapledon, one of the most significant British SF writers of the interwar period, composed his future history of the human species, *Last and First Men* (1930). In this novel, the First World War (in which Stapledon served as part of the ambulance corps) is reduced to little more than a footnote in the two-billion-year evolution of humanity, revealed finally to be a cyclical process destined to return to its origin. A greater diversity of SF authors began at this time to be prevalent in the genre: W.E.B. Du Bois, for example, imagines a (temporary) end to racial discrimination in a post-apocalyptic US in 'The Comet' (1920), while Charlotte Perkins Gilman revises the familiar tropes of lost-world fiction to develop a critique of the failures of patriarchal capitalist imperialism in *Herland* (1915) and its sequel, *With Her in Ourland* (1916), which depict a utopian society that has rejected harmful gender stereotypes. Feminist themes of sexual equality, or of more militant matriarchal revolution, became prevalent in interwar SF, further popularised in such stories as Francis Stevens' 'Friend Island' (1918) and M.F. Rupert's 'Via the Hewitt Ray' (1930). Elsewhere, Conan Doyle, whose son Kingsley was killed at the Battle of the Somme, turned increasingly away from the scientific themes of his earlier stories, instead expounding on the (as he saw it) imminent embrace of spiritualism in the west in such works as 'The Vital Message' (1919) and *The History of Spiritualism* (1926). Indeed, one of his final novels, *The Land of Mist* (1925), sees even so devoted a materialist as Professor Challenger embrace 'psychic science' and ends with a call for 'the rebirth of the world—of the true world, the world as God meant it to be', in which the early twentieth century becomes a mere bump on the road towards 'peace and glory unutterable' (Doyle, 2010: 398).

At the same time, the scepticism and uncertainty that marked the 'Age of Catastrophe' inform many speculative works from the period. Even the title of Stapledon's *Last and First Men*, for example, suggests its apocalyptic tone—there will indeed be a 'last' man, who 'shall make after all a fair conclusion to this brief music that is man' (1978: 314)—while in Stapledon's later novel, *Star Maker* (1937), the universe is eventually revealed to be simply one of many experiments in creation undertaken by an inscrutable and indifferent deity. A similar scenario is found in *A Voyage to Arcturus*, a 1920 work of 'symbolic fantasy' by Scottish writer David Lindsay who, like Stapledon, had served in the British Army during the war. The novel, which depicts an allegorical journey across the planet 'Tormance' circling the star Arcturus, examines an array of philosophical and mythological systems before finally arriving at an image of all creation as the product of a pleasure-seeking deity called 'Crystalman', and of human life as a 'horrible war ... against all that is most shameful and frightening, against sin masquerading as beauty, against baseness masquerading as nature' (2003: 279). The meaning of life, the novel suggests, is that there is *no* meaning beyond the basic experience of pain, and specifically of pain 'masquerading' as pleasure. In the US, meanwhile, the works of H.P. Lovecraft, Edmond Hamilton, and other writers of 'weird fiction' also took up this theme of universal indifference, instilling it with a sense of dread at humanity's seeming inability to control its own fate and the indifference of an unsympathetic cosmos.

Alongside the social upheaval caused by the war and the emergence of new social and political movements, the interwar period was also a time of tremendous technological advancement. Much of this progress was linked to the preparation for and conduct of military conflict, with the pre-war arms race among the European powers fuelling the expansion of heavy industries like steel and iron, and of communications and transport technologies such as flight and radio. At the same time, as Alex Goody notes, 'the efforts of Frederick Taylor ... and Henry Ford ... were fundamental in transforming the techno-economic paradigms of America, and of other Western nations' (2011: 15). Increasing automation revolutionised the shape of everyday life, alleviating the stresses of domestic labour, contributing to a post-war surge in production and consumption, and revolutionising the free time increasingly afforded, for the first time, to all classes. Yet if these developments underscored the potential for technological progress to positively alter human life, the destroyed countryside of Europe and crippled lungs of returning soldiers served as dramatic reminders of its darker possibilities.

For Gorman Beauchamp, speculative writers reacted to accelerating technological change throughout the twentieth century in two distinct ways: on one side are the 'technophobes', who feared the rapid escalation of scientific progress, 'view[ing] technology as a creation that can transcend the original purposes of its creator and take on an independent existence and will of its own'; and on the other are the 'technophiles', those who 'contend[ed] that technology is value-neutral, merely a tool that can be used for good or ill', and so embraced the new possibilities offered by emerging technologies (1986: 54). This distinction is concerned not merely with the destructive or creative capabilities generated by new technological possibilities, but also and more fundamentally with the significance of this technology for human agency:

> The question ... is this: is the technology in dystopian fiction merely an instrument in the hands of the state's totalitarian rulers, used by them to enforce a set of values extrinsic to the technology itself, or is it, rather, an autonomous force that determines the values and thus shapes the society in its own image, a force to which even the putative rulers—the Well-Doers and Big Brothers and World Controllers—are subservient? (54)

As the twentieth century wore on, this question became crucial. Adorno and Horkheimer, for example, writing in 1944, expressed fears of the growing 'technical apparatus' that escalated 'society's domination over nature to unimagined heights' while also causing 'individuals as such [to vanish] before the apparatus they serve' (2002: xvii). Conversely, the technocratic movement that emerged in the US during the interwar period asserted the need to eliminate waste in production through the rational organisation of industry by a 'soviet of technicians'. Thorstein Veblen, writing in 1919, argued that any such 'incoming directorate' would of necessity be 'of a technological nature', while its 'purpose' would be 'the care of the community's material welfare by a more competent management of the country's industrial system' (2000: 141). In this view, instrumental rationalism, seen as a value-free mode of organisation, becomes the only sensible basis on which to develop human society.

In line with such concerns, much SF from this time is concerned with the conflict between technological determinism and human agency—the question of whether technology undermines or supports a view of the human as an autonomous, self-realising entity. The most significant technophilic response to this question can be found in the magazine SF produced in the US from the 1920s onwards. The US had emerged from the First World War with the fastest-growing economy in the world, and the subsequent decade was the period of the 'New Era', a time of rising consumerism, accelerating urbanisation, greater education, and expanding developments in communications and transport. Modern SF is itself a product of such advances in media technologies, as the development of cheaper print and transport processes in the late nineteenth and early twentieth centuries contributed to a booming market for pulp fiction. Publications such as *Amazing Stories*, *Astounding Stories of Super Science*, *Wonder Stories*, and other early SF magazines standardised and marketed a newly recognisable style of 'scientific fiction', consolidating previously disparate strands of speculative fiction and scientific romance into a coherent genre and imbuing it with a distinct techno-futurist style.

As John Cheng notes, the writers and editors of the early pulp SF magazines 'genuinely believed that science held imaginative potential and progressive purpose' (2012: 83). Their mission was to explore the possibilities of future science and technology and share their 'discoveries' with their readers. Hence Hugo Gernsback, in the editorial for the first issue of *Amazing Stories*, proclaimed that stories of 'scientifiction' would be remembered 'as having blazed a new trail, not only in literature and fiction, but in progress as well' (1926: 3). The stories of 'super-science' that filled the early SF magazines routinely pitted macho scientist protagonists against the forces of nature and the universe, and were frequently (though not always) underpinned by a technocratic ideology that prioritised technical knowledge as the sole marker of human development at the expense of any engagement with wider cultural or political questions. Nor was this attitude limited to the US: within the British tradition, a more subdued version of this trend is evident in the later works of Wells, whose *Men Like Gods* (1923) and *The Shape of Things to Come* (1933) envision future utopian technocracies organised along rationalist—and often eugenicist—lines.

In contrast to the technological optimism of the American pulps, the distrust of progress provoked by the 'Great War'—famously encapsulated in the apocalyptic imagery of T.S. Eliot's *The Waste Land* (1922)—is evident in many other speculative works from this period. Some works attempt to preserve a conservative sense of human nature amid broader anxieties regarding the threat of technological and scientific progress. Karel Čapek's 1920 play, *R.U.R.*, for instance, captures the sense of anxiety surrounding new modes of industrial production, in which labourers come to be replaced by 'robots' (a Czech word which translates roughly into 'slave')—mechanised workers within ultra-rationalised systems of capitalist production. This image of the mechanised human is frequent in the speculative fiction of the 1920s and 1930s. E.V. Odle's *The Clockwork Man* (1923), for example, depicts a future in which each human is fitted with a 'clock' that dictates their thoughts and feelings, doing away with 'death and disease, with change and decay', but also with free will and agency (2013: 139). Fritz Lang's *Metropolis* (1927), too, features several iconic shots depicting the mechanisation of the human: masses of identical labourers marching to and from factories, or exhausted workers struggling to manipulate the hands of an oversized clock. Each of these works articulates a traditionalist view of human nature as requiring preservation from the distortions of mechanical rationalisation.

As Beauchamp notes, however, in such technophobic works the 'greatest threat posed by technology ... is not that man's mechanical creations will come to rule over him like some alien power but rather that he will so completely introject the ethos of technology that his highest aspiration will be to become a machine himself' (1986: 62). An example of this can be found in E.M. Forster's celebrated 1909 short story, 'The Machine Stops', which depicts a harrowing image of the technological suicide of the human race: 'man who had once made god in his image, and had mirrored his strength on the constellations, beautiful naked man was dying, strangled in the garments that he had woven' (1974: 278). A similar position is evident in Soviet author Yevgeny Zamyatin's famous techno-dystopia, *We* (1924), which appeared in English translation decades before its publication in the USSR. *We* depicts a humanity that has voluntarily relinquished all individuality and agency, reduced to a willing cog in a social machine set to undertake the 'integration of the grandiose, endless equalization of all Creation' (1977: 19). The satire of Zamyatin's novel is aimed not merely, like Kafka's *The Trial* (1925), against dehumanising bureaucratic autocracy, but more broadly against the usurpation and attempted dissolution of human historical agency— against the idea, highly relevant in the context of post-revolution Russia, that there could ever be a *final* revolution, or that history could be made to stop at the moment of revolutionary victory. The preoccupation with a changed experience of time under modernity, and with the clock as a symbol of dehumanising rationalisation, can be seen also in the works of Odle and Lang—as I will discuss in more detail with regard to Huxley, technocracy in these works is interpreted as severing the connection between the individual and any meaningful experience of time.

The figure of the trans-human encompasses both the technophobic and technophilic strains of humanist thought in SF: while some works fear the technological usurpation of human nature—evident in the robots and mechanised human labourers common to the period—others focus on the new possibilities for human advancement brought about by scientific progress. The trend towards technophilia is most evident in the early US pulp stories, in which 'human' frequently becomes a byword for the rational command of space and time. Conversely, the anxieties of the technophobic tradition centre not on the threat posed by Frankenstein's monster, but on the fear that modern humans may be unwittingly remade as monsters themselves. With such sinister possibilities in mind, I turn now to Huxley's *Brave New World*.

The 'life-worshipper' and the end of time in Huxley's *Brave New World*

Brave New World, described by Edward James as 'the best-known work of British SF from between the wars', is also perhaps the most famous technophobic work in twentieth-century SF (1994: 35). Its remarkable popularity no doubt stems, as John Clute has noted, from its ready 'compendium of usable points and quotable jibes' (2019: par. 6) on the subject of technological saturation, a theme that was to become of ever-greater importance within both SF and wider culture as the century advanced. Even in its own day, Huxley's novel was critically regarded as a prescient critique of the twinned dangers of technological materialism and political apathy: Rebecca West, reviewing the novel in 1932, noted that 'the book describes the world as Mr. Huxley sees it may become if certain modern tendencies grow dominant' (West, 1997: 197) while Bertrand Russell noted that, 'while Mr. Huxley's prophecy is meant to be fantastic, it is all too likely to come true', arguing that the novel offers a much-needed warning against the 'illusion of freedom' engendered by material comfort (Russell, 1997: 212).

Set in the year 2540 AD, or 632 'AF' ('After Ford'), *Brave New World* depicts a dystopian Britain organised along principles of technocratic social engineering that have matured from their embryonic forms within Huxley's own time. Following first Bernard Marx, an 'Alpha' (i.e. highly intellectually developed) worker disenchanted with the superficiality of life in the 'World State', and later 'John the Savage', a 'primitive' yet eloquent member of a 'Savage Reservation' brought to Britain to experience the wonders of technological advancement, the novel offers a satirical caricature of the human utterly subsumed beneath an ideology of technological efficiency and normalisation. The novel has traditionally been read as a bleak summation of Huxley's views regarding the dehumanising impacts of capitalist consumerism and scientific management—as the archetypal example of what Zygmunt Bauman (borrowing from Nigel Thrift) calls a 'Joshua discourse', a narrative world characterised by 'monotony, regularity, repetitiveness and predictability' (2000: 55).

Yet, as I will argue, despite the novel's preoccupations with the adverse consequences of contemporary industrial and consumerist practices, it also contains an early expression of Huxley's philosophy concerning the 'best' or 'truest' form of human individual. This human type, which Huxley terms the 'life-worshipper', does not wholly reject either the materialism or rationalism depicted in *Brave New World*, but rather seeks to achieve a balance between the material–biological and rational–intellectual aspects of the human being—between humanity's 'spiritual' and 'animal' natures. This is not, however, another version of the 'supreme' masculinist human figure of Conan Doyle and London. Huxley's ideal of the human, as will be shown, emphasises communality, rather than conflict, between the human and non-human worlds. In *Brave New World*, it is the 'primitive' John the Savage who comes closest to achieving the synthesis of animal and spiritual that Huxley saw as marking the truly 'human' individual.

The genesis of *Brave New World* appears, initially at least, to have been Huxley's desire to poke fun at his contemporary, H.G. Wells, of whose all-too-utopian outlook and technocratic views Huxley was a frequent critic. Sybille Bedford, in her biography of Huxley, describes how the novel began 'light-heartedly enough' in this sardonic fashion: Huxley was required to produce another work but 'felt like holding back from another straight novel' (Bedford, 1993: 243), and so decided, as Arthur Goldsmith puts it, to have 'a little fun pulling the leg of H.G. Wells' (quoted in Bedford, 1993: 244). *Brave New World* marks a transition point for Huxley as an author: David Leon Hidgon notes that, '[as] late as 1929, Huxley had no interest in and even no sympathy for utopian or futuristic fiction' (2013: 1), instead focussing on plaintive works of gentle satire chronicling the disenchantment and nihilism of the post-war generation. Nevertheless, throughout his works of the 1920s, there is a clear strain of cynicism directed towards the Wellsian technocratic viewpoint. In *Point Counter Point* (1928), for instance, the artist Rampion paints a visual chronicle of history 'according to H.G. Wells', consisting of an ascending line of human figures, 'growing larger and larger at every repetition', moving in 'a triumphant spiral clean off the paper, towards Utopian infinity'—this contrasts with Rampion's (and Huxley's) own classicist view of history as peaking in ancient Greece (1974: 290–1).

As David Bradshaw has argued (in Huxley, 1994: 31–43), however, it is important not to overstate the differences between Huxley and Wells. The former's views on Wellsian social engineering, despite his famous denunciation of the principle in *Brave New World*, are never wholly consistent: if Huxley did not approve of Wells's overtly utopian stance towards scientific advancement, neither did he advocate a Luddite position on technology. Huxley's concerns in his novel, like Zamyatin's in *We*, centre not simply on technology itself, but on the capacity for technology to negatively determine the human. Christoph Bode even argues that, far from being technophobic, Huxley views technology in an instrumental way: 'it all depends on who uses [technology and] to what extent' (1990: 366). Hence the scientific procedures of *Brave New World* 'are explicitly presented as *means* to an end and not ends in themselves' (352, emphasis in original). Indeed, Huxley later incorporates many of the same procedures—used to extremely different effect—into Pala, the utopian society of *Island* (1962). Given this, Bode argues, Huxley must then be understood primarily as an idealist: the shape of society, he believed, is largely a reflection of human thought, and therefore the only effective way to influence social development is to try and change how people think.

Yet such an assessment seems only partially accurate. Huxley is indeed extremely critical of the bland philistinism and superficial materialism of western culture and condemns contemporary forms of leisure for failing to provide intellectual stimulus or, as he terms it in an essay from 1936, 'psychological rewards' (Huxley, 1994: 232). Yet he is equally critical of any tendency towards idealism or abstract intellectualism that has lost touch with the material world. Hence Rampion, in *Point Counter Point*, denounces his friend Philip Quarles—a self-portrait of Huxley himself— for 'whoring after abstractions', arguing that 'if you allow yourself to be influenced by non-human, absolute considerations, then you inevitably make either a fool of yourself, or a villain, or perhaps both' (1974: 559–60). Later, in *Ends and Means*, a 1937 study into the 'nature of ideals', Huxley argues that 'children should be taught to examine all personifications, all metaphors, all abstractions occurring in the articles they read, the speeches they listen to. They must learn to translate these empty words into terms of concrete contemporary reality' (1938: 215). For Huxley, there is a necessary balance to be struck between human thought and the objective external environment: 'Good education', he argues in the above 1937 work, 'will be fully effective only when there are good social conditions and, among individuals, good beliefs and feelings; but social conditions will not be altogether satisfactory until there is good education' (180). This relationship between society and the human individual indicates that, for Huxley, the material and social worlds never cease to matter—to address the spiritual crisis that he believed was afflicting western civilisation, it was necessary to examine both the crisis of intellectual stultification *and* the material–social conditions contributing to this crisis.

Brave New World is particularly concerned with what Huxley perceived to be the numbing superficiality and materialism of 1920s American culture. During the 'Roaring Twenties', the US was fast becoming the dominant cultural producer of the western world, fuelled by the advent of Hollywood cinema and a US economic surge which increasingly brought American cultural commodities to European markets. (Arthur C. Clarke, for example, growing up in Somerset, would encounter his first American SF pulp magazine, a copy of *Astounding Stories*, in 1930.) Nor was Huxley the only British speculative writer concerned with the growing influence of American economic and cultural trends: Olaf Stapledon predicted the eventual 'Americanization' of the globe in *Last and First Men*, warning against a materialist mindset 'wholly concerned with the values of individual life', driven by 'a crude materialistic dogma' and 'a denial of all those finer qualities which had emerged to be the spirit of man' (1978: 54–5). Stapledon's critique of American values—in which 'God was the supreme Boss, the universal Employer ... and to be wealthy, therefore, was to be respected as one of God's chief agents' (54–5)—demonstrates a shared fear with Huxley of the corrupting materialism of American culture.

Huxley's fears, however, are more concrete than Stapledon's abstract anxieties regarding the 'American' mindset. While Huxley's sardonic targets in the novel are wide-ranging and complex, one unambiguous focus is the dehumanising conditions of nascent industrialisation and the massification of human individuals stimulated by the processes of industrial production and consumption. Such processes are symbolised in the novel by the figure of Henry Ford—a frequent target of criticism in Huxley's essays—who even comes to replace God as the principal deity of the 'World State'. In an essay written concurrently with *Brave New World*, Huxley noted that 'English motor factories [were] not quite so completely rationalised as the corresponding thing in America'—yet 'the difference [was] only one of degree, not of kind' (1994: 77). The alienating implications of the Fordist assembly line were, for Huxley, clear: such intense rationalisation of the workplace under Taylorist and Fordist principles was, as he remarks in *Brave New World Revisited* (1958), fundamentally anti-democratic, since 'democracy can hardly be expected to flourish in societies where political and economic power is being progressively concentrated and centralized' (2004: 251–2).

This centralisation was evident both at the micro-level—in the strict hierarchies of atomised workplaces that stripped 'the Little Man' of both skill and responsibility in their labour—and at the macro-level of monopolistic corporations, as 'more and more economic power comes to be wielded by fewer and fewer people' (252). The result was a society in which:

> The Power Elite directly employs several millions of the country's working force in its factories, offices and stores, controls many millions more by lending them the money to buy its products, and, through its ownership of the media of mass communication, influences the thoughts, the feelings and the actions of virtually everybody. To parody the words of Winston Churchill, never have so many been manipulated so much by so few (252).

This passage highlights, in Huxley's view, the most serious consequence of economic and political massification: the complete loss of agency experienced by the human subject. With the advent of mass production, any attempt to organise the workforce must necessarily be carried out on a scale at which the individual will cease to matter. The resulting alienation of the labourer within industrial production, 'condemned to psychological poverty' as opportunities for creativity are more and more removed from the daily experience of factory life (1994: 78), is satirised in *Brave New World* in the mass production of actual workers themselves in the World State: 'standard Gammas, unvarying Deltas, uniform Epsilons. Millions of identical twins. The principle of mass production at last applied to biology' (2004: 19).

In giving expression to these anxieties, Huxley anticipates Foucault's argument that, since the late eighteenth century, political power has been characterised by a 'biopolitics ... that is directed not at man-as-body but at man-as-species' (2003: 243). Under such a system, Foucault argues, 'bodies are replaced by general biological processes', managed by 'a technology which brings together the mass effect characteristics of a population, [and] which tries to control the series of random events that can occur in a living mass' (249). Biopolitics shifts the political emphasis from individual to species—from developing social structures designed for the needs of individuals towards the technocratic manipulation of individuals for the benefit of social stability. The governance of the World State in *Brave New World* resembles an extreme form of biopolitics: each individual of the World State is conceived, developed, and 'decanted' in a state laboratory, manipulated by external factors such as temperature and duration of gestation that determine whether the individual will be a lowly Delta labourer or bright Alpha scientist. The goal of such processes, as explained by the Director of the 'Hatchery', is 'social stability': 'Standard men and women in uniform batches. The whole of a small factory staffed with the products of a single bokanovskified egg' (2004: 18). In *Brave New World*, Huxley laments the taming of the multiplicity of human nature into reproducible units under a socio-economic ethos bent on standardisation and stability—the 'reduction of [human] multiplicity to unity', as he described it in 1958, by the implementation of scientific rationality within human processes (254).

These anxieties concerning developments in industrial production are linked with the other (for Huxley) major corrupting force in technocratic capitalism: mass consumer culture. Huxley was a 'critic ... of civilisation' (Adorno and Horkheimer, 2002: xvii) and particularly the popular leisure activities—cinema, radio, and even newspapers—that he saw as mere escapist distractions from more pressing social and intellectual questions. In an essay from 1929, in which he describes his first visit to a 'talkie' cinema show, Huxley links this new form of entertainment to an array of concerning developments in both culture and economics, stemming particularly from the impacts of American capitalism and cultural influence:

> It [the cinema] is a corruption as novel as the régime under which ... all the rest of us now live—as novel as protestantism and capitalism; as novel as urbanization and democracy and the apotheosis of the Average Man; as novel as Benjamin-Franklinism and the no less repulsive philosophy and ethic of the young Good Timer; as novel as creation-saving machinery and the thought-saving, time-killing press; as novel as Taylorized work and mechanized amusement (1937: 48).

The implications of routinised leisure are, for Huxley, clear: such outlets are 'addictions', 'instruments of information and persuasion' that surreptitiously rob the individual of agency by reducing them to 'reading-addicts, hearing-addicts, seeing-addicts' (1938: 212–13).

Correspondingly, in *Brave New World*, the citizens of the World State regularly indulge in 'soma', a hallucinogenic drug distributed by the government, while enjoying an abundance of non-reproductive sex enabled by government-mandated sterilisation and birth control. Huxley also depicts a satirical version of the cinema—the 'feelies'—that aims at stimulating the bodily sensations of viewers. The 'feelies' are framed as a successor to the 'talkies', which began to appear in the late 1920s—a development that, as Laura Frost notes, Huxley found disturbingly 'corporeal': 'For Huxley, far from being a technological advancement, cinema is symptomatic of cultural degeneration, and the introduction of sound was a particularly alarming development because of its implications for bodily pleasure' (2006: 447). The true risk of such fleshly satisfactions, Huxley warns, is political apathy: they provide an all-too-easy escape from the complexities and ambiguities of the real world. Hence the characters featured in his erotic 'feely', *Three Weeks in a Helicopter*, materialise to spectators as 'incomparably more solid-looking than they would have seemed in actual flesh and blood, far more real than reality' (2004: 154). Frequent indulgence in such escapist pleasure, as with that of other 'mechanized amusements' of the 1920s, comes at the cost of genuine contact with the 'real', a category that would come to preoccupy Huxley more and more after the publication of *Brave New World*, as he began to explore Eastern mysticism and, famously, to experiment with hallucinogens.

The crucial point, however, lies with the belief of World State citizens that their detached enjoyment of such activities reflects their own free will, as demonstrated in this exchange between Bernard and Beta worker Lenina:

> 'Don't you wish you were free, Lenina?'
> 'I don't know what you mean. I am free. Free to have the most wonderful time. Everybody's happy nowadays.'
> He laughed, 'Yes, "Everybody's happy nowadays." We begin giving the children that at five.' (2004: 90)

Lenina's automatic responses here resemble a machinic process, reproducing encoded propagandist ideas without intellectual effort. Yet Huxley viewed such a process as already ongoing within consumer capitalism, which conditioned individuals into 'that race of perfect producers and consumers of which industry has need ... producing and preserving that stability and uniformity without which machines cannot be used to their maximum advantage' (Huxley, 1994: 110). This image of individuals as 'machines' whose purpose is to maintain social stability, and the wider subjugation of the human individual to the biopolitical needs of the species, is satirised in *Brave New World* by the 'conscription of consumption' enforced by the World State: 'Every man, woman and child compelled to consume so much a year. In the interests of industry' (2004: 54). As Huxley wrote in 1939, such 'incessant stimulation from without is a source of bondage', one to which citizens within a materialist–capitalist society, consciously or unconsciously, sacrifice their agency (1980: 94).

Brave New World thus offers a version of the trans-human—a being whose ontology is rooted in the technological as much as biological realm—that is far from the utopian vision of transcendent consciousness propagated by More or by Huxley's brother Julian. *Brave New World* paints a grim picture of a social totality engineered with scientific precision: the World State is a clockwork social body whose rhythms have been standardised within a narrow, predetermined spectrum of possibilities, wherein the human species, reduced to a mechanised mass of producing and consuming individuals, has itself been rendered technologically reproducible. The novel thus offers a critical imaginative response to key socio-economic developments of the early part of the century, particularly industrial Fordism and the growth of conspicuous consumption stimulated by advertising 'propaganda'.

Yet, notwithstanding this dark sketch of technological saturation, it is clear from both *Brave New World* and Huxley's other writings that technology does not *inevitably* degrade the human. If Huxley is not a pure idealist in his attitudes towards social and technological change, neither is he a straightforward materialist. Indeed, the novel contains various characters who resist the machinic indoctrinations of the World State: Bernard Marx, the discontented yet superficial Alpha; Helmholtz Watson, a creative writer and dissident, ironically employed at the 'College of Emotional Engineering' to pen 'feely scenarios' and 'slogans and hypnopaedic rhymes' (Huxley, 2004: 71); and Mustapha Mond, one of the 'World Controllers', who recognises the shortcomings of the civilisation over which he presides, yet who nevertheless argues that agency and creativity are worth sacrificing since they are 'incompatible with happiness' (202). Mond, in fact, recognises the threat posed to the World State by intellectualism and idealism: when questioned as to why all individuals are not designed to be high-functioning Alphas, Mond responds that '[a] society of Alphas couldn't fail to be unstable and miserable' since such individuals, 'capable (within limits) of making a free choice and assuming responsibilities', would come into conflict with a society based on the relinquishing of individual will (200).

Yet the most significant character to oppose the technocratic operations of the World State is 'John the Savage', an idealistic young man raised in a 'Savage Reservation'. The Reservations are 'primitive' communities which, 'owing to unfavourable climatic or geographical conditions', have 'not been worth the expense of civilising' (149), and are instead used as tourist destinations for citizens of the World State. On one such trip, Bernard and Lenina encounter John, whose mother Linda, a British Beta worker, had been stranded in the Reservation years before. Bernard and Lenina bring John and his mother back to Britain, and the latter half of the novel chronicles John's exposure to, and increasing disillusionment with, the hedonism and moral decadence of modern society. It is through the character of John that Huxley undertakes his most thorough-going criticisms of the superficiality and nihilism of contemporary western life—the novel famously ends with a bleak image of John's suicide, having failed to escape from the nightmare of happiness in the World State and recover some sense of existential meaning.

The Savage Reservation is far removed from the mechanised, sterile civilisation of Fordist Britain. As Bernard and Lenina arrive, they are greeted by a ritualistic ceremony involving 'a ghastly troop of monsters ... masked or painted out of all semblance of humanity', who engage in a 'strange limping dance' before collectively whipping a teenage boy into unconsciousness (2004: 108). When questioned on the purpose of the ceremony, John's explanation reveals a fertile mixture of spiritual influences and nature worship: it is, he states, for 'the sake of the pueblo—to make the rain come and the corn grow. And to please Pookong and Jesus' (111). As with the World State, sexuality is to the fore in the social and cultural life of the Reservation—but far from the fruitless couplings of the sterile workers, the sexual engagements of the 'Indians' are infused with libidinous significance: 'the men's deep savage affirmation of their manhood' is followed, 'in a neighing treble, [by] the women's answer' (108). The citizens of the Reservation also struggle with exposure, starvation, disease, old age, and finally death— phenomena long since banished from the social life of the World State. Hence Lenina is shocked at the sight of an 'almost naked Indian ... profoundly wrinkled and black ... [his] body bent and emaciated to the bone', or the 'spectacle of two young women giving breast to their babies', or a 'dead dog lying on a rubbish heap' (105–7).

The Reservation, then, is configured as the *yin* to the World State's *yang*, a vibrant and violent culture antithetical to the sophisticated yet impotent society of soma and feelies. Given the more 'natural' mode of life experienced in the Reservation, it would be easy to interpret this space as a positive rural alternative to the dehumanising urbanism of the World State. Yet social life in the Reservation is underpinned by a set of superstitious beliefs that are just as intellectually and emotionally disengaged as those of 'civilised' society. For all its contrasts, the Reservation parallels the World State in its intolerance of difference and diversity: the inhabitants of the Reservation refuse to accept John's fierce individualism, instead making of him an outcast, a 'white-hair' denied participation in the social rituals of Reservation life. If Huxley condemns the corruption of humanity by the intense technologisation of modern life, then, he equally rejects any glib suggestions of a 'return' to nature, or the notion that the mechanical rhythms of factory and cinema could be replaced *en masse* by the more 'organic' traditions of pueblo and plain. What is needed, he proposes, is a social system in which both the mind and body can flourish, which will not come about by means of either the logic of techno-rationality or naïve notions about the 'purity' of pre-technological life.

Hidgon argues that the inspiration for the episode in the Savage Reservation sprang from materials gathered during a round-the-world trip that Huxley undertook from September 1925 to June 1926. This trip took Huxley and his wife Maria through India and a host of south-east Asian countries to Japan, where they crossed the Pacific to America, taking in San Francisco and New York as well as the more rugged terrains of Arizona and New Mexico (see Hidgon, 2013: 143–94). The extreme contrasts in human existence encountered in the nine months spent travelling from the 'somewhat Extreme Orient' (quoted in Bedford, 1993: 174) to the booming United States left Huxley with 'many exploded convictions, many perished certainties' (Huxley, 1926: 287). Following one memorable incident during a sailing trip down the coast of Borneo—in which a sailor armed with a knife threatened mutiny—Huxley commented on 'the precarious artificiality of all that seemed most solid and fundamental in our civilisation, of all that we take most for granted' (221). He returned finally to London with an increased appreciation of the dualisms that defined the human being:

> In one country, [the traveller] will perceive, the true, fundamental standard is distorted by an excessive emphasising of hierarchic and aristocratic principles; in another by an excess of democracy. Here, too, much is made of work and energy for their own sakes; there, too much of mere being. In certain parts of the world he will find spirituality run wild; in others a stupid materialism that would deny the very existence of values (290–1).

The implication here is of a need to balance spiritualism with materialism—to 'create ... a standard of values that shall be timeless, as uncontingent on circumstances, as nearly absolute' as can be made (291).

This is a preoccupation that would steadily grow in importance in Huxley's writings. In *After Many a Summer*, for instance, Huxley dramatises some revealing conflicts between a variety of worldviews, not one of which is attentive to the full range of authentic human capacities and needs. The novel centres on Jo Stoyte, an ageing business tycoon obsessed with extending the duration of his life through scientific means. After uncovering a record of an aristocrat who discovered the secret to eternal life, Stoyte tracks down the man, only to discover that he has degenerated into a mute ape-like being. Such base materialist concerns, Huxley suggests, lead only to a neglect of the spiritual cultivation of the self. Against this limited viewpoint, Huxley sets the wise Mr. Propter, who insists that human nature embraces both the 'animal' and the 'spirit' and insists that 'men's business is to make the human world safe for animals and spirits' (1980: 123). The most complete expression of this philosophy may be found in Huxley's final novel, *Island*: set on Pala, an island utopia founded by a Scottish doctor and a Palanese monarch, the novel advocates a mix of western scientific pragmatism and eastern intellectual spiritualism. The 'modest ambition' of the Palanese way of life, as one citizen explains, is simply 'to live as fully human beings in harmony with the rest of life on this island', free from 'those senseless pointless cockfights between Man and Nature, between Nature and God, between the Flesh and the Spirit! Wisdom doesn't make those insane separations' (2005c: 210, 193). Huxley here suggests that a balance of spirit and matter is necessary for the true realisation of the human self.

John the Savage offers an early prototype for the later citizens of Pala. An inchoate mix of spiritualism and classical western culture, John is free from both the strict social conditioning of the World State and the uncritical superstitions of the Reservation. Indeed, in his preface to a 1946 edition of *Brave New World*, Huxley suggests that, if he 'were to rewrite the book, [he] would offer the Savage a third alternative. Between the Utopian and primitive horns of his dilemma would lie the possibility of sanity' (2005b: 7). This 'sanity' resembles the society of Pala:

> Science and technology would be used as though ... they had been made for man, not (as at present and still more so in the *Brave New World*) as though man were to be adapted and enslaved to them. Religion would be the conscious and intelligent pursuit of man's Final End, the unitive knowledge of immanent Tao or Logos, the transcendent Godhead or Brahman. And ... the first question to be asked and answered in every contingency of life [would be]: 'How will this thought or action contribute to, or interfere with, the achievement, by me and the greatest possible number of other individuals, of man's Final End?' (2005b: 7).

It is John who comes closest to the ideal combination of animal and spirit in *Brave New World*. Born of the Savage Reservation yet conversant with the technological feats of the World State, John's worldview embraces conflicting impressions from both sources: 'Lying in bed, he would think of Heaven and London and Our Lady of Acoma and the rows and rows of babies in clean bottles and Jesus flying up and Linda flying up and the great Director of World Hatcheries and Awonawilona' (2004: 120).

More important than these two influences is John's identification with a western literary culture which predates the World State itself, symbolised by the battered copy of Shakespeare's collected works discovered in the Reservation. Through his reading of these texts, John forms a crucial link to a cultural past that has elsewhere been suppressed in the name of social stability. In one sense, Shakespeare acts as a synecdoche for a set of conservative western values—honour, nobility, transcendental suffering, sexual prudence, and so on—that provide John, as Mario Varricchio argues, with 'a transcendental idea of culture, which he sees as natural heritage, an old wisdom transmitted throughout the centuries' (1999: 101). But it is also significant that Shakespeare is viewed by Huxley as a 'life-worshipper'—someone who balanced the animal and the spiritual sides of life in his works. Shakespeare, as Huxley wrote in 1936, along with a host of other artists and thinkers throughout history, 'is at one moment a positivist and at another a mystic: now haunted by the thought of death ... and now a Dionysian child of nature: now a pessimist and now ... an exuberant believer that God's in his heaven and all's right with the world' (1937: 234). The life-worshipper is a 'manifold and discontinuous being ... he is many different people' (234): 'a series of distinct psychological states, a colony of distinct personalities' (338), who is not beholden to any particular ideology, set of presuppositions, or form of sensual experience at the expense of all others. They thus achieve, Huxley argues, the balance of oppositions necessary for the fullest appreciation of the 'primary fact of existence' (234). Hence the significance of Shakespeare's works in *Brave New World* goes beyond the merely literary: these works also provide a model for the balanced form of being—'so subtly refined and yet so brutal, so sensual and yet so spiritual' (226)—that Huxley viewed as most favourable to the realisation of human potential.

John's inability to integrate into the World State stems precisely from its lack of balance in this regard: in prioritising the sensual life, the World State has denied itself access to the spiritual, while in its commitment to rationalism it has sacrificed human freedom. Unable to cope with the lack of any familiar moral or spiritual life in the World State, John eventually finds himself rebelling against spiritual death— against the vacuity of a purely materialist existence. In his conversation with Mustapha Mond, John attempts to outline his dissatisfaction with life in the World State. Moving first through the loss of religion, then through a vague notion of suffering as the necessary 'cost' for the proper alignment of the soul, John finally claims from Mond simply the right 'to be unhappy':

> the right to grow old and ugly and impotent; the right to have syphilis and cancer; the right to have too little to eat; the right to be lousy; the right to live in constant apprehension of what may happen tomorrow; the right to catch typhoid; the right to be tortured by unspeakable pains of every kind (2004: 215).

John's rebellion against the World State is expressed particularly through the category of *time*. Each of his grievances against the World State—his anger at Lenina's attempted seduction of him, his revulsion at the lack of sexual restraint, and his final desire to be allowed to age, catch diseases, and finally die in accordance with his own physical nature—is ultimately rooted in time. For John, such things are only worth attaining if one must strive or suffer to attain them, since 'tears are necessary' for virtue (213).

In two essays published in 1936, 'Pascal' and 'Time and the Machine', Huxley outlines what he saw as some of the major consequences of industrialisation for western perceptions of time, as well as the mode of time most proper to the life-worshipper. Like Mumford, Huxley views time as a 'recent invention', a concept 'hardly older than the United States' that was co-created with the 'locomotive', the 'factory', and the 'office' (1937: 122). In conforming to the fast-paced rhythms of industrialised society, Huxley argues, western society sacrificed 'the majestic movement of cosmic time'—of 'sunrise, noon and sunset; of the full moon and the new; of equinox and solstice; of spring and summer, autumn and winter' (124). As a result, time is transformed within such societies into an 'artificial, machine-made' category (124): 'a collection of minutes, each of which must be filled with some business or amusement' (123). Yet the 'mechanized labour and mechanized leisure' that filled the working or leisure time of most western citizens are 'mere substitutes for life'—a way of *escaping*, rather than spending, time (229). 'For a modern American or Englishman', Huxley writes, 'waiting is a psychological torture'—in contrast with life in the 'Orient', where individuals have 'not lost the fine art of doing nothing' (123). Huxley then defines the mode of time proper to the 'life-worshipper' as the 'present eternity of ecstatic timelessness which is the consummation of intense living' (230). Rather than constantly striving towards future possibilities or dwelling on past events, Huxley argues, the true life-worshipper will strive towards a state of mindfulness in which 'present eternity' is prioritised over past and future, which is for Huxley the true goal of human existence.

In other words, time for Huxley must be *experienced*—to attempt to escape from time (whether through leisure or work) or to invest too heavily in either past or future is to cut oneself off from profound human existence in the present and, by extension, from a fully rounded sense of reality. This clearly influences Huxley's representations of time in *Brave New World*. For citizens of the World State—as for those of western capitalist societies—waiting is antithetical to happiness: whereas John views unfulfilled desire as a virtue, Lenina is puzzled by John's wish to postpone their sexual union, simply asking 'what for?' (2004: 156). For Lenina, the lapse of time between identifying and satisfying a desire is simply unnecessary. As Varricchio argues, '[desire] is dead in *Brave New World*' since 'to admit the existence of it would be to recognize the failure of the ideal State' (99). When confronted with 'the slings and arrows of outrageous fortune', as John states to Mustapha Mond, the World State and its inhabitants 'neither suffer nor oppose them' but sidestep them altogether (214).

At the same time, the social structures of the World State adhere to 'machine-made time' that extends even to the level of biological processes. Foetuses are no longer born but 'decanted' according to strict social need, while death takes place according to a stipulated plan that sees all individuals perish at sixty. In this context, 'mother' and 'father' have become dirty words, suppressed alongside any notions of family, monogamy, history, or anything that would imply a connection to a collective or biological past. The forward movement of time, in both individual and socio-historical senses, effectively does not exist: every day in the individual's life is identical to both the day before and those of their peers, organised around cycles of work and leisure. The justification for such mechanisms is, as always, social stability: as Mond states, there can be 'No civilisation without stability' and 'No social stability without individual stability' (47). Such stability necessarily entails temporal stasis—from the individual stasis of soma-addicted individuals to the historical stasis achieved by the suppression of the cultural past. As Mond reiterates, in the words of '"that beautiful and inspired saying of Our Ford's: History is bunk. History," he repeated slowly, "is bunk"' (40).

In his yearning for 'constant apprehension', then, John is really lamenting the death of time—'true' time, experienced as creative and mindful engagement with the present—in the World State. This understanding of time as creation, furthermore, is linked to the loss of agency under capitalist modernity discussed earlier. For Huxley, human freedom came under threat from habits of uncritical production and consumption. By participating in mechanised labour in Taylorised factories and offices and then indulging in equally thoughtless leisure pursuits such as cinema or radio, individuals denied their own creative faculties and diminished their capacity to experience time in an active and meaningful way.

It is thus significant that John's final attempt to escape from the World State involves a moment of creative endeavour that emphasises this sense of human-meaningful time. After seeking isolation in a disused lighthouse, John sets about creating a garden. During this work, he experiences a fleeting unity of the animal and the spirit, a moment of bodily and intellectual harmony described in a remarkable passage:

> He was digging in the garden—digging, too, in his own mind, laboriously turning up the substance of his thought. Death—and he drove in his spade once, and again, and yet again. And all our yesterdays have lighted fools the way to dusty death. A convincing thunder rumbled through the words. He lifted another spadeful of earth. Why had Linda died? Why had she been allowed to become gradually less than human and at last ... He shuddered. A good kissing carrion. He planted his foot on his spade and stamped it fiercely into the tough ground. As flies to wanton boys are we to the gods; they kill us for their sport. Thunder again; words that proclaimed themselves true—truer somehow than truth itself. And yet that same Gloucester had called them ever-gentle gods. Besides, thy best of rest is sleep and that thou oft provok'st; yet grossly fear'st thy death which is no more. No more than sleep. Sleep. Perchance to dream. His spade struck against a stone; he stooped to pick it up. For in that sleep of death, what dreams? (2004: 226–7)

Here, John's actions harmonise with his thoughts, his physical movements corresponding closely with his stream-of-conscious reflections: the act of turning over the earth reflects his internal reality, in which memories, ideas, literary references, and emotions are 'turned over' as he works through his recent experiences. At the same time, the 'thunder' of Shakespeare's words, echoed by the thunder in the surrounding landscape, underlines that John has the resource of a historical and cultural hinterland behind him. His familiarity with the work of one renowned artist enables John to nourish his private self and achieve a more profound sense of grief and loss. As a result, he forms a connection with that broader human history (or, at least, that of European society) which has been utterly repudiated by the World State: 'those specks of antique dirt called Athens and Rome, Jerusalem and the Middle Kingdom ... *King Lear* and the *Thoughts* of Pascal' (41).

To suggest, then, that the novel does not offer an alternative to its bleak technophobic picture is not accurate. Certainly, the question of how best to address the unchecked advance of technology is left unanswered—but in this fleeting moment at the close of the novel, Huxley does at least sketch out the kind of harmony of 'animal' and 'spirit' that he deemed necessary to the spiritual and material salvation of the human. *Brave New World*, reacting against the subversion of human nature by ever more pervasive technocracy, falls back on a conservative notion of human agency as needing to be preserved from technological corruption. Yet, at the same time, Huxley's notion of the 'life-worshipper', epitomised in prototypical form by John the Savage, accounts not merely for the intellectual and spiritual being of the human, but for its material and sensual being as well. Huxley thus roundly rejects any notion of the trans-human as a utopian figure—instead, he stresses the preservation of human agency from technology and rejects any approach towards human life that prioritises either the intellectual or material worlds at the expense of the other.

Early pulp SF: *Skylark* and 'a universe ruled by the human mind'

At first glance, Huxley's *Brave New World* has little in common with the early space operas of E.E. 'Doc' Smith. Smith's *Skylark* series is the quintessential early work of technophilic SF in the US tradition, vibrantly capturing the sense of utopian possibility so often linked in the pre-'Golden Age' pulps with technological and scientific speculation. Published in Gernsback's *Amazing Stories* from August to October 1928, *The Skylark of Space* appeared at the very beginning of magazine SF: *Amazing Stories* had begun publishing only two years beforehand, and in 1928 was still the only US magazine dedicated to 'scientifiction'. The genesis of Smith's story, however, predates the consolidation of SF as a market genre, having been written in stages between 1915 and 1920 while Smith was working as a chemist and studying towards a Ph.D. in that field (Moskowitz, 1967: 20–2). *The Skylark of Space* was rejected by many magazine publishers before being accepted by *Amazing Stories* editor T. O'Conor Sloane (for the meagre fee of $75). Following its publication, Smith quickly became one of the most popular authors in pulp SF, producing two sequels—*Skylark Three* (*Amazing Stories*, Aug–Oct 1930) and *Skylark of Valeron* (*Astounding Stories*, Aug 1934–Feb 1935)—that extended the action of the original tale to other galaxies and even dimensions. During this time, Smith also published *Triplanetary* (*Amazing*

Stories, Jan–Apr 1934), a story of interstellar alien invasion that would eventually be reworked as a prequel to his renowned *Lensman* series (1934–1948).

Smith is thus a key author in the pre-Golden Age era of American SF, a time in which the utopian possibilities of technology were of central concern to American SF writers. *The Skylark of Space* established a much-borrowed narrative framework featuring larger-than-life scientist–adventurers acting as torchbearers in a universal conflict between progress and decadence, with technology as their instrument and nature as their resource. The series centres on Richard Seaton, a scientist–inventor who inadvertently discovers a new metal, called simply 'X', which when brought into contact with copper and an electric current induces a cataclysmic liberation of atomic energy. Seaton channels this energy into a propulsion mechanism with which to power a series of ever larger and more sophisticated flying crafts—the titular 'Skylark' spaceships—which he uses to explore the galaxy alongside his wife Dorothy and friends Martin Crane and Margaret.

Smith's notion of the trans-human differs significantly from that of Huxley's *Brave New World*. The latter, drawing on a European tradition of utopian satire stretching back to Swift, expresses anxieties concerning contemporary industrial developments. Smith, conversely, drawing on the episodic yet flexible format of the early pulp magazines, inflates those developments to (literally) galactic proportions, imbuing technology with a utopian appeal and casting it as a powerful instrument for self-realisation. Yet some crossover between Huxley and Smith can nevertheless be identified: both, as I will argue, are concerned with shielding the autonomy and agency of the human individual from the more extreme tendencies of capitalist modernity. For both, furthermore, the means of achieving this lie in adopting the most fruitful attitude towards technological processes. For Smith, in contrast to Huxley, technology is not an oppressive system external to the human but a practical means of individual self-expression—his protagonists are not the victims but the propagators of a technological rationalism aimed, like the House of Salomon in Bacon's *New Atlantis*, at facilitating humanity's ever-deepening command over non-human nature.

In particular, technology in Smith's *Skylark* stories is equated with the rationalisation of space and time, a process of abstracted 'enframing' in which matter itself becomes the final frontier to be breached. The 'human' in these works is divorced from mere individual biology, instead becoming shorthand for a number of key humanist traits: a rationalist worldview, adherence to a set of conservative moral values, a belief in technological progress and in human dominion over nature, and a prioritisation of individual, as opposed to social, identity. Hence, and in sharp contrast to the humans of Conan Doyle and London, to be 'human' in these texts does not really mean to be *biologically* human—rather, the term points to the possession of elevated intellectual and moral qualities used as qualitative markers in a broader process of identification and Othering.

I will begin this analysis by examining the literary genealogy of Smith's series. *The Skylark of Space* is one of the earliest 'space operas', a subgenre centred on interstellar travel and encounters with alien life forms. 'Space opera', as David Pringle notes, 'was the subgenre, above all else, that the genre magazines could call their own; and it was also the first subgenre to remain, for decades, purely the property of genre SF' (2000: 45). Examining its origins, Pringle identifies several influences on the formation of space opera, including future-war and naval stories, philosophical interplanetary fiction such as Voltaire's *Micromégas* (1752) and Camille Flammarion's *Lumen* (1872), and the planetary romances of such writers as Burroughs. Its most significant predecessors, however, were surely the earlier forms of pulp fiction printed in magazines such as the *Argosy* and *All-Story*, of which Smith was a 'regular reader' (Moskowitz, 1967: 21). In the late nineteenth and early twentieth centuries, such pulp magazines were the mainstay of cheap reading material for increasingly literate populations, offering stories of 'the Wild West' and 'American detective[s]' of the sort that enthral James Joyce's young narrator in 'An Encounter' (1914).

Given this lineage, it is possible to view *Skylark* and other early works of SF as ambitious projections of earlier modes of pulp fiction onto an interstellar backdrop. Notwithstanding its key role in the consolidation of SF, however, early space opera has a controversial place in the history of the genre. Suvin, for example, dismisses much 'Gernsbackian SF' as tending towards a 'regression-to-womb stage', rehashing tropes from other sub-literary genres in innovative but reactionary guises (1979: 23–4). Indeed, like the works of imperial lost-world fiction discussed in the last chapter, early space opera often exhibits an unattractive and dated chauvinism: as Jerome K. Winters notes in his study of the 'New Space Opera' that has emerged within SF in the last three decades, earlier works are often characterised by a 'quasi-fascistic fascination with supermen and super weapons, ... abiding racism, sexism and class bigotry, as well as [a] juvenile wish-fulfilment fantasy' (2016: 13). Brian Aldiss offers a succinct summary of a view of space opera that tends to dismiss the genre as trivial: 'Science fiction is for real. Space opera is for fun. Generally' (1973: 9).

Notwithstanding this disparaging view of early SF stories as the mere 'hyping-up of the old grape juice into the new wine' (Suvin, 1979: 24), pulp SF stories held an undeniable appeal for their early readers. This appeal, as Joyce's narrator puts it, derives from 'the escape which those chronicles of disorder alone seemed to offer' (2000: 12). Pulp SF, which thrived particularly during the Depression years of the late 1920s and 1930s, offered its readers the chance to step out of the complex and often dreary circumstances of everyday life and enter a diverting world of manly adventure, uncomplicated romance, and clear-cut moral choices. Isaac Asimov, who first encountered SF at his father's newsstand in Depression-era New York, writes that pulp SF 'gave [him] the joy of life at a time and in a place and under conditions when not terribly many joys existed' (1988: 10). Jack Williamson, describing the effect of such stories on a 'green farm kid' growing up in rural southern America, describes the ideological significance of pulp SF for its early readership: 'to me— … hungry for life and ignorant of nearly everything—and to a whole generation of wondering young Americans, those disdained publications came to reflect our awe at the strangeness of the universe, our readiness to challenge all we didn't understand, our hope of better worlds to come' (2014: 539). Early SF works offered readers a tangible 'sense of wonder': 'the sudden opening of a closed door in the reader's mind' (Nicholls and Robu, 2019: par. 5). That that opening was, in the cases of Asimov and Williamson, an escape from a world of limited economic opportunities and cultural outlets to one of near-unlimited possibilities accounts for the amplified emotional response of many writers and readers to the genre.

Williamson was particularly struck by the unlimited scope for science and technology to improve human life. In a guest editorial for *Amazing Stories Quarterly* in 1928, he described his vision of a future technocratic utopia and the role of SF in its realisation:

> A universe ruled by the human mind. A new Golden Age of fair cities, of new laws and new machines, of human capabilities undreamed of, of a civilisation that has conquered matter and Nature, distance and time, disease and death. … The idea of the final product of evolution is beyond us. But a sublime picture it is that scientifiction may build through the ages, and that science may realize for the ultimate advancement of man (2014: 575).

The ideological commitments of Gernsbackian SF are on full display here: Williamson's 'Golden Age', like Julian Huxley's, stresses the tenets of Enlightenment positivist humanism, characterised by a utopian stance on scientific development, a progressive view of historical change, a commitment to a universal abstraction called 'man', and an anthropocentric view of non-human nature as an external object to be harnessed by an omnipotent, if benevolent, human intellectual subject.

Such ideas percolated, with varying degrees of emphasis, throughout the tales published in *Amazing, Astounding, Wonder Stories*, and the other early SF magazines. The space-operatic works of such well-known writers as Edmond Hamilton frequently fall back on a normative framework that encodes the conflict between humans and non-human life forms as a straightforward clash of good versus evil. These ideas even find expression in works that adopt a more ambiguous or muted stance on technological change or human development. Hamilton's 'weird' stories, for example, initially seem more invested in ideas of human evolutionary degeneracy than utopian technocracy: 'The Man That Evolved' (1931) depicts a future of human evolution in which, after passage through various stages of physical and intellectual excellence, the human circles back to end in a grey protoplasmic slush, while 'Devolution' (1936) reveals humanity to be the product of evolutionary regression among a race of disembodied extra-terrestrial intellects. For all their pessimism, however, these stories nevertheless retain an emphasis on the intellect as the key site of human evolution, over and above the natural–material world, and a view of human evolution as tending always and everywhere towards the same human figure.

In depicting encounters between the human and the non-human, then, the typical narrative of early magazine SF is concerned with a moral conflict between chaos and order—between decadent forces seeking to disrupt the orderly progress of human development and progressive forces committed to its continuation. Even so circumspect a story as John Campbell's 'Twilight' (1934)—in which a sterile and infantile humanity quietly fades out to extinction amid the luxury of its own technological creations—extends a specifically western anxiety concerning technological dependence to encompass the whole of humankind, and ends with a hopeful transfer of humanity's 'uniquely' creative faculties to 'those wondrous machines, of man's triumphant maturity ... The wondrous, perfect machines' (1972: 56). Even in its more pensive modes, early magazine SF remains committed to a universal human condition, technology as the key measure of human development, and a teleological view of human history as culminating in the appearance of white, intellectually advanced males.

At the same time, however, such stories as Frank Belnap Long Jr.'s 'The Last Men' (1934), in which humans have become the slaves of super-intelligent insects, or Sophie W. Ellis's 'Creatures of the Light' (1930), which depicts the artificial production and later destruction of a race of super-evolved yet amoral humans, evince an anxiety familiar from *Brave New World*: that the tendency towards rational order and human perfection may rob humanity of its creative potential or lead to a stultifying world of sterile technological reproduction. The response of these American writers to such concerns, particularly in the case of early space opera, differs strikingly from Huxley's critical re-evaluation of the most appropriate modes of human life. Far from retreating from instrumental rationalism to recapture some essential element of human experience, early space-operatic works typically valorise technology as the only effective means of achieving true human potential. Furthermore, technology in these works is often shaped and manipulated not on the social but on the individual level—a neutral tool deployed to radically extend, rather than subvert, individual agency. Any anxieties regarding the individual's capacity to act in a meaningful manner within industrial mass society, conversely, are redirected outwards towards external social authorities, conceived as negative restraints on individual creative enterprises.

This dynamic can be seen in a common narrative trope of the pulp SF stories of the 1920s and 1930s: the development of utopian technologies that exploit the power of nature in new ways. This trope is evident in numerous stories: in M.F. Rupert's 'Via the Hewitt Ray' (1930), which depicts a matter transporter capable of operating at the speed of light; in S.P. Meek's 'Submicroscopic' (1931) and Henry Hasse's 'He Who Shrank' (1936), which feature matter-reduction technology; and in Campbell's 'The Battery of Hate' (1933), in which a device that can produce electricity 'so cheaply nothing can compete' is developed by a lone experimenter in his basement (Campbell, 1975: 116). These technologies have the clear capacity to revolutionise the experience of everyday life—yet each story also stresses the tension between the radical inventor–pioneers, committed to progress, and a conservative society that resists or suppresses technological change. As a result, in each case the radical potential of the technology to change society becomes stifled—whether by a public suspicious of too-rapid advances in 'Via the Hewitt Ray', or by the hostility of an entrenched scientific old guard in 'Submicroscopic', or by the aggressions of a jealous capitalist baron in 'The Battery of Hate'—and it is instead left to the resourceful and provident individual to explore the full ramifications of their discovery.

This dynamic can also be seen at work in the use of technology and scientific discourse within Smith's *Skylark* series. Although well versed in the scientific idiom—a result of his professional work as a 'chemist of high standing and an excellent mathematician' (see introductory note to Smith and Garby, 1928b)[2]—Smith is nonetheless rather loose in his use of scientific discourse: his tales frequently and flagrantly disregard the laws of nature even as they were understood in his own time, and ignore fundamental assumptions regarding the nature of matter. The mysterious metal 'X', for example, is offered to the reader with barely a smattering of scientific explanation, while one breezy exchange between Seaton and his millionaire co-adventurer Crane does away with the whole of Einsteinian relativity: when Crane protests that Seaton's plans to travel at a speed approaching 'the velocity of light' are impossible, Seaton replies that Einstein's 'theory' is no more than that and proceeds to send special relativity 'to pot' by careening through the galaxy at superluminary speeds (Smith and Garby, 1928b: 531).

Smith's disregard for accepted scientific knowledge is typical of pulp SF of the era: as Andrew Ross notes, such 'fanciful scientific "errors" were tolerated as "superscience" conventions in order to explain the interstellar plausibility of the generic "space opera"' (1991: 420). Deviations from established fact were in most cases treated not as blunders but as speculation—as 'super-science', defined in *Astounding* in August 1934 as 'the projection of inventive thought into the realm of unexplored realism'. Hence, even so extravagant a story as *The Skylark of Space* could be interpreted as speculation on future possibilities: as Gernsback writes in an introductory note to the second instalment of *The Skylark of Space*, 'We know so little about intra-atomic forces that this story, improbable as it will appear in spots, will read commonplace [*sic*] years hence'.

As well as liberating SF stories from a strict adherence to realistic scientific extrapolation, however, this tendency to reject or subvert orthodox knowledge also reflects a certain ambivalence regarding the authority of established science. Responding to reader criticisms that the faster-than-light travel in *The Skylark of Space* was implausible, Smith made his position on the distinction between theory and empirical fact clear: 'Please bear in mind that we KNOW very little. It has been widely believed that the velocity of light is the limiting velocity, and many of our leading authorities hold this view—but it cannot be proved, and is by no means universally held' (1930a: 389). These 'leading authorities', Smith

---

[2] *The Skylark of Space* was partially co-written with Lee Hawkins Garby, a neighbour of Smith, who drafted the romantic elements of the story while Smith handled the remainder. Upon its publication, the story was attributed to 'Edward Elmer Smith, in collaboration with Lee Hawkins Garby'. The story then underwent significant revision by Smith before its 1946 republication by Fantasy Press, with Smith as sole author. Since I am referring to the original magazine publications, I will list both Smith and Garby when citing *The Skylark of Space*.

suggests, do not possess a monopoly over scientific wisdom—indeed, having previously '"proved" that the transatlantic cable and the airplane were scientifically impossible', it seems the best attitude to adopt towards such authorities is a wary scepticism (389). As Robert Heinlein (a close friend of Smith) later wrote, any theoretical model should 'be judged ... for what it [is] worth—precisely nothing, until confirmed by experiment' (Heinlein, 2014: 66). It is only human 'assumptions', Smith insists, that limit the scientific imagination, which is why the only respected 'facts' in his stories are the 'mathematical proofs whose fundamental equations and operations involve no assumptions', supported by the empirical validity of the individual human senses (389).

This refusal to accept established scientific knowledge at face value— to prioritise the socially accepted viewpoint over and above what may be empirically verified by the individual—is informed by the broader socio-economic context of the United States in the early decades of the twentieth century. This was the era of the Fordist factory, exploding consumerism, mass production, and the technological transformation of everyday life, driven by massive corporate conglomerates and captured in Coolidge's famous declaration in 1925 that 'the business of America, is business' (quoted in Beaud, 2001: 183). Alongside such trends, the growing commercialisation of scientific research and design led, as Ross argues, to an increasing overlap between scientific and economic power. 'Scientific knowledge', Ross states, 'had come to govern the processes of production':

> the goal of modern industrial use of technology had become one of transforming science into capital. Control of science itself became an industrial monopoly: confined to the new corporate research laboratories, or to university locations where research worked hand in hand with corporate interests (1991: 425).

Smith himself was no stranger to industrial America, working throughout his life as a chemist for a variety of donut-mix companies and also as an inspector at an ordnance plant during the Second World War (a role from which he was dismissed for refusing to certify defective weapons). And indeed his protagonists, Seaton and Crane, do not shy away from the benefits of scientific commercialism: barely has the miraculous 'X' been discovered when its commercial potential is being exploited by the 'Seaton-Crane Company', which can 'sell power for less than one-tenth of a cent per kilowatt-hour and still return twenty percent annual dividends' (Smith and Garby, 1928a: 403). In his 1946 revision of *The Skylark of Space*, Smith is even more explicit on this point: Crane, after learning about the kinetic properties of 'X', imagines the financial rewards that may be reaped if they could 'control that power ... put it into a hull ... harness it to the wheels of industry' (1974: 18), having secured their private control over the metal with a 'clear title, signed, sealed, and delivered' (19).

Yet, despite the far-reaching applications of the marvellous 'X' or the new frontiers of knowledge opened by Seaton's interstellar travels, the science that makes these marvels possible remains known only to a select few pioneering individuals. The effort to overcome barriers to human progress is, in the *Skylark* series, an individual effort—Seaton's conservative fellow scientists pour scorn on his claims to have discovered a revolutionary new power source, insisting that his discovery 'came out of either a bottle or a needle' (that is, was born of alcohol or drugs), thus provoking him to develop the technology himself (Smith and Garby, 1928a: 390). As Ross argues, such 'rugged individualism', so often valorised in the SF pulps, offers a response to 'the increasingly Taylorized culture industry': like 'the cowboy and the private detective', the 'genius-inventor' was an 'anachronistic [hero] increasingly employed to criticize the loss of individual autonomy in a bureaucratically organized corporate culture' (1991: 417, 427). Seaton is, in this sense, not a rogue scientist but a figurative embodiment of anti-Taylorist sentiment, while his escape into outer space represents a means of 'escape [from] the new Taylorist tyranny of organized and quantified time and space that had come to preside over the contemporary workplace'—a 'utopian version ... of the desire' to escape a principle of rationality increasingly coming to dominate lived space and time under capitalist modernity (427).

Hence early pulp SF stories such as *Skylark*, Ross argues, react against the capitalist trends of Taylorist management, the corporatisation of scientific development, and the mechanisation of labour. Seaton and Crane rail against the stuffy corporate conformity of the capitalist workplace, preferring to 'be off exploring new worlds' than taking an active part in the running of the Seaton-Crane Company (Smith and Garby, 1928a: 403). It is also telling that the primary villain in the *Skylark* series—the amoral scientist DuQuesne, who seeks exclusive control of 'X'—does so with the co-operation of 'the immense World Steel Corporation'. DuQuesne insists on the subordination of individuals to the species in the service of progressive historical change, demanding to know 'what ... a few lives amount to' compared with the technological advancement of all humanity (395). When later faced with a deadly plunge into a super-sized star, DuQuesne's primary concern is that Seaton should not follow him into the abyss, since to do so would be to lose 'the greatest discovery the world has ever known ... for perhaps hundreds of years' (538). The purposes to which each directs the super-advanced technology gained from their travels to other worlds is also significant: in *Skylark of Valeron*, DuQuesne attempts to establish a global autocracy dedicated to the management of a rational and technologically efficient world, while Seaton devotes himself to overthrowing this autocracy in the name of individual human liberty—to 'the government of right instead of by might' (Smith, 1935b: 151).

DuQuesne's Darwinian outlook—an understanding of his own insignificance in the larger scheme of human endeavour—therefore stands in sharp contrast with Seaton's fierce individualism. DuQuesne and Seaton embody the mass and the individual respectively: while DuQuesne considers the generality of humankind, Seaton is concerned with his own personal self-actualisation. Where the former is committed to biopolitical stasis and the perpetuation of the species, the latter is devoted to the values of individual growth and the exercise of individual agency. Through the characterisation of his independent and resolutely self-directed protagonist, Smith thus rejects the tendency within capitalist modernity towards massification and the subordination of the individual to the biopolitical primacy of the species.

It is thus useful to compare the vastly different works by Huxley and Smith on this basis: they clearly share some key concerns about the effects of capitalist modernity on individual agency and creativity. Smith's works share with *Brave New World* a concern about the consequences of the scientific and corporate management of human individuals. In response to this, Smith, and other writers of pulp SF, recast technology as a manifestation of individual human potential rather than an expression of corporate or economic power—a highly individual mode of empirical control over the natural world. Seaton, the archetypal hero of pulp SF, represents the new face not of *homo economicus*, but of *homo faber*, the tool-building human individual. They are trans-humans, deploying technology as a utopian means to overcome human biological limitations, yet in such a way as to valorise and universalise, rather than transform or overturn, the traditional subject of western humanism. Pulp SF was thus populated by scientific supermen who use their extensive knowledge of scientific and technological principles to almost miraculously shape the natural–material world.

Indeed, it is significant that matter itself in these works comes increasingly *not* to matter at all, substituted by a series of ever-more penetrating 'forces', 'rays', 'waves', 'beams', 'radiation', and other kinds of *non*-matter. Smith's *Skylark Three*, for example, concludes with an interstellar conflict that deploys 'fields of force extending for thousands of miles', between two vessels 'better than two hundred thousand light-years apart', while *The Skylark of Valeron* features a 'projector' that can transmit a person's words and physical likeness across vast distances of space (1930c: 657). As a result, not even the unimaginable reaches of interstellar space—'millions on incandescent millions of miles', distances that are 'absolutely meaningless, even expressed in parsecs' (1930c: 658, 632)—can present a permanent obstacle to human expansion. Early SF narratives are awash with such immaterial forces: the 'cosmic rays' of Campbell's *Islands of Space* (*Amazing Stories Quarterly*, Spring 1931)—'COSMIC RAYS! HIGH CONCENTRATION! Get up the screens!' (173)—or the 'barrier rays' of Williamson's *The Legion of Space* (*Astounding*, Apr–Sep 1934)—'Particles dancing away—radiation—beating through us—disintegrating—our bodies' (128)—or the 'Martian paralysing rays' of Cummings' *Brigands of the Moon* (*Astounding*, Mar–Jun 1930) offer just three of many possible examples.

This focus on intangible forces rather than tangible matter in these narratives offers a response to the unsettling of traditional understandings of space resulting from the techno-economic developments of the early twentieth century. As David Harvey notes, western cultural perceptions of space had undergone a rapid process of collapse since the late nineteenth century as a result of the development of new forms and networks of transportation and communication, the growth of global imperialism, accelerated modes of production, and so on (see Harvey, 1992: 260–83). The global economic catastrophe of 1929, and the spread of American culture lamented by Huxley and Stapledon, revealed the tightly integrated nature of the global economic and cultural field. The 'time–space compression' brought about by this integration, Harvey argues, stimulated a struggle among artists to generate coherent frames of reference through which these rapid spatial changes could be confronted.

One response to these conditions was the tendency towards spatio-temporal 'unity'—the collapse of traditional, local times and places and their replacement with a 'global space bound together through mechanisms of communication and social intervention' (Harvey, 1992: 270). Such unified spatial and temporal frameworks are highly evident in the space-operatic works of the period: the increasingly vast frames of spatial reference in Smith's *Skylark* series reflect this trend towards western globalisation—a tacit acceptance of time–space compression and the unification of previously distinct spaces as facts of contemporary life, and of the need to harness such processes in pursuit of unified human progress and the Enlightenment goal, as Harvey puts it, of 'universal human emancipation' (270). In these works, the expansion is not horizontal—a move that would implicate his characters in the geopolitical complexities of global power relations—but *vertical*, towards the blank frontiers of interstellar space. The extreme collapse of space as portrayed in space-operatic works thus reflects the real-world process of unifying all space within a single, all-encompassing frame of (western) human reference.

In this manner, space opera reflects American fantasies of global domination and its associated imperialist attitudes: in addition to the literary precursors of space opera outlined by Pringle, it is clear that the journeys undertaken by Seaton and his companions owe as much to the lost-world works of Conan Doyle and Kipling as to the westerns and detective stories of earlier pulps. Indeed, the narrative overlap between *The Skylark of Space* and such a work as *The Lost World* is significant: each depicts a group of scientist–adventurers departing from a comfortable life in the prosperous west to undertake a voyage into the unknown, discovering strange new worlds and encountering unfamiliar creatures and lifeforms—a 'jolly journey' that can take place only because the protagonists' command over space guarantees their safe return. In a segment that could have been modelled on the plot of *The Lost World* (and which, incidentally, is later repeated in Campbell's *Islands of Space*), Seaton and his co-adventurers even intervene in a war on another planet: the adventurers aid the 'Kondals', a sympathetic race of aliens native to the planet of 'Osnome', to overcome their mortal enemies, the ruthless 'Mardonales'. In each case, the intervention of a technologically superior race is deemed necessary to the advancement of civilisation: as with Conan Doyle, Smith's depictions of human–non-human relations take the form not of coexistence between equal species but of a technological clash between superior and inferior forms of being.

In answer to Conan Doyle's question as to 'where the romance writer is to turn when he wants to draw any vague and not too clearly defined region', then, space opera points to the blank spaces of the interstellar map, rendered imaginatively available by the technological advances and soaring national confidence of the United States in the 1920s. Furthermore, the encoded hierarchy of the human in *The Skylark of Space* can be understood in similar terms to Conan Doyle's novel. The Mardonales are depicted as a treacherous, slave-owning, and therefore 'bad' race, while the Kondals are the repressed, fundamentally 'good' humans. The symbolism of the conflict is registered in the racial imagery associated with the opposing groups: whereas the antagonistic Mardonales 'shone a dark, livid, utterly indescribable color' (Smith and Garby, 1928b: 554), the friendly Kondals are a 'light, soft green' (615)—representative respectively of their 'dark' and 'light' natures.

The bloody overthrow of the Mardonales, like that of Conan Doyle's ape-men, is thus provoked by their lack of adherence to a recognisably western moral framework. The liberated Kondals herald the encounter with humans as 'the meeting on terms of mutual fellowship and understanding of the inhabitants of two worlds separated by unthinkable distances of trackless space and by equally great differences in evolution, conditions of life, and environment' (Smith and Garby, 1928c: 626). Yet, notwithstanding this noble proclamation, the supremacy of the earth-humans over Osnome is made clear as they become, like the Englishmen on the plateau, the necessary means by which another species secures its evolutionary future. In a final twist, the Kondals go on to pronounce Seaton as 'overlord, the ultimate authority on all Osnome', an instance of imperialist wish-fulfilment—the voluntary submission of the more 'primitive' race to their technological superiors—familiar from *The Lost World* (Smith and Garby, 1928c: 635). The euphoric transcendence of material limits in *The Skylark of Space* expresses an imperialist confidence familiar from Conan Doyle: a belief in the possibility of western dominion over space and in the western *telos* of human advancement to be directed by a benign imperialist force.

So, is *The Skylark of Space* simply *The Lost World* writ in large galactic terms? It certainly shares the confident imperial humanism of Conan Doyle's novel—yet *Skylark* also adheres to a more extreme, and explicitly Cartesian, form of humanism than that of *The Lost World*. Smith's understanding of the term 'human' extends beyond the boundaries of the human body or, indeed, of the biological species—that is, beyond the bounds of *homo sapiens*—encompassing *any* being that exhibits recognisably 'human' qualities. Consider, for example, Seaton's remark on first encountering the Mardonales: 'They're *human*, right enough, but ye gods, what a color!' (Smith and Garby, 1928b: 554, my emphasis). This seems a highly curious remark—how could the Mardonales be considered 'human', given their utterly alien origins? At the same time, we find DuQuesne, an undeniable member of the species *homo sapiens*, described as a 'cold, *inhuman* sort of a fish' (Smith and Garby, 1928a: 404, my emphasis). The meanings assigned to 'human' here extend beyond the merely biological or material, instead privileging abstract moral and intellectual qualities. This use of the term is present throughout Smith's SF works. Roger, the human antagonist of *Triplanetary*, for instance, who resembles DuQuesne in his calculating and amoral manner, is described as being 'scarcely human', 'an over-brained, under-conscienced human machine—a super-intelligent but lecherous and unmoral mechanism of flesh and blood' (1934b: 26). In the *Lensman* series, too, the biologically inhuman alien races that make up the 'Lensmen'—an elite interstellar police force—are united by a common dedication to the advancement of civilisation: a mission 'of paramount importance to all the intelligent peoples of all the planets in space' (1979: 54).

This understanding of 'human' as emphasising shared intellectual and moral, not biological, qualities is a recurring facet of space opera, as in this passage from Edmond Hamilton's 'Crashing Suns' (*Weird Tales*, Aug–Sep 1928):

> Beings there were among those thousands from every peopled sun in all the Galaxy's hosts, drawn here like myself to represent his star in this great Council which ruled our universe. Creatures there were utterly weird and alien in appearance ... —creatures from Aldebran, turtle-men of the amphibian races of that star; fur-covered and slow-moving beings from the planets of the dying Betelgeuse; great octopus-creatures from mighty Vega; ... these, and a thousand others, were gathered in that vast assemblage, forms utterly different from each other physically, but able to mix and understand each other *on the common plane of intelligence* (1965: 93, my emphasis).

This final phrase—the 'common plane of intelligence'—underscores the precedence granted to the intellect as the key site of human development and advancement in early magazine SF. This is not to suggest that the body is disregarded: Seaton, the archetypal pulp SF hero, is a superman in a physical as well as intellectual sense, with 'muscles writhing and rippling in great ridges under the satin skin of his broad back' (Smith and Garby, 1928b: 559). But the significance of the body is consistently downplayed in comparison to the mind.

It is necessary, then, to distinguish between the 'human' in its physical and intellectual manifestations: whereas the evil Fenachrone race in *Skylark Three* are *physically* humanoid, 'with recognizable features', they are nevertheless equipped with a 'gigantic and *inhuman* brain', the result of a 'monstrous and unspeakable culture' (1930b: 546, my emphasis). Conversely, when, in *Skylark of Valeron*, Seaton declares 'Humanity *über alles—homo sapiens* against all the vermin of the universe', he is referring to the *intellectually* human: those beings committed to progress and the 'march ... towards civilisation' (1934a: 140). The epilogue of *Skylark Three* makes the distinction clear:

> Varied are the physical forms and varied are the mentalities of our almost innumerable races of beings, but in Civilization we are becoming one, since those backward people who will not co-operate

with us are rendered impotent to impede our progress among the more enlightened (1930c: 658).

To resist the forward march of intellectual 'enlightenment' is to be considered 'backward', regardless of biology—to be, like the Mardonales and the Fenachrone, atavistic throwbacks in the progressive evolution of an abstracted and (literally) universal 'humanity'.

The popularity of the motif of telepathy within pulp SF neatly illustrates this preoccupation with corporeal transcendence. Like many pulp SF writers from the period, Smith assumes that the development of telepathic powers—literally, the abstraction of thought from its physical basis—will be a natural step for humankind. In Smith's fiction, telepathy enables the transcendence of the human body, offering a universal medium of communication with which alien beings can transcend differences in biology and culture and connect 'on the common plane of intelligence'. Central to the *Lensman* series, for example, is the notion that beings from different planets, wildly different in bodily composition and linguistic facility, can communicate easily and swiftly with each other using a universal telepathic code, thus dissolving contingencies of culture, language, and custom within the universal 'language' of higher intellectual thought. Since only beings of a high degree of intellectual and moral calibre can qualify as 'Lensmen' in the first place, telepathy, and the capacity for higher thought that enables it, thus becomes reconfigured as a shared and essential quality of all 'advanced' and 'civilised' beings.

In their use of telepathy, Smith's stories and wider early pulp SF precisely prefigure concepts later associated with transhumanism, which privileges 'informational pattern over material instantiation, such that embodiment in a biological substrate is seen as an accident of history rather than an inevitability of life' (Hayles, 1999: 2). Transhumanism, as Robert Ranisch and Stefan Lorenz Sorgner note, constitutes 'a contemporary renewal of humanism': an intensified humanism which 'embraces and eventually amplifies central aspects of secular and Enlightenment humanist thought, such as belief in reason, individualism, science, progress, as well as self-perfection or cultivation' (2014: 8). Transhumanism is thus committed to technological transcendence—a furthering of human evolution through ever-greater interface with technological systems. The transcendence depicted in the *Skylark* series is of a similar type, privileging the abstract qualities of the mind (telepathy, the constant drive for ever-deeper intellectual control over nature) and immaterial natural forces ('rays', 'waves', 'radiation', and so on) over the material substance of the body and the material space of nature.

There are, then, differing notions of the human in the *Skylark* series. On the one hand, there is the fierce individualism and technological autonomy of Seaton—on the other, the communalism and universalism of the 'human' mind, by means of which all 'civilised' beings march towards teleological unity under the flag of intellectual and civilisational progress. Seaton represents both 'versions' of humanity: he is both a self-possessed and self-actualising individual *and* an abstracted incarnation of the 'human' kind of intellectual being (as opposed to a 'human being', a biological member of the species *homo sapiens*).

This dialectic is dramatically depicted, for example, in the conclusion of *The Skylark of Valeron*. Following a dizzying series of adventures, Seaton and his co-adventurers find themselves confronted with a group of disembodied 'Intellectuals'—literally, a group of incorporeal individuals, with no tangible or material components, who roam the galaxy seeking other powerful minds to add to their number. To combat these ghostly figures, Seaton invents a literal thinking machine—a 'towering mechano-electrical Brain'—to be utilised in a mental duel against these enemies. The Brain amplifies Seaton's own intellectual powers: with it, as he says, 'I can see anything I want to look at, anywhere; can hear anything I want to hear. It can build, make, do, or perform anything that my brain can think of' (1935a: 74). After using the Brain to defeat the Intellectuals, Seaton turns his invention over to the newly formed 'Galactic Council' who, it is implied, will use it to guide the future course of galactic affairs.

In one sense, the Brain is the pinnacle of Seaton's intellectual evolution throughout the *Skylark* works, a climactic and Herculean synthesis of his comprehensive knowledge into a device destined 'soon to become the most stupendous force for good ever to be conceived by the mind of man' (1935a: 73). The Brain also serves, however, as a metaphorical species-brain, a repository of all human knowledge, history, and experience—as the *telos*, in Aristotle's terminology, of human command over time, space, and life:

> All the pangs and all the ecstasies, all the thoughts and all the emotions of all evolution of all things, animate and inanimate, are there; of all things that ever have existed from the unknowable beginning of infinite time and of all things that shall ever exist until time's unknowable end. It covers all animate life, from the first stirrings of that which was to vitalize the first universe in the slime of the first world ever to come into being in the cosmos, to the last cognition of the ultimately last intelligent entity ever to be (1935b: 146).

In the icon of the Brain, we have circled back to Williamson's vision of a 'universe ruled by the human mind ... of a civilisation that has conquered matter and Nature, distance and time'. The Brain makes possible a utopia of human rule over matter—western technocracy writ in galactic terms—while Seaton comprises both a self-actualising human individual and an allegory for the advancement of the whole 'human race'. Seaton thus figures, as described by his wife Dorothy, as both 'man' and 'god' (1935b: 154)—both a lone pioneering figure *and* a collective emblem of the human's imperial sway over nature.

In Smith's *Skylark* series, then, 'humanity' encompasses meanings co-extensive with the 'humanity' of Enlightenment thought. The human in Smith is an intellectual phenomenon, present within the physical body yet also reflective of a universal, progressive and rational 'mind' that extends beyond biological barriers, incorporating each new entity it encounters—human and non-human alike—into a steadfastly human-centred narrative of teleological progress.

Conclusion

We end with two vastly different visions of the trans-human. On the one hand, there is Huxley's dystopic image of technological determinism, with the human individual rendered powerless by technological systems beyond their control. On the other, there is Smith's utopic image of human self-actualisation, evincing ever-greater technological control over the material world in the service of human biological transcendence and emancipation.

Huxley's notion of the 'life-worshipper' is the most useful concept for transformative posthumanist thought to emerge from the preceding discussion. In the introduction, I mentioned Halberstam and Livingstone's concept of 'someness'—a quality of hybridity, rejecting both unities and dualisms. This quality is at work in Huxley's fiction: his insistence on the need to balance the animal and spiritual aspects of human nature, and his deep distrust of universals, abstractions, and absolutes, demonstrate the concept of 'someness' in action. The relationship between mind and matter in Huxley's thought is one not of domination but of synthesis.

Huxley can be clearly distinguished from such a writer as Smith—or, indeed, Conan Doyle or London—on this basis: the complete mastery of the body in such characters as Seaton, Everhard, and (to a lesser extent) Challenger and Roxton—products of nineteenth-century notions concerning the ideal 'Man'—expresses a broader imperial impulse of mastery over nature. Nature, in the works of these writers, is something simply to be conquered or instrumentalised. Huxley, conversely, stresses an organic relationship between mind and matter, or culture and nature, in which neither is permitted to rule over the other. Invested in the tradition of western intellectual thought, yet critical of instrumental rationalism as a threat to core human values, Huxley rejects old universals and narratives in favour of new forms of meaning (hallucinogenics, eastern humanist religions) and more dynamic and critical human communities. This is not a fully posthumanist image—Huxley rejects older forms of humanism but seeks to reform rather than overturn them while remaining committed to a universalist notion of humanity—yet it does prefigure certain preoccupations that would later come under that heading.

The broadly optimistic tone and assimilative technocratic outlook of American pulp SF, meanwhile, would continue right up to the 1940s, when world events would force a revision of such technophilic attitudes. The United States, as I will examine in the next chapter, becomes the undisputed centre of SF production in the mid-century period—a time when questions about individual agency and autonomy in the context of mass society would come ever more to trouble SF, leading to diverse new forms of the human.

Chapter Three

Homo Gestalt: Atomics, empire, and the supra-human in Isaac Asimov's *Foundation* and Arthur C. Clarke's *The City and the Stars*

> Their memories, their projections and computations flooded in to Gerry, until at last he knew their nature and their function; and he knew why the ethos he had learned was too small a concept ... Here was why and how humanity existed, troubled and dynamic, sainted by the touch of its own great destiny. Here was the withheld hand as thousands died, when millions might live. And here, too, was the guide, the beacon, for such times as humanity might be in danger; here was the Guardian of Whom all humans knew—not an exterior force, nor an awesome Watcher in the sky, but a laughing thing with a human heart and a reverence for its human origins. ...
>
> He saw himself as an atom and his *gestalt* as a molecule. He saw these others as a cell among cells, and he saw in the whole the design of what, with joy, humanity would become (Sturgeon, 1968: 188).

In his 1953 novel, *More Than Human*, Theodore Sturgeon depicts a radical new kind of human being. *Homo gestalt* is a compound individual: a group of persons who, over the course of the narrative, 'blesh'—that is, 'blend' and 'mesh'—to form a composite consciousness. Each individual within *homo gestalt* retains their self-identity, yet the group also functions as a hive mind with a single subjectivity. Initially, the *gestalt* comprises only six individuals, but by the novel's close this group has joined a throng of other minds acting as a single *gestalt* consciousness. The function of *homo gestalt*, as indicated in the above passage, is one of benevolent guardianship, guiding humanity along a course of progressive historical development and influencing figures as diverse as William Morris, Enrico Fermi, and even Henry Ford. With *homo gestalt* as custodian, it is suggested, humanity is safe from annihilation: '*in terms of the history of the race',* the *gestalt* consciousness states, *'atomic war is a ripple on the broad face of the Amazon!'* (188, emphasis in original).

Sturgeon's novel depicts a version of the 'supra-human', the archetypal human figure of this chapter, which becomes an important vehicle for the exploration of posthumanism in mid-century SF. As the twentieth century advanced, traditional notions of possessive individuality, agency, and autonomy came under ever-increasing threat from the growth of bureaucratic systems and mass social, political, and technological regimes. The bombings of Hiroshima and Nagasaki, and the concentration camps of Europe, presented the horrifying consequences that could result from such anonymising processes. The supra-human emerges in response to these concerns: it is a composite human figure, an aggregate body comprising a huge mass—indeed, often a galaxy—of individuals. This human 'figure' both encompasses and surpasses the individual—yet, significantly, the supra-human is also paternal, acting, like Sturgeon's *homo gestalt*, as a custodial figure to nurture humanity towards a higher level of development or consciousness. Accordingly, the supra-human is also motivated by concerns familiar from the humanist tradition: human progress and evolution, technological advance, and the conflict between biological individualism and technological transcendence.

I will examine two major works from the mid-century period: Isaac Asimov's *Foundation* series (1942–1949) and Arthur C. Clarke's *The City and the Stars* (1956). Asimov was one of the most influential writers to emerge in the Golden Age of SF, and his subsequent impact on the field has been profound—as John Clute notes, 'his was the default voice of the genre, the voice of SF speaking to itself' (2005: 365). Like London's *The Iron Heel*, *Foundation* brings two opposing ideas of the human individual—as both free and active social agent *and* passive victim of socio-historical forces—into conflict. *Foundation* depicts the emergence of a biopolitical 'Empire' (in Hardt and Negri's use of that term) in which the needs of the individual are subordinated to those of the social mass. The alienation inherent in this system, however, is modified by paternalistic institutions that safeguard humanity from the violence of fascist rule. In this way, Asimov assimilates the bureaucratic tendencies of mass society into an optimistic vision of progressive and technocratic humanism.

I will then turn to the works of Arthur C. Clarke, the writer who, after Asimov, has had perhaps the greatest influence on the course of post-war SF. Clarke arrived to the field as the Golden Age was coming to an end, and was a major contributor to the more brooding mode of SF that emerged in the late 1940s and 1950s. Clarke's works demonstrate a sense of ontological 'humility': humanity, he suggests, must acknowledge both its own technological shortcomings and the possibility of beings radically more advanced than itself. This humility informs his vision of the galactic empire: as in Asimov's *Foundation*, it is a technological empire, made possible by ever-greater human command over the material world—yet it is also distinguished from the empire of *Foundation* by its symbiosis of individual and society. Whereas Asimov stresses the need for external controls that trade individual agency for social stability, Clarke instead envisions a transcendent cosmic 'body' made up of active and co-operating individual 'cells'.

Before examining these authors, I will briefly consider the broader context of mid-century SF. The works of this period can be divided into two broad categories corresponding to the technophilic and technophobic traditions identified in previous chapters. Whereas Golden Age SF adheres to the technocratic precepts and Enlightenment rationalism inherited from pulp SF, the SF that appeared after the Second World War exhibits a more reflective and anti-progressive outlook. I will then examine the significance of the technoscientific 'Empire' in mid-century SF, which provides a flexible icon with which to allegorise the human relationship to mass society.

Atomics and empire in the 'Golden Age' and beyond

In the introduction to *Adventures in Time and Space*, their important 1946 anthology of magazine SF, Raymond J. Healy and J. Francis McComas make some remarkable comments on the political and technological developments of their age:

> Our time is both conditioned and challenged by the quiet men in the laboratories. The war demonstrated that God is no longer on the side of the heaviest battalions, but on that of the heaviest thinkers. The atomic explosions have destroyed more than Japanese cities; they have broken the chains that have held man earthbound since his beginnings. The universe is ours. Over and above all problems of imperialism, racism, economic and political instability, is the question: what shall we do with that universe? For once in his history, the most average of men is concerned with more than his own immediate future (1974: par. 2).

Many of the sentiments expressed in this brief passage echo the discussion of pulp SF in the previous chapter. There is the appeal to the 'quiet men in the laboratory', recalling the larger-than-life scientist–engineers who propelled humankind, willingly or otherwise, to the stars in the early space operas. There is the prioritisation of abstract thought over mere matter—of 'thinkers' over 'battalions'—in the history of human achievement. And there is a familiar sense of imperial chauvinism: the 'universe', we are assured, is 'ours', ready to be exploited for the sake of human progress. The precise demography of 'we' is never explored: the uncomfortable 'problems' resulting from the long history of white patriarchal imperialism are as ever dismissed in the service of 'universal' human progress, codifying a western, and particularly US, imperial fantasy as the destiny of an abstracted and globalised 'man'.

Yet this passage also reveals certain forebodings regarding humanity's apparent destiny in the stars. The year before the publication of the anthology saw the detonation of (as Truman put it) 'the most terrible bomb in the history of the world' (quoted in Glover, 2001: 101). In his editorial in *Astounding* in November 1945, John W. Campbell heralded the arrival of the 'Atomic Age', writing that 'the civilization we have been born into, lived in, and indoctrinated with, died on July 16: 1945' (1945: 5). Healy and McComas' offhand reference to the destruction of Hiroshima and Nagasaki recalls a familiar spectre that runs through much post-war SF: the destruction or corruption of humanity by means of atomic technologies, whether through radiation poisoning, mutation, or the ever-present threat of 'mutually assured destruction' between global superpowers. Little wonder, then, that 'average men' were turning their thoughts to the future: the shadow of the Cold War meant that the future was no longer certain.

In this section, I will be treating Healy and McComas' 1946 anthology as a watershed text, marking a culmination of the tropes and ideas that defined the 'Golden Age' of SF. This is the period beginning in or around 1937, the year in which Campbell took over as editor of *Astounding Science Fiction*, one of the most popular SF pulps of the 1930s. Following his appointment, Campbell moved quickly to remake the magazine into a more mature SF publication. In the process, he also helped to establish or consolidate the reputations of several significant writers, including Isaac Asimov, Robert Heinlein, A.E. Van Vogt, Clifford Simak, Lester del Rey, and Theodore Sturgeon. The term 'Golden Age' is used here as a convenience: there is no universal agreement as to when the period began or ended, and the relevance of the term has often been disputed. Yet, as James Gunn remarks, 'the phrase itself is not as useful as the attitude towards science fiction that it implies' (1979: viii). The term 'Golden Age' serves a useful purpose in this regard: notwithstanding its dubious connotations regarding the quality of the work produced during this time, the term usefully distinguishes between the outlandish super-science stories of the 1930s and the more thematically complex and self-consciously sociological works that characterised the 1940s.

The Golden Age stories appeared in a context of growing technological hegemony that had characterised social life in the United States since the 1920s and which, following the slump of the 1930s, was reinvigorated in the years prior to and during the Second World War. As Michel Beaud notes, the global economic system of the mid-twentieth century was 'hierarchical ... with the United States as the dominant imperialism in the economic, monetary, technical, military, political, and ideological domains, as well as its way of life and diffusion of information' (2001: 251). The post-1945 economic boom—which for other developed nations, as Eric Hobsbawm remarks, constituted a period of 'catching up'—was for the US merely 'a continuation of old trends' (2006: 263). By the middle of the century, the US was firmly established as the world's dominant imperial superpower, and 'effectively exercised control of national politics in the states of the Caribbean and Latin America, the Pacific and Asia, the Middle and Near East, Africa, and to some extent even Europe' (Hobsbawm, 2006: 12).

Moreover, as Carroll Pursell notes, the first decades of the twentieth century saw the gradual emergence in the US of a 'social hegemony' dominated by 'American technology' (2007: xiv). During the period from the 1920s up to the Second World War, US social attitudes towards technology were characterised by the slogan of the 1933 'Chicago Century of Progress' World's Fair: 'Science Finds—Industry Applies—Man Conforms' (quoted in Pursell, 2007: 230). The technocratic bent of this slogan, and the peculiarly passive human figure that it conjures up, emphasises the assumed centrality of science and technology to twentieth-century human life, with the implication that humanity need only submit itself to the needs of technological development to achieve social and political harmony. Even following the economic turbulence of the 1930s, Pursell goes on, attitudes towards technological progress in the US were 'still understood in terms of cultural lag—that is, that society was lagging in its ability to deal with the material changes wrought by science and technology' (268). Progress was evident not only in the ever-growing variety of consumer goods that had been appearing in American homes since the 1920s, but also in the gradual shift, after 1933, of scientific expertise in the natural sciences away from Europe towards the US (Hobsbawm, 2006: 523).

The Golden Age thus coincided with a period of US global domination during which the transformation of everyday private and political life by advanced technology, far from being exceptional, was assumed. Atomic technology in Golden Age works symbolised both the apex of human collective scientific effort and a springboard from which to launch the next stage in human development. If the atomic bomb highlighted the dangers of human technological hubris, it was nevertheless, as Raymond F. Jones put it in 1946, 'boundless in its resources' (Healy and McComas, 1974: 965). Atomic technology featured in magazine SF as the 'central component of the belief that technological innovation was the principal revolutionary force in the world' (Berger, 1979: 121). Hence even those stories depicting the social and psychological costs of exploiting atomic technology—Heinlein's 'Blowups Happen' (1940), for example, or Lester del Rey's 'Nerves' (1942)—stop short of questioning whether such technologies should exist. In other stories, technology is directly equated to social and civilisational progress: in Van Vogt's 'The Weapons Shop' (1942), for instance, in which an underground organisation of arms dealers combats the decadent 'Empress' of the solar system, or in the stories of Heinlein's future history, *The Past Through Tomorrow* (1939–1962), which depict the dynamic effects of various technologies—'rolling roads' and 'atomic piles'—on the political and economic shape of US society. As Walter J. Miller put it in 1954, 'A man could change his politics, his friends, his religion, his country, but Men's tools were a part of his body ... Trading it for a stone would be like cutting off his arm. Man was a user of tool, a shaper of environments' (2010: par. 3).

This utopian view of technology, however, came increasingly into question after the Second World War, and particularly following the 'single, instantaneous Let There Be Death' of Hiroshima and Nagasaki (Disch, 1998: 80). Paul Boyer argues that 'Hiroshima ended the luxury of detachment' that had characterised cultural perceptions of atomic technology (1994: 258). Far from equating technology with social advance—as in the Golden Age works of Asimov, Heinlein, Van Vogt, and others—post-Hiroshima SF was forced to confront the possibility of mass human self-immolation by means of atomic weaponry. There thus emerged a more circumspect and pessimistic strain of SF with its roots in the works of Wells, Huxley, Čapek, and Zamyatin. Indeed, many of Campbell's own stories from the 1930s (published under the pseudonym 'Don A. Stuart') pre-empted the concerns of 1940s and 1950s SF regarding human technological suicide, whether through nuclear holocaust or the subversion of human creativity and agency through technological means.

This dynamic is evident in many SF texts from the period. The threat of atomic holocaust, for example, looms large in George Pal's Cold War reimagining of Wells's *The War of the World* (1953), with its scenes of mass global panic and urban destruction, and in more muted form in Ray Bradbury's evocative short story, 'There Will Come Soft Rains' (1950), in which the peaceful image of an automated house, mindlessly preparing breakfast for its absent occupants, is contrasted with the silhouettes of children blasted in ash upon its exterior wall. Neville Shute's popular *On the Beach* (1957) disdains explicit images of violence or destruction in favour of the quiet gloom of a post-apocalyptic world, as a lethal cloud of radioactive dust makes its inexorable way across the southern hemisphere towards the last remaining survivors of a nuclear conflict. Two other works, Simak's *City* (1952) and Leigh Brackett's *The Long Tomorrow* (1955), emphasise the long-term psychological and social consequences of atomic weapons for human society. Urban life in both works is rendered untenable by the menace of the 'atom bomb'—as Simak writes, 'if the cities of the world had not been deserted, they would have been destroyed' as they offered all-too-easy targets for mass civilian casualties (2011: 22). The result in each case is a fundamental upheaval of human society. *City* depicts the entropic extinction of humanity as it escapes into 'The Sleep' (a form of suspended animation) or else undergoes the material and psychological transformation required for posthuman existence on Jupiter. *The Long Tomorrow*, by contrast, depicts the emergence of radical anti-rationalism and anti-progressivism in the US as a fundamentalist Christian revival sweeps across a newly pre-technological American southwest. In both cases, atomic technology renders untenable the familiar social structures of the twentieth century.

In other works, the fear is not holocaust but physical and psychological mutation. Atomic mutation replaces eugenics as the primary means of imagining disability in mid-century SF: where disabled individuals were before treated as evolutionary aberrations that threatened to pollute the human gene pool, they now figured as symbols, tragic and threatening, of humanity's technological hubris. This can be detected in two important stories: Judith Merrill's 'That Only a Mother' (1948) and Richard Matheson's 'Born of Man and Woman' (1950). Each story features a child victim of mutation: in the former, a disabled child and her emotionally vulnerable mother are depicted as hapless by-products of nuclear fallout, while in the latter the mutated child, initially a helpless victim of parental abuse, becomes by the end of the narrative an alarming and alien threat to the stability of one suburban household. Nuclear mutation also figures as a trope in the 1954 SF film, *Them!* In this film, concerns about mutations are generalised into an anxiety concerning human supremacy over nature. Given the radical possibilities generated by nuclear technologies in the 'Atomic Age', symbolised by the giant ants and prehistoric beasts of 1950s SF films, the future of human dominance on the planet became, as one character puts it, something that 'nobody can predict'.

One of the most widespread anxieties in mid-century works, and one that I will explore in relation to Asimov and Clarke, is the apparent subjugation of the individual to the needs of mass society. This is reflected, as Scott Sanders argues, in the growing sublimation of character to thematic or ideological concerns in much SF of the twentieth century. Sanders argues that, as a genre, SF assumes the inconstancy of social forms and, as a result, '[theme] replaces character as the organizing principle' (1977: 14). In particular, SF emerges in response to the 'dissolution' of the individual within mass society, taking as its starting point the assumption that social processes, rather than individuals, are the key sites of dynamic change in society and that the significance of the individual in society is correspondingly diminished (15). Hence, SF can be read as a symptom of the increasing bureaucratisation and massification of US society in the twentieth century:

> the science fiction novel offers an extension and restatement of the central problem with which the modernists wrestled—namely, the fragmentation and anonymization of the self in modern society ... The primacy of system over individual appears formally in the genre in the subordination of character to plot; in the use of stereotypical characters; in the preference for technical and discursive (and therefore anonymous) language (15).

Sanders overstates the insignificance of character in SF, particularly as the genre became more stylistically and thematically sophisticated in the post-war period—yet his assessment offers a useful way of thinking about the context of mid-century works. The intensifying mechanisation that characterised the interwar years, culminating in the unprecedented industrial warfare of the Second World War—a conflict typified, as Alex Goody remarks, by 'aloof perpetrators and an undifferentiated mass of victims' (2011: 85)—did much to emphasise the intense vulnerability of the individual to large-scale, anonymous social processes. As Daniel Bell argues, the 'pervasive cultural theme' of the 1940s and 1950s 'was the depersonalization of the individual and the atomization of society' (1972: 20). There could be no more effective demonstration of this than the dropping of atomic bombs over Japan. Indeed, Jonathan Glover suggests that the very decision to deploy nuclear weapons was at least partly enabled by the 'fragmentation of responsibility' within the distributed power networks of modern political systems. As a result,

Glover remarks, 'the sense of personal responsibility' in the atomic bombings 'was reduced by the way agency was fragmented' (2001: 103). Both facets of the bombings—the decision-making process and the atrocious outcome—demonstrate a shattering of the individual as the primary site of, respectively, social agency and human value.

Such themes are explored in many works of the period. The dampening effects of mechanisation on human creativity, for example, are explored in Jack Williamson's 'With Folded Hands...' (1947), in which the spread of benevolent helper robots causes the infantilisation of humanity. Conversely, the mechanisation of the human itself can be seen in such stories as C.L. Moore's 'No Woman Born' (1944), William Tenn's 'Child's Play' (1947), and Cordwainer Smith's 'Scanners Live in Vain' (1950), each of which depicts the penetration of the human body by various technological systems. The suppression of individuality and persecution of deviancy also appear in a variety of works. In Van Vogt's *Slan* (1940), for instance, a race of telepathic, physically powerful humans are hunted down and slaughtered by a dictatorial government in a clear allusion to the treatment of the Jews in Nazi Germany (Mullen, 1975: 284)—in each case, the persecution rests on the assumed inhumanity of the suppressed population, which is then recast as a threat to the social and cultural 'purity' of the dominant 'race'. Themes of social conformism and alienation may also be found in Jack Finney's *The Body Snatchers* (1954, filmed in 1956 as *Invasion of the Body Snatchers*) and Philip K. Dick's 'The Father Thing' (1954), each of which expresses a fear of oppressive social and cultural conformity suggestive of McCarthy-era persecution. Such anxieties are further expanded in works such as Richard Matheson's *I Am Legend* (1954) and John Wyndham's *The Chrysalids* (1955) to encompass a broader fear of assimilation into an anonymous and sterile mass society. And, finally, Poul Anderson's *Brain Wave* (1954) laments the growth of invasive bureaucratic systems: scientific research in the mid-century, Anderson writes, suffers from 'projectitis' (2013: 9), that is, the stultification of creativity by mass bureaucratic and administrative systems, a theme also evident in William Tenn's 'The Brooklyn Project' (1948) and Raymond F. Jones's 'The Person from Porlock' (1947).

Istvan Csicsery-Ronay Jr. offers one potentially useful way of thinking about the subjugation of individual to social forces in SF. Drawing on Michael Hardt and Antonio Negri's *Empire* (2000), Csicsery-Ronay argues that SF 'has been driven by the desire for the imaginary transformation of imperialism into Empire': 'a technological regime that affects and ensures the global control system of de-nationalized communications' (2003: 232). Following the First World War, the SF empire increasingly came to take the form, as Csicsery-Ronay argues, of 'technoscientific Empire—Empire that is managed, sustained, justified, but also riven by simultaneously interlocking and competing technologies of social control and material expansion' (236). It is, in other words, an increasingly post-nationalist empire, one underpinned by a recognisably US ideology of technocratic imperialism whose expansion is registered in its ever-growing command over matter, particularly interstellar space—'a cosmos', as Csicsery-Ronay puts it, 'governed by the laws and right of technoscience' (238). Such empires can, of course, take on both utopian and dystopian qualities: indeed, as Csicsery-Ronay argues, 'Most serious sf writers are sceptical of entrenched power, sometimes because of its tyranny, sometimes because it hobbles technological innovation' (241). Hence, while writers such as Heinlein or Smith celebrate the libertarian possibilities generated by technocratic principles, others such as Huxley or Čapek warn of the existential cost of substituting technological for political or cultural power in society.

The key phrase in Csicsery-Ronay's outline of the SF 'Empire' is 'technological regime'. In this study, I have been interested in how technology underpins humanist and posthumanist conceptions of nature, society, and humanity itself. SF can be read as an aesthetic response to the overlapping ontologies of human and technology—a relationship between 'man and machine ... in which neither can be reduced to the other', both having instead to co-exist in 'a reciprocal relationship' (Armstrong, 1998: 86). As Andreas Huyssen remarks, the experience of technology in the first half of the twentieth century can be divided into the 'aestheticization of technics ... on the one hand and the horror of technics inspired by the awesome war machinery of World War I on the other' (1986: 10)—what Peter Childs describes as 'a championing as well as a fear of technology' (2000: 4) that echoes the distinction between technophilic and technophobic works that has informed this study. These contrasting perceptions of technology are incorporated in various ways into the SF works I have examined so far: in the valorisation of technology in the works of Verne and Smith, the authority granted to scientific and technical discourse in Verne and Doyle, and the contrasting condemnations (from quite different standpoints) of the technological and industrial transformation of human nature in Huxley and London. Each of these works must be understood as an aesthetic response to the conditions of modernisation in the nineteenth and early twentieth centuries.

The rapid growth of technological and bureaucratic systems in the lead up to the Second World War and beyond produced an alteration in SF notions of the individual. Within the 'technoscientific regimes' of many SF works—as in the real biopolitical regimes of the mid-century—the question becomes how the relationship between individual and society is to be imagined or realised. The liberal humanist model of the active and autonomous subject, endowed with the capacity for meaningful social action, seems ill-equipped to deal with the realities of mid-century mass society. One potential alternative, as in the works of Asimov and Clarke, may be found in the figure of the supra-human. The supra-human is the natural citizen of the SF 'Empire': by transferring the capacities and anxieties of the individual human being to the mass social body, the supra-human allegorically resolves the conflict between humanist individualism and mass, anonymous social and political forces. To explore this notion in more detail, I turn first to Asimov's *Foundation*.

Benevolent biopolitics in Asimov's *Foundation*

In a 1987 interview, Asimov outlined his views regarding the significance and fate of the human species. Responding to the possibility that robots may one day become 'sufficiently intelligent to replace us', Asimov responds:

> I think they should. We have had many cases in the course of human evolution, and the vast evolution of life before that, in which one species replaced another, because the replacing species was in one way or another more efficient than the species replaced. I don't think Homo sapiens possesses any divine right to the top rung ... As a matter of fact, my feeling is that we are doing such a miserable job in preserving the Earth and its life-forms that I can't help but feel the sooner we're replaced the better for all other forms of life (quoted in Ingersoll, 1987: 69).

Asimov here summarises two distinct narratives of human progress. The first is biological, situating humanity as the dominant species of evolutionary history with the responsibility of 'preserving' the rest of nature. The second, in contrast, is technological, looking ahead to a time when technological artefacts have gained the sentience required to sustain themselves and may opt to supersede humanity as the rulers of the earth. For Asimov, this is no Frankensteinian moment of terror: an unapologetic 'rationalist' (1995b: 13), Asimov is committed to embracing humanity's overthrow if it arises as the logical outcome of an evolutionary process.

Asimov's words suggest a great deal about his views concerning the human being and human society, and his beliefs concerning paternalism, rationality, mechanism, and his prioritisation of species over individual. These themes inform Asimov's *Foundation*, one of the best-known series in western SF (beating even Tolkien's *The Lord of the Rings* to claim the Hugo Award for 'Best All-Time Series' in 1965). Patterned on Gibbon's *The Decline and Fall of the Roman Empire*, the series centres on the rise and fall of the 'Galactic Empire', an imperial system comprising the millions of inhabited worlds of the Milky Way. At the beginning of the series, Hari Seldon, a mathematician on the planet of 'Trantor' (the central planet of the Empire), has developed a set of mathematical and sociological techniques for predicting the future evolution of any given society. After applying the principles of 'psychohistory' (as he terms his new science) to the Galactic Empire, Seldon realises that the Empire is on the verge of social and political collapse. In response, he establishes a colony of intellectuals on an isolated planet, with the ostensible aim of collating and preserving the massed knowledge of the galaxy before its collapse. This colony, called the 'Foundation', is intended to act as the germ for the second Galactic Empire, with its historical development following the course of a secret 'Plan' devised by Seldon himself.

The original trilogy then follows the fortunes of the Foundation over the first four centuries of its development. The first *Foundation* novel depicts the early years of the colony, as the inhabitants of Terminus establish control over their more powerful neighbours and overcome a series of economic and political 'crises' predicted by Seldon. In the follow-up novels, *Foundation and Empire* and *Second Foundation*, the citizens of the Foundation face further crises, both predicted and unforeseen, including a final confrontation with the dying Empire, the rise of the 'Mule'—a mutant who can manipulate the emotions of those around him and who threatens to seize control of the galaxy—and the discovery of the 'Second Foundation', a community of telepaths secretly established by Seldon to guide the course of the First Foundation along the 'Seldon Plan'.

As I will argue, *Foundation* advocates a biopolitical social system in which the desires of the individual are sublimated to the continuation of the species, guided by benevolent, rational, and paternalistic institutions. The view of the individual that emerges in Asimov's works is mechanistic: like his famous robots, constrained by the 'Three Laws' that dictate their range of possible behaviours, Asimov's humans are determined by fixed, calculable behaviours, and subject to mass biopolitical control by faceless organisations. In the end, *Foundation* offers a vision, not of posthumanism, but rather of *supra*-humanism, in which the central focus of the humanist narrative shifts from the level of the individual to that of the whole species while retaining the central emphasis on reason as the key principle for human progress.

I begin this analysis by examining the genesis of Asimov's series, which, as with his famous *Robot* stories, appeared early in his writing career. Like many Golden Age writers, Asimov was a protégé of Campbell, and *Foundation* first appeared as a series of stories in the pages of *Astounding* between 1942 and 1949. Campbell had a major impact on the drafting of the works: Asimov had originally intended to write only a single story about the collapse of a 'Galactic Empire', but Campbell encouraged him instead to produce a 'long open-ended saga' covering thousands of years of galactic history (1995b: 117). This proposal accorded well with Asimov's own literary preoccupations: he had a keen interest in history (Asimov briefly considered undertaking a Ph.D. in that subject before switching to chemistry), and was interested in using SF to explore not only social and political ideas but the evolution *over time* of such ideas (1995b: 116). In a 1995 essay, Asimov distinguishes between narratives concerned with developing 'an insight into the characters of the individuals who people the story' and those concerned with 'ideas' (1996: 314–15). Asimov places his own works squarely in this latter category: 'I am so intent on presenting my opposing ideas', he writes, 'that I make no serious attempt to characterise brilliantly' (315), instead using his characters to represent specific ideological viewpoints and 'champion alternative views of life and the universe' (315).

The *Foundation* trilogy thus takes in a broad focus on social and historical evolution that differs markedly from the SF of the 1920s and 1930s. Such a theme—the dynamic movement of human society through time—was for Asimov the natural subject of SF. In a 1953 essay, Asimov writes that, if SF is to amount to anything 'more than let's-pretend object lessons', then writers must grapple seriously with the idea that 'human society not only could change but that it did' (1971: 273). He then goes on to define three types of SF—'gadget', 'adventure', and 'social'—before situating his own works in the final category. Donald M. Hassler makes a similar point regarding the depiction of technology in the *Foundation* series: Asimov, he argues, by declaring his major interest to be 'the influence of social change and history' and thereby fixing his interest on the 'why' of social forces rather than the 'how' of purely technological wizardry, 'effectively disassociates himself from the "gadget" materialism of [other] SF writers' (1988: 40). In doing so, he locates his interests in descriptions neither of richly realised human characters nor of new technologies, but in the human societies in which such technologies have 'already [been] perfected' and are therefore 'already a problem' (Asimov, 1971: 266–7).

This is a claim that warrants some investigation. Throughout his fiction, Asimov displays little serious interest in exploring the impacts of technological advancement on the human condition or human society. Even his *Robot* stories, which explicitly focus on the development of revolutionary new technologies (the robots themselves), do not seriously interrogate questions of technological or human ontology, being mostly exercises in inventive problem-solving as Asimov works his way through a host of scenarios involving the Three Laws. Berger, as noted in the previous section, places Asimov's works squarely within a mode of SF writing that treats technology uncritically, accepting its role as the primary driver of social change over and above other human institutions or ideologies. Indeed, despite the evident dangers associated with it, Asimov was a firm believer in the widespread deployment of atomic technology until the end of his life, maintaining a clear distinction between constructive and destructive uses of such technology. In his *New Guide to Science* (1987), for example, after lamenting the possibility of 'all-out thermonuclear war between the two superpowers' (1987a: 444), Asimov goes on to describe the various ways that 'fission products can be put to good use', including such small-scale innovations as atomic batteries that would not look out of place in his *Foundation* universe (451).

Consequently, in *Foundation* there is a clear emphasis on technology as an emblem of human civilisational power. At the outset of the trilogy, for example, Trantor, the central planet of the collapsing Galactic Empire, has been entirely enclosed within a cocoon of 'lustrous, indestructible, incorruptible metal' (1987b: 75)—an image of the total technological enclosure of human environments that Asimov was later to reuse in his *Robot* novels, *The Caves of Steel* (1953) and *The Naked Sun* (1956). Trantor is described as 'the mightiest deed of man: the complete and almost contemptuously final conquest of a world' by means of advanced tools and machines (1977: 14). Following the collapse of the Empire, however, and the subsequent looting of the great machinery of Trantor by nearby worlds, the planet is transformed into a barren wilderness whose citizens are forced to return to the soil, selling off the metal of their planet 'for seed and cattle' and returning the planet 'to its beginning [in] primitive agriculture' (1979: 152). The symbolism here is blatant: human civilisational progress is equated with extensive or sophisticated technological capacities, without which human populations are exposed to both the aggression of hostile enemies and the ravages of nature.

In a similar way, the eventual conquest of the galaxy by the Foundation is driven by its superior knowledge of nuclear science, which allows the tiny colony to swiftly establish economic control over the surrounding 'Four Kingdoms' despite vastly inferior material resources and a near-total lack of military assets. The takeover of the despotic planet of Korrell, for example, exploits the appeal of superior technology as a means for establishing the relative dominance of human populations: having made the Korellians dependent on the products of their culture—'the machines in the factories', as well as the 'household gadgets', the 'woman's atomic knife' and 'Automatic Super-Kleeno Atomic Washing Machines' (1977: 185–6)—the Foundation succeeds in fostering a culture of technological consumerism without relinquishing the means or method of production. They can then use the threat of technological embargo as an effective means of economic control over the planet.

Asimov's insouciant deployment of a vast galactic setting for his stories of imperial intrigue also suggests his uncritical acceptance of the continuation of human—and particularly American—technological and imperial capacities. The conquest of space is, of course, a recurrent trope of much early SF: the move from earthly through interstellar to galactic dimensions could be viewed as simply the next logical step in expanding the spatial frameworks of SF since the *Voyages* of Verne. But Nemo's twenty thousand leagues take time to clock up—ten months, to be precise—while even Smith's *Skylark* works stress the cognitive dissonance produced by contrasting scales of human and galactic spatial experience.[1] There is, in other words, a tangible 'sense of wonder' in the sudden enlargement of human spatial frameworks in these earlier works. This sense diminishes significantly in later SF: the prevalence of interstellar travel, and particularly the trope of the galactic empire that forms the background to much mid-century SF—in Asimov's *Foundation* and *Empire* series but also in Smith's *Lensman* (1934–1948), James Blish's *Cities in Flight* (1955–1962) and *A Case of Conscience* (1958), Clarke's *The City and the Stars*, films such as Fred M. Wilcox's *Forbidden Planet* (1956), and stories such as Van Vogt's 'Black Destroyer' (1939), Fredric Brown's 'Arena' (1944), and Tom Godwin's 'The Cold Equations' (1954), to name only a few examples—indicates the diminishing role of space within SF as a perceived limitation to human technological or

---

[1] 'Awed by the immensity of the universe, the two at the window were silent, not with the silence of embarrassment, but with that of two friends in the presence of something beyond the reach of words. As they stared out into the infinity each felt as never before the pitiful smallness of even our whole solar system and the utter insignificance of human beings and their works' (Smith and Garby, 1928b: 546).

imperial advance. For Asimov, as for many writers of the Golden Age, it is no longer necessary to describe or examine the material means by which humanity fulfils its galactic ambitions—it is simply assumed that the technology will be available when needed.

Indeed, the vast expanse of *Foundation*'s galactic setting, the fleeting sketches of entire planets and worlds, and the sweeping scale of its narrative timelines all suggest a worldview that has left behind embedded or material experiences of time and space. Asimov's Foundation dramatises the '[v]iolent ... overcoming [of] obstacles placed in its way by "nature"' that Csicsery-Ronay describes as characteristic of techno-scientific SF 'Empires' (2003: 238). In *Second Foundation*, for example, Asimov describes 'the Lens', a piece of cartographic apparatus that can generate 'a reproduction of the night sky as seen from any given point in the galaxy' (1979: 26). The authority bestowed on the Galactic Empire by the Lens, Asimov writes, must be understood 'scientifically and culturally' rather than 'politically' (26). The Lens takes the modernist concept of the 'destruction of space through time' to its logical limits: the reduction of the galaxy to a set of discrete, interchangeable, and easily negotiated worlds is an extreme example of the 'conquest and rational ordering of space [which] became an integral part of the modernizing project'—a demonstration of what David Harvey terms 'time-space compression', the 'overcoming of spatial barriers' to the extent that 'the world sometimes seems to collapse inwards on us' (1992: 249, 240). Space as a phenomenological category—that is, as a material obstruction to human action that must be overcome through the forward motion of time—is thus effectively neutralised in Asimov's *Foundation* works.

So far, then, the *Foundation* trilogy recapitulates the buoyant techno-humanism of the earlier space operas of Smith, Hamilton, and Campbell, in which technology provides the material and ideological means to extend (western) human hegemony beyond the terrestrial plane and enact humanity's imperial destiny among the stars. Whereas Conan Doyle's *The Lost World* uses evolutionary theory to dramatise the civilising mission underpinning moral narratives of European colonialism, Asimov's trilogy enacts the 'manifest destiny' of US economic and technological imperialism. It is telling that the primary drivers of imperial expansion in the Foundation are the 'traders'—domineering merchants whose wares are shrouded in religious 'mummery' intended to instil a reverential attitude towards technology among the subjects of the Foundation (1977: 73). The eventual evolution of the traders into sovereign 'merchant princes' completes an image of linked economic–political and technological supremacy which typifies the era. In contrast to Asimov's self-identification as a 'social' SF writer concerned with the 'problem' of technological development, then, technology seems *not* to be a problem at all in his *Foundation* works, instead functioning as an unexamined narrative motif underpinning a vision, familiar from Smith's *Skylark* series, of human galactic imperialism.

Despite these echoes of earlier pulp SF, however, the actual human figure that populates the *Foundation* series is of a vastly different order from those earlier works, inflected by Asimov's preoccupations with grand social and historical narratives as well as the troubled context of the mid-twentieth century. According to Asimov, it was Campbell who was primarily responsible for the exclusive focus on *human* society and individuals, as opposed to non-human beings or worlds, in the works. The editor of *Astounding* was, Asimov states, intensely chauvinist in his attitudes towards SF and would not publish any story suggesting that white humanity might not be the supreme race of the universe:

> John could not help but feel that people of northwest European descent (like himself) were in the forefront of human civilization and that all other people lagged behind. Expanding this view to a galactic scale, he viewed Earthmen as the 'northwest Europeans' of the galaxy. He did not like to see Earthmen losing out to aliens, or to have Earthmen depicted as in any way inferior. Even if Earthmen were behind technologically, they should win anyway because they invariably were smarter, or braver, or had a superior sense of humor, or *something* (1996: 243–4).

Asimov, a child of Russian Jewish immigrants to the US, did not necessarily share Campbell's chauvinist viewpoint on Anglo-Saxon superiority, particularly as he fell victim to the anti-Semitic prejudice widespread in the US in the lead-up to the Second World War. To sidestep Campbell's dogmatic insistence on human triumph in the stories published in *Astounding*, Asimov decided simply not to include any aliens at all in his *Foundation* works. Instead, he depicts an 'all-human galaxy', a format which allowed 'the play and interplay of human beings [to] be followed on an enormous canvas' (1996: 246). (In *Foundation's Edge*, the 1982 sequel to the *Foundation* series, the absence of non-human entities is revealed to have resulted from galactic engineering by the 'Eternals', a secretive group of human individuals who exist outside of time.)

Asimov's reluctance to depart too radically from Campbell's strict prejudices is perhaps the reason that, despite the vast spaces and times of the *Foundation* stories (the Galactic Empire is described as having persisted for more than twelve thousand years), Asimov's human characters remain as familiar as if they had stepped straight out of his own 1940s New York. These characters conform to a recognisable 'type' to be found throughout Golden Age SF, and particularly the stories published in Campbell's *Astounding*: they are conservative, pragmatic, and technically minded males, able to overcome any difficulty through a combination of rational thought and witty dialogue. In this, Golden Age SF betrays its pulp ancestry: the heroes of such stories are the natural successors to the Seatons and Arcot-Morey-and-Wades[2] of the early space operas, although the super-science elements of the 1920s and 1930s pulps had, by the mid-century, been toned down in favour of 'softer' sociological themes.

Because of Asimov's devotion to this type, all the human characters depicted in the *Foundation* series appear remarkably and implausibly alike. As Charles Elkins argues, despite the incredible technological and scientific innovations depicted in the series—'traveling faster than light, developing atomic technology, predicting and controlling human events, controlling minds'—'Man' in Asimov's series 'remains essentially the same; the springs of human action are unchanged' (1976: 27). Even the cadences of speech throughout the vast reaches of the galaxy remain firmly rooted in Asimov's mid-century vernacular: Salvor Hardin, for instance, mayor of the Foundation in its early years, warns his fellow council members against 'jolly[ing] along' a neighbouring enemy planet (1977: 46), before lamenting that *'the Galaxy is going to pot!'* (48, emphasis in original). Such an unwavering attachment to one very local version of the human may partly stem from Asimov's self-confessed lack of knowledge concerning human psychology: 'I have to make my characters act according to my own feel, my own intuition, which isn't good enough. I haven't studied people that well ... I wish better maps were drawn' (quoted in Freedman, 2005: 104). James Gunn defends the 'strategic narrative value' associated with the 'maintenance of contemporary characteristics' in Asimov's depictions of human individuals in *Foundation*: by assuming the existence of an unchanging human nature, Gunn argues, Asimov frees himself to instead focus on the 'evolution of an idea' (1982: 47).

The format of his *Foundation* series—a collection of nine stories comprising snapshots of a four-hundred-year history—obviously limits the extent of characterisation feasible within the series. As Hassler puts it, 'the real hero of the trilogy is the sublime history of humankind itself' (1988: 44)—yet this shift in emphasis also diminishes the significance of the human individual, sacrificed to grander notions of historical

---

[2] Arcot, Morey, and Wade are the protagonists of Campbell's space-operatic series of stories and novels, originally published in the 1930s.

evolution and progress. Hari Seldon, for example, despite his prominent role in the overarching mythology of the Foundation universe, directly appears in only one story while the primary antagonist of the series, the 'Mule', features in only two. Such shift in narrative focalisation—from one central character to multiple protagonists—is evident in many SF works of the mid-century, most clearly seen in the abundance of 'future histories' within the genre in the mid-century—works such as Simak's *City*, Heinlein's *The Past Through Tomorrow*, Cordwainer Smith's *The Instrumentality of Mankind*, and James Blish's *Cities in Flight*.

This erosion of the significance of the individual human is best exemplified in *Foundation* in the science of 'psychohistory'. Psychohistory is defined as 'that branch of mathematics which deals with the reactions of human conglomerates to fixed social and economic stimuli' (1977: 16). By applying theories of sociology, history, and statistical mathematics to human society, the theory suggests, it becomes possible to predict future events on a galaxy-wide scale. Such predictions are underpinned by 'the mathematics of human behaviour that can neither be stopped, swerved, nor delayed' (1987b: 31). Furthermore, as described by the *Encyclopaedia Galactica* (a fictional work within the series), the 'conglomerate' under psychohistorical observation must be 'sufficiently large for valid statistical treatment' (1977: 16). The comparison is made between populations and gases: although the actions of individual humans cannot be predicted 'any more than you could apply the kinetic theory of gases to single molecules', when dealing with 'mobs, populations of whole planets', social progress can be charted with apparent precision (81). The manifold permutations of human existence are thus reduced to a set number of predictable variations derived from the primary ordering principle of human progress: human history itself. It is from history that Seldon extracts his 'Plan' for the future progress of humanity, while the periodic 'Seldon crises' that threaten the Foundation are, predictably enough, 'not solved by individuals but by historic forces' (184).

If the soma and 'feelies' of *Brave New World* threaten the 'courageous individuality' of liberal humanism, then the psychohistory of *Foundation* turns away completely from human individuality in favour of social and historical determinism. Under the Seldon Plan, the whole of the galaxy becomes a quantitative problem to be managed by technological means. Biopolitical technologies, as Foucault notes, operate in relation to 'phenomena' that, like the gas cloud metaphorically employed by Asimov, 'are aleatory and unpredictable when taken in themselves or individually, but which, at the collective level, display constants that are easy, or at least possible, to establish' (2003: 246). The Seldon Plan functions as a 'technology of security' (Lemke, 2011: 36–7): a regulatory tool to ensure the normalisation of the 'mechanics of life' within a society, judged according to an aggregate of parameters that diminish the significance of individual deviation or nonconformity (Foucault, 1978: 139).

Similarly, the 'calculated management of life' (Foucault, 1978: 140) undertaken by the 'Second Foundation'—a secret society of telepaths committed to preserving the Seldon Plan—reveals its biopolitical function: its role is not to actively govern but to ensure the normalisation of the galactic population so that social progress is not interrupted. Hence it is the Second Foundation that successfully neutralises the 'Mule', an unpredictable mutant who threatens to overthrow the Seldon Plan. The Mule is a social aberration whose distorted body—he is described as 'not a man to look at without derision', 'one hundred and twenty pounds ... stretched out into his five-foot-eight length', with 'bony stalks' for limbs and 'a fleshy beak that thrust three inches outward' from his face (Asimov, 1979: 14)—highlights his biological (hence his name) and historical redundancy. For Foucault, the material body constitutes the final site of resistance in biopolitical regimes, the location upon which technocratic discipline and surveillance is enacted and from which liberation must begin (see Harvey, 1992: 213–14). Yet biopower, as Hardt and Negri argue, works to 'alienate' individuals from a 'sense of life' by imposing pervasive external controls that overrun the very material–biological processes—the 'brains' and 'bodies'—of 'bare life' itself (2000: 23). The overthrow of the Mule by the Second Foundation in *Foundation* dramatises the suppression of the biological body in favour of abstracted systems of technocratic control. The telepathic powers of the Second Foundation are significant in this regard: telepathy in *Foundation*, as in *Skylark*, offers an index of the prioritisation given to intellectualism over and above the material world and the human body. (The Mule also demonstrates telepathic powers, but these are dismissed as a 'freak' accident of nature [1979: 167].)

Not only the masses but also the individual human is subject to rational manipulation in *Foundation*. For Asimov, the human mind is characterised by a set of 'rules' equated with 'the [emotions] and impulses of humanity: hate, love, fear, suspicion, passion, hunger, lust, and so on [that] will not change while mankind remains Homo sapiens' (quoted in Gunn, 1982: 47, bracketed content in original). Correspondingly, the human brain in *Foundation* is conceived not as an organic mass but as a piece of electrical apparatus that may be both known and improved upon through technological intervention. Hence the 'electroencephalographs' of the First Foundation can, with 'feathery electrodes' and 'vacuum-encased needles', 'reveal the thoughts and emotions of the subject, to the last and least', transcribed onto 'neatly squared paper' (Asimov, 1979: 94–5). Similarly, the telepathic abilities of the Second Foundation are derived from 'mental science' developed from 'the facts of neural physiology and the electro-chemistry of the nervous system' all the way down to 'nuclear forces' (84).

This view of human behaviour as mechanically predictable recurs throughout Asimov's fiction, routinely providing the basis for resolving narrative conflict. Indeed, Asimov himself says as much, stating that he 'tend[s] to see the world mechanistically. I don't want to suppose that there are problems that are inherent and insolvable' (quoted in Ingersoll, 1987: 104). The typical Asimovian story pits mutually opposing antagonists against one another in a game of logical one-upmanship and is resolved only when one party succeeds in accurately pre-empting the behaviours or responses of the other. Asimov's Robot stories, for example, take the form of 'continual games of "if this, then the next"' by means of which Asimov can explore all the 'combinations and permutations' of the Three Laws of Robotics (1988: 39). This is also the structure of the two stories in *Second Foundation*: each of these tales features a twist ending revealing that Preem Palver, leader of the Second Foundation, has successfully predicted the actions of his antagonists—the Mule in the first story, the First Foundation in the second—and arranged appropriate counter-responses.

The human that thus emerges from Asimov's SF works is a mechanistic being, determined by fixed 'rules' of behaviour and thought. The individual human being, as one general of the Galactic Empire indignantly notes, is equated to 'a silly robot following a predetermined course into destruction' (1987b: 31). Psychohistory, meanwhile, applies the principle of reason on a galactic scale, treating the population of the galaxy in supra-humanist terms: as a composite body whose individual components move, or are made to move, in harmony with one another. Individual agency is subsumed within mass biopolitical structures, administered from afar by omniscient authority figures such as Hari Seldon and Preem Palver. This shift in emphasis—from the sanctity of the individual to that of the mass population—is condensed in Asimov's formulation of the 'Zeroth Law of Robotics', which expands the focus of the First Law from the individual human to the whole of humanity: 'No robot shall injure humanity, or, through inaction, allow humanity to come to harm'.

So, does the *Foundation* trilogy express an outright rejection of the human as political and historical actor—a mid-century expression of biopolitical fatalism, written in an age of mass oppressive regimes, in which the survival of the population eclipses the agency of the individual? This question cannot be answered with a simple affirmative. As noted already, Asimov's focus on *human* societies and individuals in his *Foundation* works was a response to Campbell's glorification of European humanity while his characters—active, rational, pragmatic men—reflected a common 'type' in Golden Age SF. Asimov did not, however, share Campbell's northern European ancestry, and indeed the emergence of National Socialism in Germany during the 1930s meant that he was 'no great admirer of ... northwest European stock' (1996: 244). Asimov experienced 'mild' anti-Semitic prejudice (as he describes it) in his youth, and during the 1930s was keenly aware, as 'no American Jew could fail to be ... that the Jews, first in Germany, then in Austria, were being endlessly humiliated, mistreated, imprisoned, tortured, and killed, merely for being Jewish' (1995b: 20). In his autobiography, he likens the persecution of the Jews in Europe to that historically suffered by African Americans in the US, even long after the abolition of slavery (1995b: 21–2). Asimov was, then, acutely aware of both the possibility and consequences of oppressive political regimes and of the violence necessary to maintain these—he felt that any response to such disquieting trends should not only ensure the survival of the species but also, and more importantly, protect the individual from institutional violence.

One way of achieving this was through the simple application of reason. As Gunn notes, 'the theory of psychohistory was for Asimov a way to make Hitler's persistent victories bearable': no matter how cruel or senseless events may appear, 'reason had to eventually prove its supremacy' (1982: 46). Yet reason alone is not enough to guarantee human happiness or survival—indeed, the 'final solution' undertaken by the Nazis, as Davies argues, sounded a death knell for a certain understanding of rational humanism since, unlike the carnage of the First World War, the systematic, structured, and ultra-rational operation of the Holocaust could not be viewed as 'the result ... of some inexplicable descent into irrational, atavistic barbarity' (1997: 51). Such reason must also be tempered by a universal (as opposed to parochial) sense of human identity and compassion. Whereas the ideological project of the Nazis rested on a myth of biological chauvinism underpinned by social Darwinist eugenics, Asimov's rationalism is universal in its scope and benevolent in its operations. For him, not one nation or creed but all of humanity was to be subject to bureaucratic social institutions such as the Second Foundation, whose management of society was characterised by paternal stewardship rather than indifference or hatred. The manner in which the Second Foundation eventually neutralises the threat of the Mule in *Second Foundation* reflects a need for compassion in the management of social progress: the Mule is not punished but psychologically manipulated so as to simply 'forget' his plans for galactic domination, after which he returns to his home planet 'a far happier man' (Asimov, 1979: 69).

It is extremely important, then, to distinguish Asimov's biopolitical systems in his *Foundation* works from those of fascist regimes emerging in Europe in the lead-up to the Second World War. Asimov's *Foundation* is the inverse of the biopolitical regime of National Socialism: it is all-encompassing, rather than exclusive, in its outlook on the entire human species (although, as with most SF from the period, in practice overwhelmingly focussed on white males) and marked by universal benevolence rather than racist parochialism. The Seldon Plan offers a form of *paternal* biopolitics which, though alienating in its view of the human as a mechanistic being subject to anonymous manipulation by social forces, nevertheless preserves a notion of human progress that is universal in its application. The Second Foundation is the key symbol of this paternalism: in conversation with one of his 'Students', the 'First Speaker' of the Second Foundation states that, in the face of 'accidents, unforeseen and individual ... *we* will exist', as a result of which 'the huge Galaxy ... was now safe forever' (1979: 184, 187, emphasis in original). For Asimov, it was necessary to protect the individual from the violence of social, political, and technological authoritarianism. Human freedom and agency may be relinquished to ensure continued biological survival—but for Asimov, in the context of the persecutions that marked the 1930s and early 1940s, this was perhaps a price worth paying. Indeed, as M. Keith Booker notes, the two benign institutions—the First and Second Foundations—depicted in the novel respectively command 'precisely the technologies about which Americans in the 1950s were most anxious: atomic power and mind control', thus reassuring readers that 'we have nothing to fear from science'—provided that it is in the right hands (2001: 38).

In Asimov's view of humanity, then, individual human agency is subordinated to the will of totalitarian yet virtuous institutions. The goal, as ever, is human progress, but a vastly different kind of progress from that of the pulp SF of the previous decade. Whereas those earlier texts are concerned with the self-actualisation of heroic individuals, Asimov's *Foundation* instead focuses on the progressive development of a mass social body—a shift of emphasis from individual to social survival that is best understood in the context of the new horrors of warfare and genocide that emerged during this period.

Ontological humility and the body as metaphor in Clarke's *The City and the Stars*

In this next section, I move on to Arthur C. Clarke, one of a small number of British writers active in the field of American SF by the end of the 1950s. Although attempts had been made to establish a magazine SF tradition in Britain, such publications were still largely American affairs. C.S. Lewis, for example, after publishing his *Space Trilogy* (1938–1945), had turned largely to fantasy and, like Stapledon, was sceptical of the value of American magazine SF (see Miller, 2003: 70–81). The other major British writers of this period were Eric Frank Russell, who appeared regularly in US magazines throughout the 1940s and 1950s, and John Wyndham, who, as Edward James argues, is more properly read in dialogue with Wells than with the SF magazines to which he occasionally contributed (1994: 59–61).

Clarke is, in certain ways, a difficult SF writer to classify. Much of his fiction—such as his early trilogy of novels, *Prelude to Space* (1951), *The Sands of Mars* (1951), and *Islands in the Sky* (1952)—shows a clear fondness for hard SF themes, expounding at length, and with obvious affection and knowledge, on a host of scientific and technological themes. Clarke was a mostly self-educated expert in numerous fields of scientific inquiry and in the 1930s and 1940s was a key member of the British Interplanetary Society, where his time was spent attempting to convince a sceptical public about the usefulness of rockets and the viability of landing a man on the moon. Throughout his lengthy career, Clarke published non-fiction articles and works on diverse scientific topics, to the point where, like Asimov, his non-fiction output greatly exceeds that of his fiction.

This interest in the hard facts of science was encouraged by an early familiarity with SF writing. As a young boy, Clarke had read the works of Verne and Wells—the 'great masters', as he later described them (quoted in McAleer, 1993: 179)—and had encountered his first SF pulp magazine, a 1928 copy of Gernsback's *Amazing Stories*, at the age of eleven. Within eleven more years, he had amassed a sprawling collection, including every copy of *Astounding* printed up to that point. Through his familiarity with the SF pulps, Clarke became well-versed in 'all the clichés of pulp science fiction' (Clarke, 1989: 23). In his own works, these clichés are tempered with the more complex narratives typical of Golden Age SF, as well as a careful adherence to scientific realism. Although his tales do not resemble Gernsbackian 'tales of instruction', which sought to both entertain and educate the reader in scientific matters, his close fidelity to the accepted paradigms of scientific thought does inform much of his science-fictional *oeuvre*: from the use of time dilation in his depictions of interstellar travel in *Childhood's End* (1953), through the detailed technical descriptions of a 'space elevator' in *The Fountains of Paradise* (1979), to the attempt, in *The Songs of Distant Earth* (1986), to 'create a wholly *realistic* piece of fiction on the interstellar theme' with the aim of counterbalancing Hollywood's fantastical treatments of this theme (1986: xiv). Indeed the 'Author's Note' to this latter novel neatly summarises Clarke's lifelong attitude to writing SF: this and other works contain 'nothing ... which defies or denies known principles' (xiv).

Although Clarke dates his 'initiation to the genre' of SF to the early pulps making their way across the Atlantic (1989: 11), he was also influenced by works of British speculation from the late nineteenth and early twentieth centuries. The British writers of scientific romance, as discussed in the last chapter, were more metaphysical and circumspect than their US counterparts in their considerations of human progress and technology, evident in the works of such writers as Wells, George Allen England, E.V. Odle, and C.S. Lewis (with whom Clarke had a brief correspondence). In his autobiography, Clarke pays respect to Wells as a key innovator in SF, serving also for a time as vice-president of the H.G. Wells Society (1989: 28-30). Of greater importance for the development of Clarke's writings, however, was Olaf Stapledon: Neil McAleer, for example, identifies a clear Stapledonian influence on several of Clarke's early works, and indeed Clarke himself describes the profound effect that Stapledon's *Last and First Men* had on his young mind, writing that 'No book before or since ever had such an impact on [his] imagination' (quoted in McAleer, 1993: 21). I will return to Stapledon's influence on Clarke in more detail later in this discussion.

Clarke, then, is a product of two distinct traditions. Although well-versed in the 'technoporn' (Clarke, 1989: 99) of the US pulps—tales of spaceships, gadgetry, bizarre aliens, and masculine adventure—he was equally influenced by the more sceptical and circumspect texts of the British speculative tradition. Even his earliest works—stories such as 'Rescue Party' (1946), in which a group of aliens explore a dying Earth abandoned by humanity, or 'The Sentinel' (1951), in which a lunar explorer discovers a beacon deposited by an ancient race of aliens—demonstrate the philosophical tone, expansive spatial and temporal frameworks, and theme of human pathos familiar from the works of Wells and Stapledon. It is as a result of these highly varied influences that Clarke's works seem so effectively to straddle the divide between scientific positivism on the one hand and ontological or epistemological scepticism on the other—clearly invested in the possibility of bold and expansive human enterprise, yet also postulating the existence of worlds, entities, and realities that lie, perhaps forever, beyond the horizons of human understanding.

The twinned influence of these two traditions is evident in Clarke's *The City and the Stars*, a novel set on a barren Earth in the distant future. Following an ancient conflict with a mythical alien race called the 'Invaders', the megacity of 'Diaspar' seals itself off from the rest of the planet, remaining in isolation for one billion years and becoming, its citizens believe, the last civilisation on Earth. The novel follows the adventures of Alvin, a rebellious youth from Diaspar who is unaffected by the agoraphobia that afflicts his fellow citizens. After escaping from Diaspar, Alvin encounters another earthly society, the pastoral utopia of 'Lys', whose citizens are telepathic. The ramifications of Alvin's discovery slowly reawaken Diaspar to humanity's role in the history of the universe. It is eventually learned that, during the years of the 'Galactic Empire' in the ancient past, humanity had inadvertently created a malevolent disembodied intelligence, the 'Mad Mind', which wreaked untold havoc throughout the galaxy before being finally stopped. Soon after this, the citizens of the galaxy established contact with a powerful race of unknown beings located, it is suggested, at the far end of the universe. While most races of the galaxy set out to locate these beings, earthly humanity instead returned to its home planet, separating into the two societies of Diaspar and Lys and fashioning the myth of the 'Invaders' as a way of subduing the human impulse towards technological experimentation and galactic exploration. With this myth thus dispelled, and human curiosity reawakened as a result, the novel ends with Diaspar and Lys joining forces to undertake the regeneration of Earth and the resumption of interstellar travel.

For Tom Moylan, *The City and the Stars*, appearing in the early years of the Cold War, offers a thematic response to that conflict. In *The City and the Stars*, Moylan argues, the division between Diaspar and Lys—between a technologically advanced but spiritually void city and a utopian network of self-reliant, pastoral villages—is symbolic of that between a spiritually exhausted capitalist materialism and the reinvigorating simplicity of a rustic communist system (1977: 154). Hence, Moylan argues, where 'Diaspar is a flawed utopia, Lys is a perfectly realized one ... a medieval pastoral utopia' which, though 'it must be surpassed by the return to empire', also denotes 'the negation of the returning capitalist empire'—that is, the nullification of the alienating tendencies of capitalism by way of the mediating influence of pastoral communism (1977: 154). Clarke, by uniting Lys and Diaspar at the novel's conclusion, is seeking 'the benefits of communism without having to pay the historical price of struggle and revolution', or without sacrificing 'capitalist, "free-world" hegemony' (154).

Clarke himself has taken issue with such politico-economic readings of his novel: responding directly to Moylan's article, he points to both his own notebooks—which date the novel's inception to the mid-1930s— and to the 1968 preface to *Against the Fall of Night*, the 1948 novella later expanded as *The City and the Stars*, as evidence against such an interpretation (1978: 88–90). In the preface, Clarke identifies his own 'transplantation from the country ... to the city'—from his native Somerset to London, where he took up a post with the British Civil Service in 1936—and 'the conflict between a pastoral and an urban way of life' as the original inspiration for the story (1975: par. 4). Indeed, *The City and the Stars* at times demonstrates such a longing for a lost connection to nature—what Raymond Williams terms 'a myth functioning as memory' (1975: 43), a nostalgic longing for a past 'Golden Age' of 'peace, innocence, and simple virtue' lost to Clarke in the busy metropolis of London (1).

This preoccupation with urban and rural conflict is evident in the opposition between urban Diaspar and rural Lys. Like the 'World State' of Huxley's *Brave New World*, Diaspar is framed as a post-historical civilisation characterised by technological alienation and the loss of genuine human connection. The city comprises a single technological system: an eternal and inert 'artificial womb', 'a universe itself', monitored and preserved by an omniscient 'Central Computer' that maintains the material condition of the city in a state of perfection (2001a: 16, 9). Like the technology of the World State, the machinery of Diaspar has transformed the ontological condition of its citizens from biological to technological. Its inhabitants, for example, have left behind the 'complex and apparently uncontrollable process' of natural birth (2001a: 20)—the information required to birth any individual is instead saved in the records of the Central Computer, conducted by means of 'memory units [and] matter organisers' (20). Using such technology, the inhabitants of Diaspar have become effectively immortal: by disconnecting consciousness from its corporeal form and thereby overcoming the limitations of transient embodiment, they have remade themselves as post-historical and post-biological beings, free from ideological dissent and abstracted from the material realities of their environment. The result, however, is that the countless lives of each person lack 'real emotions ... deep passions', with parents 'assigned' to each child merely to provide material care (152).

In sharp contrast, the inhabitants of Lys, by rejecting advanced technology, have instead continued along a track of human evolution familiar from many mid-century works, developing powers of telepathy 'once common to all man' but left dormant in Diaspar owing to its citizens' total dependency on machinery. The social structure of Lys is 'based largely on the direct use of [such] mental power' (110). In the last chapter, I argued that telepathy was employed in pulp SF as a metaphor for material transcendence and the expansion of human consciousness beyond the limits of the body. Clarke's works, however, do not exhibit the technocratic triumphalism of *Skylark*: the telepathy of Lys is less a signifier of material transcendence than a tool for facilitating more immediate and profound modes of human inter-communion—as Moylan argues, it provides 'one more way to overcome individual isolation' (1977: 154). Whereas the technical achievements of Diaspar have atomised its citizens within isolated living quarters—Alvin laments that, 'In a city of ten million inhabitants ... there was no one to whom he could really talk' (2001a: 14)—the need in Lys for social co-operation in the production of material necessities has made 'mutual understanding ... the very basis of their lives' (110). Mental communion thus facilitates the development of 'love based on absolute unselfishness', free from the possibility of 'false impressions' (109–10). Telepathy in Lys, in other words, does not express human intellectual mastery over matter but instead enables more penetrating modes of interpersonal union, underpinned by and conflated with a nostalgic vision of a 'Golden Age' of pre-technological rurality.

Lys, then, functions as a foil to the technological alienation and sterile urbanity of Diaspar, which represents a mode of living that has departed radically from 'natural' forms of human life. This allegorical role is emphasised by the imagery used to describe Lys, which highlights the simplicity and wholesomeness of the pastoral life. The village buildings, for example, are of 'clean, straight-forward design', the inhabitants move with 'unconscious grace', clothed in a 'single sheet draped around the body', and the air around them hums with 'unknown, throbbing life' (90–1). Clarke makes no bones about which of the two categories—technological or biological—offers the most appropriate basis for human ontology: as Alvin examines a fish in a lake outside Lys, he realises that 'Evolution and science had come to the same answers; and the work of Nature had lasted longer' (90). The welcoming pastoralism of rural Lys suggests a normative reading of these opposing societies: the contrast between the sterile technopolis of Diaspar and the georgic communes of Lys can be understood as an opposition between a dehumanising and spiritually void urban technocracy and a revitalising rural pastoralism.

The first major thematic opposition in *The City and the Stars* is thus that between the two major utopian modes of SF up to this point. On the one side, there is technocracy, realised within the 'New Jerusalem' (to borrow Samuel Delany's terminology) of Diaspar, and on the other there is pastoralism, realised in the 'Arcadia' of Lys (Delany, 1990: 303). At the same time, however, the novel is concerned with not only these two societies but also their place within a grander cosmological order—the 'stars' of the title. Indeed, much of the narrative of *The City and the Stars* is occupied with the ambiguity surrounding Diaspar's origins and the role played by ancient humanity in the wider galaxy—a mystery that eventually takes Alvin, in a plundered spaceship, to the centre of the galaxy itself. As discussed in the last chapter, interstellar space functions in much SF as a site of imperial conquest and technological transcendence. In the case of Clarke's novel, however, the broader perspective of extra-terrestrial space moves the thematic focus of the novel from a simple conflict of city versus countryside to a more metaphysical concern for humanity's cosmic future.

For the citizens of Diaspar and Lys, the 'stars' denote the terror of the mysterious 'Invaders' whose apocryphal destruction of terrestrial civilisation one billion years earlier spurred the quarantine of Diaspar. It is eventually revealed that the Invaders are mere legend—a myth created to ensure the continued isolation of the city—and that the real destroyer of the Galactic Empire was the 'Mad Mind', a disembodied being created as a result of human technological experimentation. As a product of human innovation, it is thus possible to interpret the 'Mad Mind' as symbolising the perils of technological progress itself, specifically the capacity of such progress to unwittingly bring about the circumstances of humanity's downfall. The context of the Cold War, and the shadow of atomic apocalypse looming over the western cultural imagination, suggests the metaphorical register in which the 'Mad Mind' should be understood—as a symbol for the atomic bomb itself—while the downfall of the 'Galactic Empire' implies the human self-immolation that was an increasingly plausible outcome of the 'nightmare of an atomic arms race' (Boyer, 1994: 126). Indeed, as Clarke later wrote, after the deployment of atomic weapons in 1945 'two of the main themes of science fiction—space travel, and the ultimate weapon—ceased to be playthings of the mind', instead becoming 'realities: perhaps ... waking nightmares' (1989: 197). As a result, 'science fiction writers had ... lost their innocence'—the 'realities' of the post-atomic age 'would be reflected in all their work, whether they intended it or not' (197). In the foreword to a 2000 edition of his collected short stories, Clarke's forebodings regarding human technological suicide go even further than this: 'The dinosaurs disappeared because they could not adapt to their changing environment. We shall disappear if we cannot adapt to an environment that now contains spaceships, computers—and thermonuclear weapons' (2000: x).

These comments inform the ambiguous stance on technological progress evident in *The City and the Stars*. As with much mid-century SF, the novel is committed to a notion of galactic imperialism, depicting a 'renewal of the American frontier myth to carry on the white man's burden and establish a new empire, first in the solar system and then the entire galaxy' (Moylan, 1977: 152). At the same time, Clarke exhibits a highly guarded outlook on technological progress: the 'Mad Mind', the *telos* of human achievement whose formation constituted 'the greatest sustained effort in all history', signifies at once the apex and fatal subversion of human progress as the 'dream' of technological hegemony is quickly converted into 'a disaster that almost wrecked the Galaxy' (Clarke, 2001a: 239). The scepticism of the British speculative tradition regarding human technological and historical progress can be clearly felt here, modified by the exponential increase in human destructive capabilities made possible by nuclear weapons. Technology developed for its own sake, it is suggested, has the nasty habit of turning on its creator, and so any deployment of atomic capabilities must be underwritten by sound moral and social sensibilities. In this light, the pessimistic view of technological development outlined in *The City and the Stars* follows the pattern laid down by Carl Sagan and L.S. Shklovskii in *Intelligent Life in the Universe* (1966)—a work, incidentally, that Clarke read and praised[3]—regarding the fate confronting all 'technical civilizations': that such civilisations, as their technical capabilities increase, face the increased possibility of 'self-destruction' (1966: 358).

The figure of the 'Mad Mind', then, is inspired by fears about the atomic bomb, which problematises any view of human history as a narrative of constant growth and ascendancy. On the contrary, *The City and the Stars*, like *The Lost World* and Verne's *Voyages*, understands time in cyclical terms, evident in the images of galactic imperial collapse and renewal or of life and death in Diaspar. Yet this characteristic is not (as in the latter two writers) a reflection of bland faith in the durability of bourgeois European ideals but an attempt to salvage the whole notion of human social progress by refashioning it as cycles of progress and decadence. The germ of this impulse is found in the historical shape of the twentieth century itself, which, as Alan Bullock notes, had demonstrated a dramatic tendency towards periodic collapse and regeneration:

> For a short period from 1924 through 1928, it seemed possible that the cycle of violence and repression which had lasted from 1914 to the end of 1923 might be broken. It was not. The cycle began

---

[3] For Clarke's commendation of the work, see Clarke (1986: xv).

again with the Great Depression; Stalin's second Russian Revolution (the collectivization of agriculture and the purges); Hitler's rise to power, and the outbreak of the Second World War in 1939. At the end of that war there was no remission: the division of Europe, the Cold War and the threat of a third nuclear war followed straight on (1985: 176).

Clarke's direct experience of such events was minimal: 'If I had planned it deliberately', he later wrote, 'I could not have done a better job of avoiding World War II; at its most, it was never more than a background inconvenience' (1989: 187). Nevertheless, it is difficult not to read the cyclical timeframes of *The City and the Stars* as reflecting a desire to neutralise the violent failures of western humanity by folding them into a grander historical framework characterised by cycles of ascent and descent.

For Clarke, the appropriate response to post-war nuclear consolidation—the historical moment at which technological suicide becomes a genuine possibility for humanity—is not to suppress human ingenuity but to infuse technological and imperial expansion with a sense of critical and moral awareness. Diaspar's shortcomings as a mode of human civilisation lay in the fact that, 'when power and ambition and curiosity were satisfied, there still were left the longings of the heart' (2001a: 250–1). The role of pastoral Lys is to infuse 'warmth and understanding' into the technological might of Diaspar, thereby guiding humanity towards a more organic relationship with 'his world' (252). The key, as Clarke writes in *Imperial Earth* (1975), is to recognise that nature 'was not designed for the convenience of Man, and that presumptuous creature's attempt to use it for his own advantage would often be foiled by laws beyond his control' (1977: 86). Far from the Enlightenment ideal of a 'human empire' over nature, then, Clarke implicitly recognises human vulnerability to the destructive capacities of both natural law and technological progress.

Indeed, in *The City and the Stars*, Clarke further subverts the Enlightenment scientific narrative by questioning the limits of human epistemology at the level of the body itself. It is impossible, he writes, for any one race—including the human race—ever to obtain a 'true picture of the Universe', since 'a race's world-picture depended on its physical body and the sense organs with which it was equipped' (2001a: 239). Clarke here rejects scientific empiricism as a path to 'true' knowledge: the human mind, he argues, is a 'by-product of an immensely intricate arrangement of brain cells' (239)—material entities that limit the human mind as a tool for gathering objective information about the external world. As Clarke writes, 'the eye had to be educated before it could pass intelligible impressions to the brain' (1975: 107). Human knowledge will thus always be partial, incapable of ever realising total dominion over nature.

This quality of Clarke's fiction—its emphasis on the necessary partiality of human knowledge—is evident in many of his works, often taking the form of an encounter between humanity and some inhuman *thing*—be it an entity, being, concept, or otherwise—that falls beyond the parameters of human knowledge. It can be seen, for example, in the 'Overmind' of *Childhood's End*, a powerful and enigmatic being that instigates a process of evolutionary transcendence among the children of Earth, destroying the planet—and the last remnants of terrestrial humanity—in the process. It is evident again in *2001: A Space Odyssey* (1968), in the unexplained transformation of astronaut David Bowman into a powerful immortal being, the 'Star-Child'. And it can be detected again in *Rendezvous with Rama* (1974), in which a huge alien cylinder passes through the solar system, resisting all human attempts to comprehend its origin or function before disappearing again into interstellar space. In these examples, Clarke's works generate a clear tension between the 'known unknowns', to borrow a famous phrase, of human empirical and rational knowledge and the 'unknown unknowns' of the wider universe—those sudden encounters with some element of the universe located outside the boundaries of human epistemology.

Clarke, then, rejects any notion of unquestioned human authority over nature. The union between the Diaspar and Lys in *The City and the Stars* suggests the need to temper technocratic hegemony with an organic humanism that emphasises the value of human communion and the independence of nature and prioritises the social and moral use-value of technological artefacts. The incorporation of interstellar space, meanwhile, in contrast to earlier pulp fiction, recontextualises human evolution within an expansive universal framework in which humanity, far from being the pinnacle of evolution, is instead merely one of a multitude of—often radically more advanced—races and beings. Clarke's humanism thus exhibits a sense of 'ontological humility'—a recognition of human limitations amidst the expanses and mysteries of the cosmos. As he writes in *Childhood's End*, 'The stars are not for Man' (1970: 184). Yet, at the same time, Clarke's works also consistently employ certain metaphysical or mystical themes which imbue his use of the terms 'Man' or 'Humanity' with more transcendental meaning. *Childhood's End*, for example, though it ends with the destruction of terrestrial humanity, also depicts the children of humanity undergoing a transcendental evolution that takes them *beyond* matter: *'they're* on their way at last, to become part of the Overmind. Their probation is ended: they're leaving the last remnants of matter behind' (1970: 186, emphasis in original). The children of Earth undergo a sublime process of material disembodiment that leaves Jan—the last remaining biological human, who witnesses the transcendence—with a 'sense of fulfilment, achievement' (187).

Such a division between 'human' as referring to *material* beings and 'human' as referring to a set of abstract qualities has already been identified in the works of Smith and other early pulp writers. Yet this concept also has a rich heritage in British philosophical thought, stretching back to Arnold, Huxley, and Spencer in the nineteenth century, each of whom stressed the 'higher' qualities of the spirit— 'those gifts of thought and feeling', as Arnold put it—that distinguish humanity from the rest of nature (see Mandelbaum, 1974: 203). A more direct influence on Clarke in this regard may be found in Olaf Stapledon. Like Smith, Stapledon abstracted the concept of 'human' from its specific biological basis, instead conceiving of humanity as a set of 'higher' intellectual qualities that may be realised in a diverse range of biological sensoria. The narrative of *Star Maker* (1937), for example, tracks an ever-more-expansive abstraction of this intellectual 'spirit' from its basis in material entities. Beginning with a single human individual who finds himself suddenly and inexplicably disembodied, the novel depicts the gradual merger of this individual with other floating consciousnesses throughout space, converging towards a group consciousness made up of an ever-larger number of sentient entities (including, eventually, the stars and galaxies themselves, revealed to be sentient beings), and resulting in a final 'cosmical mind' comprising the shared consciousness of all thinking beings in the universe. This mind then encounters the 'Star Maker', an impartial deity who created the universe as simply an experiment in world-building. (The influence of this novel on many facets of Clarke's works—the 'Overmind' of *Childhood's End*, for example, or the 'Star-Child' of *2001*—is clear here.) *Star Maker* thus expresses both a radical anti-humanism—humanity, it is suggested, is by no means the apex of all creation—*and* a radical humanism: humanity, unlike the rest of terrestrial nature, contains within itself the germs of the 'cosmical mind' and humans are participants in a universal process of (to borrow a phrase from Mandelbaum) 'spiritual Evolutionism' (1974: 223).

In a lecture delivered (at Clarke's invitation) to the British Interplanetary Society in 1948, Stapledon is even more explicit on this point. The individual human, Stapledon remarks, 'is very small, an inconceivably minute parasite on a minute planetary grain floating in an immense void' (1948: 223). What separates humanity from 'the sub-human creatures', however, is 'the power of abstraction, of attending to a particular character and relating it to other instances of the same character, and giving the identity a name, such as "red," "two," [or] "pleasant"' (224). The highest form of such abstraction, for Stapledon, is that of 'the spirit, the ideal way of life ... which is implied in, and emerges from, the actual experienced nature of personal beings' (227). This 'spirit', Stapledon argues, 'is essentially the way of life in which we strive towards full, comprehensive, and true awareness of the objective universe', and is furthermore underpinned by 'the distinctly human social relationship, in which individuals are united in mutual respect for each other *as persons*' (227–8). In other words, Stapledon imagines the spirit as an expression of the 'higher' human values, abstracted from the lived experience of interpersonal communion and fellowship. From here, it is a short step to imagining a 'cosmical community of worlds' throughout the galaxy, united in spiritual communion and striving towards 'the final result of the cosmical process': 'the complete awakening of consciousness in the cosmos', which is the *telos* of Stapledon's spiritual evolutionism (231).

The dialectic between the social and the individual that informs Stapledon's cosmic transcendence can be clearly detected in Clarke's work. On the level of the individual, *The City and the Stars* reaffirms the role of the material body in ontologies of the human, a quality evident in the opposing depictions of Diaspar and Lys. The city of Diaspar offers an illustration of what Rosi Braidotti calls 'the trans-humanist fantasy of escape from the finite materiality of the enfleshed self' (2013: 91). The citizens of Diaspar flit from body to body, their intellectual existence immortalised in electronic form within the memory banks of the Central Computer. In Diaspar, in other words, the body has become little more than a temporary ampule for the artificially immortal consciousness. It is this consciousness that provides continuity to the 'human', while the material form remains in constant flux. However, the price paid for technological empowerment is social atomisation, since the body is not merely a resting place for the mind but also a site of intergenerational connection. Hence, although each person is free 'to shape his own amusements and his own life' (Clarke, 2001a: 14), Alvin nevertheless reflects that 'he would give all his achievements if he could hear the cry of a new-born child, and know that it was his own' (251). The citizens of Lys, conversely, embrace embodiment: they are embedded within a network of familial and social relations, instances of inimitable spatio-temporal materiality. Here Alvin encounters old age, infancy, and the other visual and physical markers of the effects of time on the human body—yet he also recognises the value of 'the cycle of life and death' (250), and particularly of progeny, which arouse in him 'a feeling he had never known before ... tenderness' (106). The decision at the end of the novel, in the union of these societies, to shut down the memory banks of Diaspar thus reaffirms the role of the transient, material body in individual and social fulfilment.

In addition to this, however, the human body functions in the novel not merely as a material instantiation of each human individual, but also as a reference point through which all other forms of life in the novel may be understood. Consider, for example, the disembodied entities created by the ancient Galactic Empire: the Mad Mind and childlike 'Vanamonde' encountered by Alvin during his journey to the centre of the galaxy. These beings exist in a post-material state: their 'brain[s]', Clarke writes, are comprised of 'components [that are] not material, but patterns embossed on space itself ... completely free from the tyranny of matter' (239). The intelligences are thus 'not located anywhere—perhaps not even *anywhen*' (224, emphasis in original)—yet their ontological condition is described using a comparison with the human body: the intelligences, Clarke writes, are 'embossed' upon space much like the human mind is embossed upon 'an immensely intricate arrangement of brain cells' (239). A similar metaphor is used to describe the Central Computer of Diaspar, the 'all-but-infinite intellect' that form the administrative core of the city and which 'possesses at least as much awareness and self-consciousness as a human being' (66). The Central Computer, though 'not alive in a biological sense', nevertheless possesses a fully flexible consciousness, distributed throughout the network of computers and robots that populate Diaspar (66). As Clarke writes, just as a 'brain was the sum of many billion separate cells, arrayed throughout a volume of space a few inches across, so the physical elements of the Central Computer [are] scattered through the length and breadth of Diaspar' (161).

And, finally, there is the 'protean polyp' encountered by Alvin as he travels through the lands outside Diaspar (130). Consisting of 'a colony of independent creatures' operating as a single intelligence (130), the polyp is a cyclical creature, existing for a time as a single intelligent being before degenerating into its constituent parts—'tiny, greenish specks [no] larger than an inch across' (138). In due course, the polyp will be 'reborn' as its constituent specks reassemble, acting under the influence of 'unknown forces that had never failed to do their duty in the past' (138). The polyp, Clarke writes, suffers under the 'tyranny' of material forces, tied forever to one location and helpless to end its cyclical existence. Though it tries without success to 'force its dissolving body to obey its will', it nevertheless crumbles helplessly into its home lake (138). The polyp is perhaps as physically inhuman as a being can be—yet Clarke once again resorts to a human analogy to illustrate this peculiar entity: was the bizarre lifecycle of the polyp, though 'a strange and wonderful phenomenon ... so much stranger than the organization of the human body, itself a vast colony of separate, living cells?' (138).

This recurring recourse to the human body as a metaphor to describe the lifeworlds of inhuman entities—the intelligences, the computer, and the polyp—illuminates the dialectical relationship between individual and society that informs Clarke's works. The body, as Clarke's numerous examples above demonstrate, is a composite unity: a mass of individual units acting in unison towards the achievement of a shared goal. The same may be said about the social organism, viewed in Clarke's works neither as a mere collection of atomised units nor as a singular entity that transcends its individual parts. The social body, like the human body, exists in dialectical accord with the individual being—as in the example of Lys, individuals exist, not in tension, but in harmony with the social order, each directed towards a commonly shared goal. The human body is the arch-metaphor that informs Clarke's notion of the ideal human society as an association of co-operating individuals whose self-realisation accords with the realisation of the mass social organism.

Hence, we arrive at the 'supra-human' as the culmination of human civilisation in Clarke's novel. The supra-human pervades Clarke's works. The polyp or Central Computer of *The City and the Stars*, for instance, are unitary consciousnesses comprised of millions of individual beings. The Overmind of *Childhood's End*, too, invoking Stapledon's 'cosmic consciousness', is described as 'Potentially infinite, beyond mortality ... absorbing race after race as it spread across the stars' in an evolutionary culmination experienced not as 'tragedy, but fulfilment' (1970: 178). And the Star-Child of *2001*, though 'master of the world', is 'never ... alone', but exists instead in constant communion with the beings that made it (1988: 224, 222). Clarke turns away from national, political, or economic ideologies towards post-ideological technological empowerment, evident in the figures of the Overmind, the Star-Child, or the 'Great Ones' of *The City and the Stars*. Yet it is a power infused with a humanist ethos: in the mode of Stapledonian 'personality-in-community', it is an organic form of technocratic rule, a humanist 'Empire' that derives its power not from the imposition of the human will *on* the cosmos but from the merger of human will *with* the cosmos—'human' here understood in both its material *and* immaterial senses. The supra-human thus offers the ideal figure for Clarke's notion of human culmination: as a Stapledonian 'cosmic consciousness', an organic union of individual and society.

Conclusion

With the supra-human, then, SF writers of the mid-century found one way of resolving the tension between the individual and mass society. In Asimov's *Foundation*, the entire population of the galaxy is guided through history by paternalistic and technocratic institutions. The agency of the individual human subject is sacrificed to preserve human society as a whole—a necessary loss in the face of fascistic biopolitical regimes that threatened to undermine *all* humanist values. In Clarke's *The City and the Stars*, conversely, the destiny of humanity lies in a conscious transcendence of materiality, leading to unification with a host of non-human entities in a Stapledonian 'cosmic consciousness'. Here the human body is writ in large galactic terms as a metaphor for the ideal form of society: a harmonious union between individual 'cell' and social 'body'.

In both cases, the supra-human provides one potential solution to the urgent need, as Braidotti puts it, to find 'new and alternative modes of political and ethical agency for our technologically mediated world' (2013: 58). Yet, as with each text that I have examined so far, it does so in a way that recoups, rather than overturns, the traditional liberal humanist subject. Even an entity as radically non-human as Clarke's Overmind or Star Child offers an intensification, rather than a rejection, of the precepts of liberal humanism. Both the biopolitical determinism of the Seldon Plan in *Foundation* and, in particular, the post-material consciousness of *The City and the Stars* must ultimately be placed on a spectrum between assimilative humanist and transformative posthumanist notions of the individual and society, gesturing towards the latter while ultimately falling back on the former.

The Second World War did not mark the end of the human's troubled trajectory in Anglo-American SF. In the next chapter, I will consider the period of the 1960s and 1970s, during which the ever-growing power of bureaucratic regimes, coupled with emerging concerns about the environmental future of the planet, gave rise to a host of hopes and fears centred on the human. The final human figure to be discussed is the 'post-human', with 'post' understood in the sense of both 'beyond'—and 'after'.

Chapter Four

Disaster and Redemption: Utopia, nature, and the post-human in J.G. Ballard's *The Crystal World* and Ursula K. Le Guin's *The Dispossessed*

> Oh my God. I'm back. I'm home. All the time, it was ... We finally really did it. You maniacs! You blew it up! Ah, damn you! God damn you all to hell!

In the same year that Charlton Heston was lamenting the end of human civilisation in Franklin J. Schaffner's *Planet of the Apes* (1968), Stanley Kubrick was imagining a different kind of 'post-human' in *2001: a space odyssey*. Whereas the former film depicts the literal demise of (one version of) humanity due to its own technological hubris, the latter presents an equivocal vision of post-material transcendence in the enigmatic 'Star Child'. Nor were these the only post-humans to be found in Hollywood in 1968: George A. Romero's *Night of the Living Dead* also hinted at a coming posthuman world, although this filmic apocalypse—with its African-American protagonist and guerrilla-style conflict between humans and newly revived 'ghouls'—owes more to the specific context of the Vietnam War and contemporary race relations in the United States than to the more general Cold War anxieties that fuel Schaffner's work.

The figure of the 'post-human', widespread in Hollywood SF movies in the 1960s, will be the subject of this concluding chapter. The SF of this period engages with some ongoing sociocultural concerns: the fragmentation of human agency and individuality amid the growth of stifling bureaucratic structures and pervasive consumerism; the explosion of hyperreal media and advertising images that undermined the distinction between 'real' and 'unreal'; and the accelerated rate of technological change that diluted the individual's capacity to cognitively adapt to their social environment. The archetype of the post-human functions within this context in two distinct and opposing ways, which will be respectively examined in two primary works from the period: J.G. Ballard's *The Crystal World* (1966) and Ursula K. Le Guin's *The Dispossessed* (1974).

Ballard is one of the most significant British SF writers of the second half of the twentieth century and achieved a level of mainstream and critical success unusual for an SF author. Ballard was a key figure in the 'New Wave', an aesthetic movement within SF that explored new forms, styles, subjects, and themes radically at odds with older SF modes. In *The Crystal World*, human civilisation is threatened by a bizarre crystallisation phenomenon that has appeared in various parts of the world. The novel, I will argue, ultimately advocates a submission to the all-encompassing force of technological rationality: the transformation of the 'inner landscapes' of his characters resulting from the natural disaster lead Ballard ultimately to envisage the end of humanity as a utopian moment of material transcendence. Yet this is a version of utopia that, in *The Crystal World*, requires the complete subordination of the natural world in the service of human fulfilment.

In contrast, Le Guin's *The Dispossessed*, I will argue, stresses holistic notions of embedded subjectivity, partial knowledges, and 'ontological parity'—the moral and ethical equivalence of the human and non-human. Le Guin is perhaps the most significant SF writer from the second half of the twentieth century and has received substantial critical attention both in SF studies and wider literary criticism. *The Dispossessed*, in turn, is one of her best-known works. As I will argue, *The Dispossessed*, inspired by the environmental politics of the 1970s, depicts a functioning human society that neither instrumentalises nor romanticises the natural world but instead treats it as a site of intrinsic value. Le Guin's novel comes closest of all the works examined here to a truly posthumanist vision—not by moving past the human nor, as in Ballard's work, by doing away with the human altogether, but by critically rethinking the basic concepts that have underpinned humanist ethical frameworks.

From these works emerge two distinct inflections of the 'post-human'— one defeatist and escapist, the other critical and productive. I will first begin with an overview of the SF of the period, examining the significance of environmental and ecological themes in SF during this period as well as the increased popularity of utopian works during the 1970s. These will inform the readings of the two central works, each of which falls uneasily on the spectrum between utopian and dystopian writing.

Utopia and the rejection of 'Faust' in 1960s and 1970s SF

'Previously', writes British SF author M. John Harrison in a 1975 essay, 'we've had a special fondness for Faust, our test tube clown':

> Now we execrate him. We trusted him, and he gave us DDT; we put up with his absent-mindedness and his cranky white haircut, and he got strontium in the milk; 'glutted now with learning's golden gifts', he invented Lewisite and the unburnt hydrocarbon. We made sure he ate his breakfast, wiped the egg off his tie and managed his bank account; he introduced us to phenacetin, to the MIRV and the core-melt ... His Magic Food all turned bad, his wings flew *us* a little too near the sun (1983: 341).

Harrison here offers a checklist of dubious technological achievements of the twentieth century, including harmful chemical agents (DDT, strontium, Lewisite, phenacetin) and nuclear technologies (MIRV, 'core-melts'). His examples—and the implication that much modern technological advancement has not, after all, been in humanity's best interests—inform the pall that, by the 1960s and 1970s, had dampened the technocratic impulses of earlier SF. Visions of unimpeded human triumph over the galaxy had, for the most part, gone out of fashion within literary SF by the early to mid-1960s.

In place of the Galactic Empires and mystic humanism of Asimov, Clarke, Heinlein, and others, we instead encounter Kurt Vonnegut's 'The Big Space Fuck' (1972), which lampoons space travel as 'a serious effort to make sure that human life would continue to exist somewhere else in the Universe' (2012: par. 2). Such enterprises, in Vonnegut's story, have become an urgent priority, underpinned not by noble motives of human destiny but by simple material necessity: unchecked capitalist production has meant that 'Everything had turned to shit and beer cans and old automobiles and Clorox bottles' (par. 2). As a result, human life simply 'couldn't continue much longer on Earth' (par. 2). To complete this ignoble image, the colonising ship in Vonnegut's story, carrying the freeze-dried semen of thousands of approved donors, is christened 'in honor of a famous space pioneer': Arthur C. Clarke (par. 3).

Vonnegut's story epitomises the more self-conscious mode of SF that gained popularity in Britain and the United States during the 1960s, informed by the social and cultural dynamics of that decade. In an afterword to a 1999 republication of Norman Spinrad's *Bug Jack Barron* (1969), Michael Moorcock summarises the impasse at which western society had found itself in the decades following the Second World War:

> Tired of the familiar hypocrisies and the empty moralising of the middle-class, bored with the sententious orthodoxy of the official Left, suspicious of the motives of big business, especially the arms trade, hearing the first intimations of a very noisy

uncontrollable cyberspace, a virtual universe of spin and image manipulation, understanding how popular media can become a sinister instrument of public brainwashing, how easily the culture of consumerism buys and sells our representatives ... Spinrad put his finger to the pulse of the times (Barron, 1999: 253).

These social and cultural developments inform the humanist concerns of the SF of this period: the 'technological earthquake' of post-war scientific research and development, including the heated 'space race' between the US and USSR (Hobsbawm, 2006: 265); the expansion of government and corporate bureaucracies; the clash between consumerism and an emerging, youth-oriented, anti-capitalist counter culture; the pervasive influence of mass media on individual and social values; and the disorientating impact—as Alvin Toffler outlines in his well-known 1970 study, *Future Shock*—of rapid globalisation and technological advancement on the experience of time and space. Toffler characterises the average citizen of post-war 'super-industrial societies' as a 'stranger in a strange land', unable to comprehend the 'novelty' and 'transience' that typified 'the most rapid and deep-going technological revolution in history' (1971: 186-7).

Such volatile conditions—the 'idea of change' that, as Daniel Bell argues, had come to dominate economics, technology, and culture (1972: 12)—had significant ramifications for the SF produced in the period. For Harrison, many SF writers and readers, unable to meaningfully engage with a rapidly changing technological society, fled into fictional worlds whose social, political, and cultural configurations were more readily comprehensible than those of the real world. Hence 'we have the World of Tolkien, the World of Michael Moorcock, the Worlds of *Dune* and *Star Trek*' (1983: 344). Other works from the period confront head-on the complexities of the age and their ramifications for human experience. Anxieties concerning overpopulation (a common concern for the 'baby boomer' generation of SF writers) recur in many works, including Harry Harrison's *Make Room! Make Room!* (1966), John Brunner's *Stand on Zanzibar* (1969), Larry Niven's *Ringworld* (1970), Le Guin's *Lathe of Heaven* (1971), and Thomas Disch's *334* (1972). These texts stress the devaluation of human life and its subjection to bureaucratic control—the 'birth controls' and 'death controls' that frame human life, as Harrison puts it—that result from ballooning populations and resource scarcity. At the same time, the familiar spectre of apocalyptic technology—nuclear weapons and the doctrine of 'mutually assured destruction', reaching its pitch in the Cuban Missile Crisis of 1962— remained a common SF motif, simmering under the surface of SF works throughout the 1960s and 1970s and contributing to the popularity of Stanley Kubrick's avowedly anti-nuclear SF satire, *Dr. Strangelove* (1964).

Many works of the period also questioned the humanist chauvinism— the promotion of white intellectual males as the 'universal' human type—characteristic of older SF. Joe Haldeman's *The Forever War* (1974), for example, a hard SF novel written in response to the Vietnam War, depicts a soldier who participates in a millennia-long war against the 'Taurans', a mysterious alien species. The lengthy duration of the war is caused by the inability of either side to communicate with the other: the Taurans are a race of clones and as such their subjectivity is based on communal, rather than individual, identity. Not until humanity also turns to cloning as a means of propagation (most individuals having become homosexual) is communication established between the warring races and the war ended. Hence, alongside depictions of the brutal nature of military bureaucracy, *The Forever War*, like Lem's *Solaris* (1961), rejects universal notions of 'mind' and emphasises the mutually constitutive relationship between subjectivity and embodiment.

Elsewhere, in *Do Androids Dream of Electric Sheep?* (1968), Philip K. Dick exposes the ethical limitations of traditional humanism through his depictions of 'androids'—sentient mechanical beings used as unpaid labour—and 'specials'—cognitively limited individuals employed as menial labourers on an ecologically ruined Earth. These 'near-human' beings are exposed to the cruelty and prejudice of 'normal' humans based on their perceived lack of 'true' (rational, biological) humanhood, revealing the fault lines in conventional understandings of 'proper' human subjectivity. In Kate Wilhelm's *Where Late the Sweet Birds Sang* (1976), conversely, the reverse may be seen. The novel depicts a post-apocalyptic world in which biological reproduction has been replaced by more 'efficient' cloning techniques. Mark, the illegitimate child of an ostracised clone, rejects the conformism, sterility, and lack of individuality that characterise the society of clones. Mark's revolt takes the form of a reactionary humanism: his goal is the reaffirmation of possessive individualism in contrast to the enforced socialism of the clone society. To this end, Mark establishes a pastoral society in which 'the joys of men and women, and their agonies, were private affairs' (2006: 250), conducted within an ostensibly utopian—although traditional and patriarchal—social framework.

Many of the new modes of SF that appeared at this time have been gathered under the banner of the 'New Wave', a movement usually dated from (in Britain) Moorcock's editorship of *New Worlds* from 1964 to 1969 and (in the US) the appearance of *Dangerous Visions* (1967), a watershed anthology of original stories edited by Harlan Ellison. The stories and novels of the New Wave turned away from the clichéd 'hard' SF tropes of scientific realism, futuristic technology, and space travel. Instead, there appeared more self-consciously literary works, committed to a more rigorous exploration of philosophical and political topics and of the 'soft' sciences of psychology and sociology. The preoccupations of the New Wave are evident in the movement's most characteristic concept, 'inner space', a term credited to J.B. Priestley. In a 1953 essay, Priestley wrote that 'society, like a rocket ship bound for some distant nightmare planet, is hurrying at full speed in the wrong direction; and ... dangerously over-extraverted, we are refusing to deal justly with the unconscious side of our minds' (1957: 25–6). The New Wave of SF is thus characterised by an intense interest in the psychological lifeworlds of individuals living in technoscientific societies. The new experiments in style, liberal explorations of sex, sexuality, race, and gender, and frequent recourse to psychedelic themes under the inspiration of the Beat Generation (particularly Burroughs) generated a quite different notion of the human than that previously encountered in SF.

Some works, for example, used non-realist prose styles to capture the cognitive experience of life in the late twentieth century. In Spinrad's *Bug Jack Barron* (1969), for example, a talk-show host finds himself embroiled in a complex conspiracy involving immortality, party politics, and racial prejudice in a media-saturated and racially segregated future US. The novel emphasises the role of the mass media in constructing and manipulating realities and draws attention to the collapsing boundaries between reality and 'realer than real' media images—the 'non-event history that existed only on the screen' (Barron, 1999: 226). This disorientation is mirrored in the frenzied vernacular style of the novel:

> the traffic inched at a foot a second toward Bleecker, past souvenir stands, bare-box strip joints, state-license acid parlours, furtive street-corner schmeck dealers local action fading Slum Goddess tourist trade whores, through a miasma of grease-fried sausage smells, pot-musk, drunken-sailor piss, open air toilet aroma of packaged disaster (72).

The clashing imagery and rapid-fire run-on phrasing of such passages imply sensory overload, as grammar and syntax are abandoned in the effort to keep pace with the flow of information from the external environment.

Another work, Dick's *Ubik* (1969), raises deeper questions concerning the epistemological blurring of reality and unreality resulting from technological manipulation. Set in a thoroughly commodified future

United States—in which individuals are liable to become trapped in their homes if they lack the toll required to activate the front door—the characters of Dick's novel experience a sense of cognitive alienation from the world around them. As the novel progresses, they are increasingly confronted with phenomena—time travel, spontaneous and inexplicable deaths, rapidly decomposing consumer items, 'ghosts' who feed on the 'half-lives' of the cryogenically frozen 'dead'—that neither they nor the reader are able to process or understand. The novel's ambiguous ending refuses even to clarify which of the characters are living and which exist in a state of hallucinatory 'half-life'. Both characters and readers are thus left, as Spinrad puts it in another story (riffing on Dylan), with 'no direction home'—that is, bereft of any means of confirming the objective basis of their psychological experiences.

Other writers rendered these processes in even more radical ways, depicting the complete dissolution of the human within technological systems. In 'The Four-Colour Problem' (1971), for example, Barrington J. Bayley describes society as an 'oven' designed to maintain individuals at a state of maximum psychological pressure: 'human society' in Bayley's story is a 'machine' in which individuals are 'translated' into 'social logic units', their behaviours in any social context understood as an outcome of binary 'vectors' such as 'Praise/Blame, Like/Dislike, Admiration/Contempt, Esteem/Disgust, Enthusiasm/Apathy, Why-hello-there/Get-out-of-my-sight-you-disgusting-little-man' (Bayley, 1983: 45). 'Humans', in any traditional sense, are absent from Bayley's story, substituted by 'vectors' that 'outliv[e] the units [i.e., human individuals] that process and transmit them' (45). Bayley's juxtaposition of standard narrative prose with passages of dense pseudo-scientific discourse, all contained within a perplexing nonlinear narrative, reproduces the sense of temporal and spatial disorientation experienced by individuals in the 'oven'. This technique is also employed in Pamela Zoline's 'The Heat Death of the Universe' (1967), Langdon Jones's 'The Eye of the Lens' (1968), Ballard's *The Atrocity Exhibition* (1970), and numerous other New Wave works.

Zoline's story is well known for its elaboration of the theme of entropy—the key concern, according to Colin Greenland, of much New Wave writing. In this story, a homemaker, Sarah Boyle, confronts the apparent meaninglessness of all existence and the universal tendency towards decay and dissipation. During her resulting existential crisis, the distinctions between Sarah and the technological environment in which she resides are subtly collapsed: her eyes are described as a 'fine, modern, acid, synthetic blue' (Zoline, 1983: 319), while the dissolution of her personal identity—'Sarah has at times felt a complete unity with her body, at other times a complete separation ... Sometimes, at extremes, her Body seems to her an animal on a leash, taken for walks in the park by her Mind. ... Sometimes Sarah can hardly remember how many cute, chubby little children she has' (322–4)—metaphorically enacts the 'heat death of the universe' as the boundaries between Sarah and her surroundings slowly dissipate.

The impact of all these works was both to critically address the humanist legacy of older SF modes and to expand the field to encompass new forms of subjective and cognitive experience. The general tone of post-war works was pessimistic: the general attitude towards notions of universal human progress, instrumental rationalism, and technological determinism is overwhelmingly a sceptical one. As Harrison puts it, from the tone of SF works in the 1960s and 1970s it would appear that 'Rationalism ... has sold us up a very muddy backwater indeed' (1983: 342). The New Wave's preoccupation with entropy, the ubiquitous threat of nuclear apocalypse, the collapsing distinctions between personal and public life, the reduction of the individual to a unit within a bureaucratically managed social equation, and the obsessive concern (as Greenland puts it) with 'the disruption of history and the end of man' (2013: ch. 11): each of these contributed to a sense of this period as (in the words of Philip José Farmer) 'The Age of the Plugged-In Man', or 'The Age of Complete Interconnectedness'.

This pessimistic outlook is particularly evident in depictions of humanity's relationship to the natural environment which, in the 1960s and 1970s, was rapidly moving to the fore of western cultural and political consciousness. The post-war period of skyrocketing production and manufacture also saw human ecological destruction on an unprecedented scale: as Marshall Berman remarks, societies in the 1970s '[had] to learn fast how to use their diminishing energies to protect the shrinking resources they had and keep their whole world from running down' (1988: 330). The publication of popular works of environmentalism—Rachel Carson's influential study of the environmental impacts of pesticides, *Silent Spring* (1962), and Stewart Brand's *Whole Earth Catalog*, an American magazine first published in 1968 that promoted anti-consumerist ecologism—generated a sharp rise in public awareness of ecological and environmental issues (the first 'Earth Day', for example, was held in 1970), and contributed to the growth of western environmental politics throughout the 1970s.

This concern is reflected in the rise of ecological themes in SF from the period. Brian Aldiss's *Hothouse* (1962), for example, depicts a far-future Earth on which human life has been brought near to extinction by environmental change. These changes lie beyond human control: lunar gravity has halted the planet's rotation, while the ageing sun has also expanded enormously, rendering the sunward side of the now-stationary planet inhospitably hot. Humans—reduced to tiny, tree-dwelling beings—fight for survival in this world against a plethora of carnivorous plant species. In certain ways, the novel is typical of New Wave fiction: the pantropic decline of the human species, the loss of higher cognitive and linguistic functions, and the passivity of protagonist Gren as he considers, at the close of the novel, the approaching extinction of the species epitomise the entropic structure of the work, an evolutionary fading-out of humanity that owes as much to Wells's *The Time Machine* as to contemporary environmental discourse. Aldiss's novel, however, is not so much defeatist as merely anti-idealist: his rejection of human rejuvenation or easy technocratic solutions to environmental crises requires a confrontation with, rather than an escape from, humanity's material place in the planetary ecosystem. By contrast, Frank Herbert's *Dune* (1965)—'one of the most influential examples of ecological sf', as Chris Pak notes (2016: 118)—although it explores themes of resource scarcity and ecological balance, ultimately advocates a 'strong instrumental approach to nature' that denies the natural world objective ontological value (Pak, 2016: 122). The arid landscape of Arrakis (the planet of the novel) becomes an instrument for human self-actualisation, subject to transformation in the service of human needs, while the extension of human control over the planet, encompassing even the giant carnivorous sandworms that inhabit the sandy dunes, subordinates nature to exclusively human needs.

In general, then, SF works from this period reflect a sense of environmental gloom, the experience of nature diminished (to borrow an image from John Brunner) to 'a design of dead leaves embedded under a clear plastic surface' (1984: 150). This gloom, however, was challenged with the resurgence of utopian fiction in the 1970s. In contrast to the pessimism of other SF works, utopian fiction during this period sought to 'keep alive the possibility of a world qualitatively distinct from this one … a stubborn negation of all that is' (24). These utopias differed significantly from their classical counterparts: Peter Fitting argues that, with contemporary utopian fiction, the central question concerns 'how to link a poetics of the future with a politics of the future' (1987: 24). Such utopian works, even as they departed towards some estranging future alternative, remained directed back towards the society from which they sprang, and hence the 'fundamental dynamic' at the heart of contemporary utopias, as Jameson argues, is 'the dialectic between Identity and Difference, … the degree to which such a politics aims at imagining, and sometimes even at realising, a system radically different from our own' (2005: xii). For Jameson, the focus in utopian writing thus shifts onto questions not of content but of form and representation, since 'what cannot be said' in a utopian text—or more accurately, what cannot be represented—is often of more significance than what can (xiii).

Hence more recent utopian works tend, as Fitting notes, to 'depict ... the struggle for utopia rather than the image of a finished and harmonious Utopian society' (1987: 25). Tom Moylan has been the most significant scholar of utopia in this regard, introducing the influential notions of 'classical' and 'critical' utopias (2014: 1–11). While classical utopias offered 'blueprints' of the perfect society which utopian practitioners had merely to put into practice, critical utopias depict instead an ongoing dialectic between 'the originary world and the utopian society', which is marked by 'difference and imperfection' (10). Hence critical utopias acknowledge 'the limitations of the utopian tradition' while retaining the 'dream' of perfection (10). This evolution in the utopian form, according to Moylan, becomes evident particularly in the 1970s:

> Inspired by the movements of the 1960s and finding new imagery in the alternatives being explored in the 1970s, the critical utopia is part of the political practice and visions shared by a variety of autonomous oppositional movements that reject the domination of the emerging system of transnational corporations and post-industrial production and ideological structure ... The new opposition is deeply infused with the politics of autonomy, democratic socialism, ecology, and especially feminism (11).

Hence the critical utopia emerges as part of the general wave of anti-authoritarian movements that marked the 1960s and 1970s.

Whereas works like Wilhelm's 'The Funeral' (1972) and Suzy McKee Charnas's *Walk to the End of the World* (1974) draw on dark visions of brutal patriarchal dystopias—in Charnas's novel, situated explicitly within an ecologically devastated world—others such as Le Guin's *The Dispossessed*, Joanna Russ's *The Female Man* (1975), Ernest Callenbach's *Ecotopia* (1975), Samuel Delany's *Triton* (1976), and Marge Piercy's *Woman on the Edge of Time* (1976) offer more holistic visions of human co-existence with the non-human world that explicitly reject masculinist or exploitative views of nature. In these works, the correct use of technology in human society, and the relationship of that society to the natural environment, became matters of urgent inquiry, while the question regarding the kind of humans that might inhabit such a society became a pressing one—not merely for critical utopias, but for all SF. With this in mind, I turn now to the first work under consideration in this chapter, Ballard's *The Crystal World*.

Alienation and human transcendence in Ballard's *The Crystal World*

The Crystal World is the last of Ballard's early trilogy of disaster novels, preceded by *The Drowned World* (1962) and *The Burning World* (1964; later revised as *The Drought*, 1965).[1] *The Crystal World* represents, according to Ballard himself, the culmination of his literary output up to that point. As noted by W. Warren Wagar, Ballard divided his early work into two distinct phases: the first, which concludes with *The Crystal World* in 1966, 'offered descriptions of "imaginary places," under the direct inspiration of the surrealist painters', while the second, which Ballard dated from the publication of *The Atrocity Exhibition* in 1970, focusses more exclusively on media and technology (Wagar, 1991: 53).

This division is somewhat misleading: while there are clear differences between these two phases of Ballard's writing, certain themes recur consistently throughout his early fiction. The most significant of these is Ballard's preoccupation with the experience of time. Despite his oft-repeated commitment to exploring 'inner space' in his works, it is time that forms the major thematic concern of Ballard's fiction. Indeed, 'inner space' itself is understood by Ballard as a function of time: he defines it as an 'internal landscape of tomorrow that is a transmuted image of the past' (1963: par. 6). In his much-cited essay, 'Which Way to Inner Space?' (1962), Ballard goes further, arguing that SF, to avoid becoming stale and uninteresting, must 'turn its back on space, on interstellar travel, extra-terrestrial life forms, galactic wars', and other standard tropes of the genre (1962: 117). In place of these tired ideas, he suggests that writers focus on 'the elaboration of such concepts as the time zone, deep time and archaeopsychic time. I'd like to see more psycho-literary ideas, more meta-biological and meta-chemical concepts, private time-systems, synthetic psychologies and space-times' (118).

---

[1] Prior to *The Drowned World*, Ballard had published an earlier work of disaster fiction, *The Wind from Nowhere* (1961). Although this was Ballard's first published novel, he had little regard for it, dismissing it as a 'piece of hackwork' (Brigg, 1985: 43) and subsequently referring to *The Drowned World* as his 'first novel' (Ballard, 2008: 84). Given the significant stylistic and thematic differences that separate this novel from the later trilogy of disaster novels, *The Wind from Nowhere* will be excluded from considerations of Ballard's disaster fiction for the remainder of this chapter.

Ballard's preoccupation with time is characterised by 'future shock': the collapse of the future into the present resulting from 'the incessant demand for change' that marked capitalist society, especially evident in the accelerated rate of technological development (Toffler, 1971: 9). In 'The Terminal Beach' (1964), for example, one character notes how thermonuclear weapons have 'fused the sands' of a nuclear testing site into 'layers', resulting in 'pseudo-geological strata' (2014a: 33). In contrast to the long durations of time required to form natural geological strata, these weapons have instead 'condensed the brief epochs, microseconds in duration, of *thermonuclear* time' (33). Ballard's blurring of geological and technological time here dramatises the accelerated temporal ontologies of the late twentieth century: the speed and dramatic impacts of technology have obliterated the course of natural time, overlaying it with the sediments of humanity's technological pursuits. Nuclear technologies— the archetypal technologies of the Cold War era—have thus 'inverted the geologist's maxim, "The key to the past lies in the present." Here, the key to the present lay in the future'—that is, the technological future of humanity, rapidly collapsing in upon the present (33).

Ballard's concern with time is highly evident in the work under consideration here. Expanding on a concept first depicted in 'The Illuminated Man' (1964), *The Crystal World* follows Edward Sanders, an English leprosy doctor, as he encounters a strange phenomenon that is slowly crystallising the rainforests of the Cameroon Republic. The crystallisation process freezes everything in its path, solidifying animals, plants, and objects within a static 'house of jewels' (1978: 69). The cause of this mysterious transformation, it is eventually learned, is time itself: the appearance of 'anti-time', a temporal corollary to anti-matter, is causing a decrease in the 'total store of time' remaining in the universe (85). In turn, this decrease is causing objects to produce 'spatial replicas of themselves, substance without mass, to increase their foothold on existence' (85). Affected matter, attempting to compensate for its sudden loss of temporal dimensions, begins instead to proliferate along spatial coordinates, causing a literal spatialisation of time. The full catastrophic consequences of this phenomenon are made apparent to Sanders when he attempts to rescue a soldier who has become encased within crystals. Sanders shatters the mineral formations covering the man's face and arms only to later realise that the crystals *were* the man—he had in fact been destroying parts of the man's body.

Indeed, Ballard's preoccupation with reversing or escaping time is evident throughout the disaster trilogy. Each of these novels features a protagonist who, following some apocalyptic natural disaster, uncovers a long-buried psychic connection to the distant biological past. Through depictions of psychological regression, Ballard thus reintroduces his characters into more meaningful (biological, evolutionary) 'time-systems' rendered unavailable by the technological and cultural conditions of the late twentieth century. Time within Ballard's fiction is thus figured as 'a primitive mental structure' (2014a: 594). In this, Ballard's works recall earlier imperialist fiction in which, as I argued in the first chapter, time becomes a meaningful category only at the peripheries of empire. Ballard, however, reverses the spatial framework of earlier imperialist SF: rather than travelling from 'advanced' to 'primitive' spaces to achieve backwards movement through time, western civilisation is itself made to regress to the 'archaeopsychic past' by invasive natural forces. As a result, Ballard's characters themselves become 'pre-humans' who must undergo psychological transformation to adapt to their new natural environments.

Each of Ballard's disaster works thus collapses familiar barriers between the human and the non-human as the fractious relationship of humanity to nature becomes unsustainable: ultimately, either industry pushes nature into an unstable condition that sparks global catastrophe or else the capitalist network itself is broken down by natural forces that science is unable to either comprehend or restrain. Nature in the disaster works could thus be regarded neither as an enemy to be defeated nor a realm of Otherness to be transcended—rather, it becomes an indissoluble component of humanity's material and psychological make-up. Nature is both dystopic, bringing about the collapse of advanced human civilisation, and utopic, creating the possibility for new formulations of what it means to be human in a natural world. Ballard, by maintaining these opposing utopic and dystopic images of nature in tension, questions the straightforward binary between culture and nature. Indeed, the argument may be made that Ballard's disaster works explore the possibility of a dialectical reconciliation of the human with the non-human and a more holistic attitude towards human–nature relations. By revealing humanity's deep ontological connection to nature, the novels attempt to overturn artificial human–non-human dichotomies.

Yet *The Crystal World* is more concerned with humanity's future than with its evolutionary past. As I will argue here, *The Crystal World* offers a response to the growth of mass technological systems in late twentieth-century western society and, in particular, allegorises the alienating processes of instrumental rationalism. The impacts of these processes for human individuals are depicted in Ballard's 1975 novel, *High-Rise*, in which he describes a 'new social type' that 'thrived like an advanced species of machine in the neural atmosphere' of the post-war period

(2014b: ch. 3). This human 'type', and the 'psychological pressures' that afflict it, is characteristic of a 'new kind of late twentieth-century life' defined by 'the invasion of ... privacy by government agencies and data-processing organizations', the 'rapid turnover of acquaintances ... a cool, unemotional personality [and] lack of involvement with others', and the 'impersonal steel and concrete landscape[s]' of urban space—built 'not for man', Ballard writes, 'but for man's absence' (ch. 2–3). The human itself exists within such landscapes not as a living being but as a cog in 'a huge machine' (ch. 1), while the offices and high-rises of the late twentieth century function as 'a social hierarchy as rigid and formalized as an anthill's' (ch. 7). Yet *The Crystal World* is also concerned with human transcendence, treating its natural catastrophe as a means for the human individual to achieve self-actualisation. These utopian qualities of the catastrophe undercut the force of Ballard's critique of the alienation and detachment of late twentieth-century life, particularly as the utopian moment, as I will argue, comes at the cost of the natural world.

Ballard's fiction is particularly concerned with the characteristic sense of estrangement from social and cultural systems that came increasingly to permeate individual life in the late twentieth century. The sociotechnological structures of the late twentieth century, characterised by pervasive bureaucratic and media institutions and structures, shifted social agency away from the individual towards massive bureaucratic systems and reduced the 'myth of man'—that is, the notion of the autonomous, self-identical, and self-actualising agent familiar from liberal humanism—'to ashes' (Althusser, 1965: 229). Ballard's introverted characters resemble Jameson's 'schizophrenic': 'isolated, disconnected', and unable either to comprehend the volley of 'discontinuous material signifiers' emanating from media images, 'which fail to link up into a coherent sequence', or to retain a hold on a personal or cultural past in the context of a constantly shifting present (Jameson, 1983: 119). These subjects are left without a 'feeling of identity' (119), because of which, as Greenland remarks, 'the mind ceases to balance itself and social communication is paralysed' (2013: ch. 7). This process is captured, for example, in the fragmented and shifting character at the centre of *The Atrocity Exhibition*. This character (whose name changes with each chapter) repeatedly fails in his attempts to 'obtain a valid unit of existence'—that is, a meaningful grasp on his personal and historical identity—by reinterpreting his subjective experience in terms of anonymous geometrical patterns (Ballard, 2006: 57).

Ballard confronts this sense of social and technological alienation through a series of images of human interactions with unsettling and ambiguous landscapes. In *High-Rise*, for example, the tenants of a forty-storey apartment block react against the pressures of their crowded living quarters by reverting to a tribal social formation that, as one character muses, makes explicit the 'ruthlessness and aggression' of twentieth-century life (2014b: ch. 16). A recurring theme of the disaster trilogy, meanwhile, is the estrangement of the individual from familiar social relations in the face of catastrophic natural forces and the resulting confrontation with a new, and initially incomprehensible, social environment. *The Drowned World*, for example, depicts a post-apocalyptic world in which the melting of the polar ice caps has severely flooded all major cities, which are subsequently transformed into lagoons. During a scientific expedition to an unnamed European city, biologist Robert Kerans finds himself becoming gradually alienated from both his companions and the increasingly absurd rituals of scientific investigation and military administration. He is haunted by dreams of psychological regression and dissolution into the environment: 'Kerans felt, beating within him like his own pulse, the powerful mesmeric pull of the baying reptiles ... he felt the barriers which divided his own cells from the surrounding medium dissolving' (2012: 71). This sense of estrangement from the self, of the collapse of previously stable boundaries between subjective self and objective world, is reflected in the contrast between the artificiality of the 'black marble basins and gold-plated taps and mirrors' of the 'Ritz' in which Kerans is staying and the 'strange mournful beauty' of the lagoon immediately outside the hotel (9–10). The ambiguous identity of the city—'had it once been Berlin, Paris or London?' (9)—and the collapse of familiar spatial distinctions echo the sense of individual disorientation that, as a result of continued globalisation, bureaucratic growth, and rapid technological acceleration, had become characteristic of all the 'unreal cities' (to borrow T.S. Eliot's term) of twentieth-century western societies.

At first glance, *The Crystal World* seems the least concerned of all the disaster trilogy novels with technological systems or, indeed, with human environments at all. Whereas both *The Drowned World* and *The Drought* take place in urban spaces, *The Crystal World* is set in the natural landscapes of the Cameroonian rainforests. (The other two sites of crystallisation mentioned in the novel—the Florida everglades and the Pripyat marshes of Russia—are also natural spaces.) Yet the choice of Cameroon as setting for *The Crystal World* serves in part to dramatise the above processes of individual estrangement from social structures. Ballard stresses the disconnect that has arisen between the familiar western structural apparatus of state and society historically imprinted on Port Matarre and the individuals that must navigate these structures. When Sanders arrives at his hotel in Port Matarre and begins making queries about Mont Royal—his destination in the region, to which all local transport has suddenly and mysteriously been halted—he is met with highly ambiguous responses from local workers and officials. The 'evasive' porter at his hotel, for example, responds to his queries with a 'studied shrug' (1978: 22) while a ticket taker in a nearby booking office tells him 'dreamily' that 'Nothing's going on' (26). Later, when he enquires to the local police chief, an 'African charge-captain', about the 'atmosphere of mystery' hanging over the town, he is met with the vague response that the locals of Port Matarre are leaving because of 'the forest ... It frightens them, it's so black and heavy all the time' (27). From the outset, then, Sanders encounters an air of uneasy bureaucratic inefficiency and dysfunction that he struggles to understand. This perception is further intensified by a bizarre event witnessed in a local market: a missionary priest, who had travelled into Port Matarre alongside Sanders, grabs a crystallised crucifix from a stall and inexplicably begins to shake it violently, evidently 'intent ... on exorcizing whatever powers it held for him' (35). The police officer and the priest, familiar social emblems of the institutions of civil and religious authority, have thus here become erratic, even volatile, figures within the defamiliarised world of the novel.

This sense of creeping individual alienation from the social and cultural institutions of western authority was in part informed by Ballard's own outlook on European colonialism. For H. Bruce Franklin, the waves of decolonisation and national independence movements that followed the Second World War are crucial to understanding the trend towards apocalyptic fiction that dominated SF in the post-war period. Following 'the devastation of the European empires' in the post-war decades, Franklin argues, there was 'an increasingly widespread belief, pulsating outward from England, ... that the world [was] coming to an end' (1979: par. 2). Just as much pre-war SF captured the technophilic impulses of the booming United States, Franklin argues, so post-war SF embodies the technophobic fears of the post-colonial and post-nuclear generation. He then goes on to declare Ballard to be the primary writer of the apocalypse, who '[more] than any other writer ... incarnates the apocalyptic imagination running riot in Anglo-American culture today' (1979: par. 1). The symbol of the crystal in *The Crystal World* is, for Franklin, emblematic of Ballard's ultimate fatalism, representing his deep-seated desire to check this process of imperial disintegration—the crystal symbolises a literal 'desire to stop time', within which is submerged a deeper desire 'to stop history' itself (par. 37).

This assessment of Ballard as both elegist for the fall of empire and herald of a new dystopian consciousness requires some investigation.

Certainly, the colonial past of Cameroon forms part of the background to *The Crystal World*: at one point, Sanders sees a 'French military landing-craft' moored in Port Matarre, while later he takes shelter in an extravagant mansion formerly belonging to a European mine-owner (1978: 11, 79). These details signal the lingering European presence within the former colony. Yet the depictions of Cameroon in *The Crystal World* also reflect Ballard's own experiences of colonialism. Ballard spent his formative childhood years in the 'bright but bloody kaleidoscope' of Shanghai, '90 per cent Chinese and 100 per cent Americanized' (2008: 4), where the 'French Concession' sat alongside his father's own textile factory, and where the incredible wealth of European and American expatriates existed alongside the bodies of starved Chinese labourers in the streets (6). For Ballard, Shanghai was a world of extremes: a 'cruel and lurid world' of 'gangsters and pickpockets ... Chinese dragon ladies [and] hawkers' in which all the excesses of human existence could be witnessed (29). In particular, Ballard recalls the 'enormous ancient alligator' of Shanghai zoo, a spectre who 'seemed to have been dragged forward reluctantly so many millions of years into the twentieth century', now absurdly surrounded by 'cigarette packets and ice-cream cartons' (1963: par. 3).

Later, in Lunghau internment camp where he and his family spent the war years, Ballard was exposed to the tales and memories of his fellow British internees who painted a nostalgic picture of the English homeland: a place of 'first nights and dancing till dawn ... a comfortable Beverley Nichols world of market towns and thatched roofs' (2008: 38). In contrast to the typical colonial narrative, which might envision such a setting as Shanghai as a fantastic and romanticised Orientalist landscape, for Ballard it was instead Britain itself that took on these 'unreal' characteristics. The reality of post-war English society, however, quickly shattered this wistful view: Ballard found England to be 'derelict, dark and half-ruined', a grim society in which 'hope itself was rationed' (122-3). Ballard's formative experiences of Britain were marked by disillusionment—he was witness not to the strength and vitality of the British empire nor its economic and technological conquests, but its decline and collapse.

Ballard's experiences of both Shanghai and England were thus characterised by a sense of unreality: Shanghai as a lurid and polarised cosmopolis, and England as a nostalgic fantasy punctured by the disappointing realities of post-war British society. Ballard's preoccupation with the ruin of society, then, must be put into its specific context. His apocalypse is informed not so much by the mournful *loss* of empire as by its *absence* in the first place—for Ballard, the British empire did not exist as a lived reality, because of which his dystopian works reflect not imperial pessimism but rather (for Ballard) the unreal qualities of empire. Ballard's apocalyptic images are thus of a vastly different order from those of the other British writer of the end of the world, John Wyndham. The choice of decolonised Cameroon as the setting for *The Crystal World*, and the sense of ambiguity and estrangement that hangs over the institutional structures depicted in the text, makes explicit the alienation that for Ballard hangs over *all* modern technological, urban, or human-made spaces. What emerges from Ballard's descriptions of Cameroon and London in his disaster novels, as much as from his recollections of the Shanghai of his boyhood, is a fundamental sense of *un*reality—of an unsettling distance between the individual and the social and cultural institutions by which they are surrounded.

Of course, Cameroon serves in Ballard's text not merely as an example of a decolonised nation state, but also as a specifically natural space, with Port Matarre being surrounded by rainforests. Here, too, a process of alienation is at work as nature itself is transfigured into an unfamiliar landscape by the crystallisation process. I have discussed how technological 'enframing', in Heidegger's sense of the term, can be understood as a process of spatialisation—that is, of situating otherwise mutable and fluctuating phenomena within the static structures of scientific and technological thought. The process of crystallisation is itself a literal draining of dynamism and vibrancy—of time itself— from the substance of the forest. Given this, the petrification of the Cameroonian rainforest more closely resembles a technological than a natural process: the merger of all the natural world into an atemporal and homogenous structure serves as an effective allegory for scientific procedure itself.

Indeed, it is significant to note the seeming facility with which the bizarre phenomenon is framed within a scientific vernacular. The process is the result of 'atomic' forces: 'this Hubble Effect, as they call it, is closer to a cancer as anything else ... an actual proliferation of the sub-atomic identity of all matter' (1978: 66). A similar scientific gloss is provided to account for each of the natural apocalypses depicted within the disaster trilogy—although, as Franklin argues, often amounting to little more than 'some vague pseudo-scientific theory, presented like a magician's patter' (1979: par. 5). As Ballard has noted, however, even though the details themselves are often vague ('Accuracy', he states elsewhere, is the 'last refuge of the unimaginative' [1962: 117]), the '*scientific imagination* is ... very, very important in [his] fiction' (Ballard and Lewis, 1991: 35, my emphasis). This imagination, he notes, is defined by amorality, detachment, and the meticulous dissection of the natural world—the 'core of science', Ballard says, 'is a shedding of all responsibility by the scientist who is just *looking* at a particular subject with a tendency to ignore the contingent links' (28, emphasis in original). It places science 'outside of time and space, and outside the social and human' (29). The crystallisation of *The Crystal World* literalises the totalising and universalising impulses of scientific thought—a process of literal objectification and petrification of the natural environment whose every element becomes rearticulated in the universal and fixed 'medium' of the crystal structure, symbolic of the sterility and detachment of scientific discourse.

The crystallisation phenomenon can thus be read as a reflection of the alienating qualities of the scientific imagination. One character, attempting to account for the phenomenon, notes that *'they'* have termed it 'the Hubble Effect' (1978: 66, my emphasis). In keeping with the ambiguity that hangs over the events of the novel, the precise identity of 'they' is left unspecified. 'They' are absent, anonymous, and ambiguous, symbols of the impersonal systems and institutions of scientific control. These systems and institutions, as Marcuse remarks in *One-Dimensional Man* (1964), are 'constituted [into] a rationally organized bureaucracy, which is, however, invisible at its vital center', and which is characterised by 'inhumanity and injustice' (2007: 74). For Marcuse, 'the relation between science and society' is one 'in which both move under the same logic and rationality of domination' (158). The human individual in society is thus conceived not as a free and responsible agent—rather, the overarching bureaucratic system comes to usurp individual expression altogether, alienating the individual even from the products of their own thought: as Davies remarks, within such alienating structures, 'I do not think, I am thought. You do not speak, you are spoken' (1997: 60).

It is significant, then, that *The Crystal World* concludes with its characters standing helpless before the crystallising forest, unable to undertake any meaningful action in the face of the incomprehensible events taking place around them. Human individuals in the novel are left unable to grasp even the meaning of the crystallising phenomenon: the enigmas that confront Sanders as he attempts to understand the changes taking place around him dramatise the barriers to individual epistemological engagement in the context of technoscientific societies. All that is left for these characters to do is become part of the phenomenon, as Sanders does when, at the close of the novel, he travels back into the crystallising forest to live 'in that transmogrified world' (1978: 167). If, then, as Rob Latham (paraphrasing Thomas Disch) has argued, Ballard's disaster novels can be read as 'prophetic visions of how an exploited nature might take revenge on its heedless exploiters', *The Crystal World* also dramatises the extent to which those processes of technological exploitation may turn back on humanity (2007: 111). Ballard's novel offers a response to the alienating tendencies of late twentieth-century life, which separated the individual from any meaningful sense of social or cultural identity. This is understood in his work as an outcome of bureaucracy and the accelerated advance of technological progress—these, in his view, threatened to swallow up both the natural world *and* humanity along with it.

Despite his recourse to dystopian subject matter, however, it is by no means clear that Ballard's works should therefore be read as warnings against instrumental rationalism and the heedless use of nature for human ends. Indeed, the disaster trilogy has frequently been noted for its distinctly *utopian* qualities. Wagar, for example, asserts that all of Ballard's disaster novels are really utopian texts in disguise:

> If 'utopia' is a place where all is well, a place of joy and perfection, then the psycho-physical landscapes of Ballard's fictions are manifestly such places. ... His landscapes are heavens; or, rather, liminal worlds through which discerning individuals—and in some Ballardian scenarios, all humanity—must pass to earn salvation. ... Escaping to a higher consciousness demands immersion in all being. Hence, in Ballard's transvaluation of the traditional Western wisdom, even dystopias are utopian (1991: 54).

In the disaster trilogy, each of Ballard's protagonists achieves transcendence as a result of the natural catastrophe taking place around them—as the natural landscape is upheaved, the characters correspondingly find themselves changed into 'a second Adam searching for the forgotten paradises of the reborn sun' (Ballard, 1978: 175). As noted by Wagar, Ballard's landscapes are 'metaphors for states of mind and soul, "psychic" or "spinal" landscape[s]' (1991: 53). Gregory Stephenson, too, remarks that the adaptation of the earth in Ballard's trilogy discloses 'a pre-existent inner landscape': 'a deep and potent image in the collective human psyche which may have the character of penance and retribution, or of paradise and transcendence' (1991: 62).

Ballard thus offers a dystopic utopia wherein the end of the human-made world corresponds to a psychological rebirth of humanity. Indeed, virtually all of Ballard's texts suggest a structure in which the physical setting of the novel becomes a metaphorical reflection of the psyche of the primary character. At one point, for example, Sanders, gazing on the glow being emitted from the bejewelled trees, is suddenly transported back to his youth, 'forgotten for nearly forty years', when 'everything seemed illuminated by that prismatic light described so exactly by Wordsworth in his recollections of childhood' (Ballard, 1978: 69). The sudden turn towards the personal and private implied by these 'thousand images of childhood', consolidated by reference to the Romantic poet, emphasises the extent to which the Ballardian disaster must be understood as a private, as much as a global, event (69). If, as Wagar suggests, 'immersion in all being' is required to achieve a higher plane of consciousness, then this is made possible in the disaster novels by the fact that the spatial landscapes of Ballard's novels are reflections of, and shaped by, the inner psychological worlds of his characters.

The primary focus of each novel is thus the transformation of the *internal* world of its individual characters as they struggle to adapt to their changed environments. Lorenz J. Firsching and R.M.P. conceptualise the action of the disaster novels as operating on three levels: the 'exterior', which encompasses the literal experience of the objective physical environment; the 'intermediatory' level, consisting of interpersonal relationships; and the 'interior' or 'psychic' level. The former two of these levels, Firsching and R.M.P. argue, are defined by an entropic movement from order towards chaos as the environmental disaster around which the novel centres is 'correlated' with a slow dissolution of all interpersonal ties linking the central character to those around him (1985: 298). On the interior level, however, the move is in the opposite direction—'from the confusion and alienation at the outset towards the appearance of a new psychic state, a "new psychology"' as the character regresses to a more primitive psychological state (298). In *The Crystal World*, this regression pushes Sanders towards an ambiguous and fundamental unity with all matter: 'some ancestral paradise where the unity of time and space is the signature of every leaf and flower' (1978: 83) and in which all humanity will one day 'become apostles of the prismatic sun' (169).

This dynamic may be seen in the novel's conceptualisation of biological time—a recurring concern, as mentioned above, of the disaster trilogy. A frequent motif in *The Crystal World* is the 'polarization' of the light around Port Matarre, which creates a startling contrast between the glittering forest and its peculiar, shadowy penumbra. The phenomenon is linked to the crystals themselves, which drain the light from the surrounding area. As one character comments, 'everything seems polarized … into black and white' around the crystallising forest, a splitting of the light that can only be 'reconciled'—that is, reversed or corrected—by entering the forest itself, whereupon light regains its customary hue (1978: 71). Yet the impression is also given that this division is not in fact an objective phenomenon in the external material world—rather, it is a psychological effect caused by a partial regression of the human mind through earlier stages of its evolutionary history (136). During the evolution of the human, as Sanders remarks, light was associated with 'the possibilities of life itself' while darkness signalled danger, a 'fundamental distinction' that 'we inherit from the earliest living creatures ... reinforced every day for hundreds of millions of years' (135). The polarisation, with its attendant symbolic connotations, is a psychological phenomenon arising from humanity's evolutionary history: as this evolutionary regression occurs, the human mind begins to perceive a sharper difference between light and dark, stimulated by its return to an 'earlier' biological stage. In this way, the objective world becomes refracted through human beings' epistemological grasp of the world—their very ability to perceive such fundamental phenomena as light a consequence of their biological and material ontologies.

Humans, the novel suggests, are thus still immersed in material biology and evolutionary time. Yet this image of apparent ontological union between the human and the organic non-human world is troubled by the broader utopian connotations of the crystals themselves. As Elana Gomel and Stephen A. Weninger argue, the crystal has traditionally been associated with perfection, but also with an anti-organicism that sets it in opposition to the vitality of the natural world. Surveying modernist critiques of Romanticism, Gomel and Weninger identify a recurring image within modernist literature that characterises the Romantic (in the words of Wyndham Lewis) as something 'gaseous and nebulous', reliant on 'the bowels and the nerves' (quoted in Gomel and Weninger, 2004: 67). In contrast to the disorganisation and impermanence believed to characterise the physical and organic, the image of the crystal becomes linked within modernism to utopian sentiments. The modernist preoccupation with abstraction and geometrical aesthetics was conceived as a way of escaping 'from the chaos of temporal phenomena' through spatialisation, a trend which manifested in a preoccupation with transparency and crystallisation as symbols of power, strength, health, and sexuality—but also of totalitarianism (67). Modernist architecture, meanwhile, often centred on an image of 'a new shining City of Glass' (80) which would stand in perfected opposition to the 'messy vitality' of life (74)—a trend which, Gomel and Weninger assert, has to some extent been realised in 'the epidemic of glass-walled structures in the mid- and late-twentieth century' (81).

The symbol of the crystal implies the erasure of both time and the organic body, along with all the unruly desires associated with embodied experience. As Gomel and Weninger note, the 'opposition between the dead beauty of the crystal and the messy vitality of the body underlies diverse Utopian dreams and dystopian nightmares', from Swift and Bellamy through Huxley and Forster right up to Ballard (74). Crystals throughout the century thus take on both utopian and dystopian qualities—yet always in opposition to the body and the natural processes of time. Accordingly, Gomel and Weninger interpret *The Crystal World* as an 'apocalypse of "crystallisation"', and Ballard's characters as 'long[ing] for the rest of this crystal paradise, in which there is no death because there is no life' (83). By escaping from 'the pain of corporeal existence' by means of crystallisation, Gomel and Weninger argue, Ballard's characters reveal that 'underlying the eschatological "crystal rest" is the fear of pain and the desire to escape the frailty of the body, which is ultimately achievable only in death' (83).

Numerous other critics have noted this emphasis on escape from the biological body in the disaster works. Roger Luckhurst, for example, reviewing several critical examinations of Ballard, notes that a common theme in these analyses is 'the narrative of transcendence' to be found in each of the disaster novels. The trilogy, Luckhurst argues, attempts 'to shift from the "wrong" (literal) death to the "right" (metaphorical) death [as] Being-towards-death is replaced by Being-beyond-death' (1994: 36). Ballard's characters, he goes on, recognise in the disasters the quality of transfiguration—rather than being a destructive force, they view the disaster as an opportunity to achieve some wholeness of being not otherwise available to them. Hence the novels depict 'the metaphorical transgression of the bounds of the bodily into an ultimate, ecstatic (re-)unification and (re-)integration', though what exactly is being re-unified and re-integrated is not always clear (36). Firsching and R.M.P. echo this argument: leprosy in the novel (Sanders is a leprosy specialist, and several characters present with the condition), they argue, is figured as a symbol of alienation, including alienation from the self, in which the body exists 'in a prolonged state of existence suspended between normal life and death' (1985: 306).

The Crystal World, then, depicts an apocalypse rich with utopian imagery, founded on the anti-organicist and anti-corporeal image of a crystal world. The novel appeals against the forces of modernisation and bureaucracy in the post-war period—yet also uses the ultra-rationalist symbol of the crystal as a utopian tool to overcome the ephemerality of the organic body and achieve psychic transcendence. This tension impacts on how the figure of the human in Ballard's works must be viewed. The human remains at the centre of Ballard's disaster trilogy— as Jonathan S. Taylor puts it, 'Ballard's goal is to create new myths of human transformation and, ultimately, transcendence' (2002: 93)—right up to the moment at which the human as such ceases to exist. In depicting the extinction of the human as we know it, the novel offers not a vision of positive social reformation but an escapist fantasy of individual bodily transcendence. By contrast, the true victims of the crystallising process are not humans but the animal inhabitants of the forest: the snakes and crocodiles whose 'blind eyes' become 'immense crystalline rubies' (Ballard, 1978: 79). Alongside the trees and streams around them, these natural beings become 'frozen into grotesque postures' within the sprawling crystal forest—an image of helpless submission to the uncanny force of crystallisation at odds with the euphoric transformation experienced by the human characters (83).

The Crystal World prioritises human psychological experience over the sanctity of the natural world, whose destruction is figured as an inconsequential side effect of the human individual's attempts at transcendence. Furthermore, by formulating this process of technologisation as a 'natural' (though clearly highly *un*natural) process of spontaneous crystallisation, the novel also relieves its human characters of all moral responsibility to act, whether positively or negatively, in relation to the disaster. Indeed, it is made clear that the process itself must be understood in terms that are fundamentally *a*moral: the breakdown of the 'intermediatory' level (as described by Firsching and R.M.P.) and the subsequent isolation of each character within their individual 'psychic landscapes' implies also an end to the moral obligations binding those characters. As Sanders notes, there is little point in associating 'moral notions with light and dark' once these oppositions have been suppressed within the petrified forest (136). Even the church in which Sanders shelters as he tries to escape from the forest is described by its priest as having 'outlived its function', since God now could 'be seen to exist in every leaf and flower' (162). Significantly, these natural elements—the 'countless ... birds, butterflies and insects, joining their cruciform haloes to the coronation of the forest', alongside the crocodiles, pythons, and even the trees themselves—are not given the choice of whether to accept or reject their immersion in the crystal lattice (162). That choice is available only to the human inhabitants of the forest while nature is denied those utopian possibilities, however vague, that the crystal forest has to offer its human inhabitants. The conclusion of *The Crystal World* thus removes the need to react in any meaningful manner to the apocalyptic or cataclysmic conditions of the late twentieth century. The novel is more entranced by the pleasures of solipsistic reflection—even to the point of masochistic self-destruction—than it is with the struggle to transcend the harmful dualisms of western thought.

Hence the ambiguous ending of the novel—in which Sanders comes to realise that 'there is an immense reward to be found in that frozen forest' and travels to become part of the bejewelled universe—is an act of allegorical surrender to the technoscientific processes of the late twentieth century (169). The characters in *The Crystal World* embrace the loss of time in the crystallising forest as inevitable and celebrate the loss of nature, too, as a necessary sacrifice to achieve individual utopian transcendence. It is, Sanders states, 'the gift of immortality, ... a direct consequence of the surrender of each of us of our own physical and temporal identities' (169). This 'gift', however, comes at the cost of both the natural world and the human itself. What emerges, then, is the post-human in quite a literal sense—to paraphrase Mark Fisher's aphorism that 'it is easier to imagine the end of the world than to imagine the end of capitalism' (2009: 2), in *The Crystal World* it is easier for Ballard to imagine the end of (western) humanity itself than to imagine the end of the bureaucratic structures that surrounded it in the late twentieth century.

Embedded identity and ontological parity in Le Guin's *The Dispossessed*

Le Guin was one of the most critically acclaimed SF writers of the twentieth century, and one of a select few whose works have received sustained attention in the wider literary and academic fields. (One indication of Le Guin's status within wider academic circles is that the 1987 collection of essays published on her 1969 novel and best-known work, *The Left Hand of Darkness*, was edited by Harold Bloom.) Le Guin became familiar with SF from an early age: growing up in the 1930s and 1940s, she read works by Lord Dunsany, an influential Anglo-Irish writer of fantasy and SF from the early twentieth century, and also sought out the 'trashiest magazines' of American SF she could find (Le Guin, 2015: 25–7). Like Clarke, Le Guin's interest in speculative fiction was informed by two distinct SF traditions—yet, unlike Clarke, the stories of 'hardware and soldiers' contained in the American SF magazines eventually proved tiresome for her. Le Guin's own SF, which she began publishing in the early 1960s, demonstrates a more explicit repudiation of the imperialist tone of much earlier American hard SF than is found in the mystical humanism of Clarke's fiction. Her literary value was recognised early within genre criticism: in 1975, *Science Fiction Studies* devoted its second-ever special issue to essays examining Le Guin's works (the first having been devoted to Dick).

In his introduction to this issue, Darko Suvin outlines some of the major literary concerns of Le Guin's fiction. As he remarks, she 'writes centripetally, in a narrowing spiral (say of a falcon circling to a swoop) delineating ever more precisely the same object' (1975: 203). Le Guin's fiction is often anthropological in nature (her father was an anthropology professor), informed by ideas derived, she has stated, from 'social science, psychology, anthropology [and] history' (quoted in Hull, 1986: 69). An anthropological impulse also informs the structure of many of her stories, which often centre on 'anthropologist-heroes' who arrive on unfamiliar planets and must learn to navigate their strange new environments (Latham, 2007: 117). This navigation is both literal and figurative: long voyages are a recurrent feature of Le Guin's works, symbolising her characters' inner journeys from youth to adulthood, ignorance to enlightenment, and so on, while their efforts to negotiate unfamiliar worlds eventually force these characters to question their own basic preconceptions, beliefs, and ideas.

In an essay published in 1996, Le Guin outlines this approach to storytelling in more detail. Many conventional stories, she remarks, propagate the myth of 'the Ascent of Man as Hero' at the expense of other, equally significant aspects of culture and history (1996: 51). To illustrate this point, she uses the analogy of the 'hunter-gatherer', the archetypal early human figure. Early cave paintings, she argues, tend mostly to depict battles between human hunters and a host of wild beasts, whereas in fact most early individuals, whose stories are *not* depicted on the cave walls, were gatherers. The cave paintings, she goes on, thus distort our perceptions of early human life: the demand for action, progression, and resolution in storytelling means that, 'Before you know it, the men and women in the wild-oat patch and their kids and the skills of the makers and the thoughts of the thoughtful ... have all been pressed into service in the tale of the Hero' (150). Expanding on this analogy, Le Guin argues that much popular literature, with its tales of 'Heroes' and adventure, has mirrored the cave paintings in this respect. Against such distortions, she insists that the 'proper shape of the narrative' should not be that of an 'arrow or spear, starting *here* and going straight *there* and THOK! hitting its mark', but rather that of a 'great heavy sack of stuff'—a 'carrier bag full of wimps and klutzes' (152–3).

Whatever its merits as an account of literary history, Le Guin's own focus on the gradual development of theme and character—her recurring 'delineation' of the 'same object', as Suvin puts it—demonstrates this shape in action: Le Guin's works eschew fast-paced narratives in favour of more considered efforts at world-building. Within the context of SF, this means a move away from 'the linear, progressive, Time's-(killing)-Arrow mode of the Techno-Heroic' to more considered works that attempt to detail the ambiguities, inconsistencies, intricacies, partialities, and dead ends of social and technological change (153).

This move is evident in many of her works. In *The Word for World Is Forest* (1972), for example, Le Guin depicts an attempted imperial takeover of 'Athshe', a forest planet, by an invading human force, which begins systematically felling trees for export to an ecologically ruined Earth against the wishes of the native forest-dwelling 'Athshenians'. The novel inverses the humanist chauvinism previously detected in Conan Doyle's *The Lost World* and Smith's *Skylark* series. In these works, as I discussed, certain moral and intellectual qualities are promoted as essential and universal human traits and are correspondingly deployed to classify certain kinds of beings as 'less than human'. In *The Word for World Is Forest*, the same structure is found—but this time it is earthly humanity that finds itself the subject of moral declassification by another race. The Athshenians deploy their own understanding of what it means to be 'human', based not on technological or intellectual capacities, but on qualities of empathy, compassion, and communion with nature. They thus conclude that the 'Terrans' (that is, earthly humanity)—who have killed or enslaved innumerable Athshenians, taking their pacifism and stoicism as evidence of their 'lazy', 'dumb', and 'treacherous' natures—cannot be 'men' or, '[if] they are men, they are evil men' (1980: 17–18, 41). For the natives of Athshe, it is they themselves who are clearly the more 'human' of the two races. *The Word for World Is Forest* was written explicitly in response to the Vietnam War, and demonstrates some key recurring tropes of Le Guin's fiction: anti-colonialism, encounters (violent or otherwise) between diverging cultures, and the possibility for the constructive union of—as opposed to destructive conflict between—opposing worldviews, demonstrated by the deep friendship that develops between the Athshenian Selver and Terran Lyubov.

These tropes are also evident in *The Dispossessed*. First published in 1974, *The Dispossessed* (subtitled *An Ambiguous Utopia*) forms part of Le Guin's 'Hainish cycle', a series of novels and short stories set in a shared universe in which interstellar travel has become commonplace. Each work in the Hainish cycle is independent of the others, yet each also forms part of an overarching history chronicling the gradual establishment of an interstellar confederacy called the 'League of All Worlds' (later renamed the 'Ekumen'). The League was founded by the 'Hain', an ancient human race, who train and dispatch ambassadors and mentors to other worlds to expand the membership and shared knowledge of the League. Key to the success of the League, and central to the plot of *The Dispossessed*, is the 'ansible', a device capable of instantaneous communication across vast distances. Before the creation of the ansible, messages transmitted between worlds would take years, decades, or even centuries to span the light-years that separated planets—the ansible instead allows the many worlds of the League to remain in instant communication with each other. Like Asimov's *Foundation*, most races depicted in the Hainish cycle are humanoid in nature: it is explained that, in the far-distant past, expeditions from Hain landed on and colonised the other planets of the galaxy, including Earth, making Hain the original homeworld of humanity.

Chronologically, *The Dispossessed* is the earliest work in the Hainish cycle. The story takes place on the planets of Urras and Anarres, both in orbit around the star Tau Ceti. Urras and Anarres are twinned moon-planets—that is, each appears as a moon in the sky of the other—yet the political structures of the two planets are radically different. Urras reflects the political shape of Cold War-era Earth, containing two global superpowers—the capitalist 'A-Io' and communist 'Thu'—fighting an ideological proxy war in the underdeveloped nation of 'Benbili' (a clear allusion to Vietnam and Korea). Anarres, meanwhile—the 'ambiguous utopia' of the subtitle—is organised along egalitarian anarchist principles laid down centuries before by 'Odo', a legendary revolutionary figure. Its citizens reject such concepts as centralised government (there is a central administration, but it does not use force of any kind against its citizens), private property (individuals sleep in shared dorms and eat in communal halls), and money.

The narrative of *The Dispossessed* centres on Shevek, a temporal physicist from Anarres, as he attempts to develop a new 'unified theory of Time' (1976: 99). Shevek is a central figure in the Hainish cycle: it is his ground-breaking research into the nature of time that enables the development of the ansible. The novel alternates between two separate timelines centred on Shevek: one depicting his childhood and maturation, as well as his growing disillusionment with the corruption seeping into Anarresti society, and the other following Shevek as he departs from Anarres altogether, travelling to Urras in order to complete his scientific work. Much of the novel is taken up with Shevek's interactions with this (to him) alien world—yet Le Guin is also concerned with depicting a functioning anarchist society and its shaping influence on the personal and political lives of her characters. Hence much of the text also examines the social and political structures of Anarres and the complexities of anarchism as a political model.

The Dispossessed is described by Moylan as 'perhaps the best known and the most popular of the critical utopias published in the 1970s'

(2014: 87). Indeed, of all the works examined in this study, Le Guin's novel is that which most thoroughly interrogates the concept of utopia, demonstrating Le Guin's 'major goal' in writing SF: 'the quest for, and indeed ... the first sketching of, a new collectivist system' (Suvin, 1975: 203). The subtitle of the novel highlights its critical utopian nature: Le Guin's concern lies not with the struggle to *achieve* utopia, as in London's *The Iron Heel*, nor with imagining a 'perfect' and static utopian society, as in Bellamy's *Looking Backward*, but rather with the ambiguities that arise in the historical evolution of utopia—the actual operational realities of the utopian project, narrated from the perspective of a single individual. The flawed and ever-shifting anarchist society of Anarres is thus vastly different from London's idealised 'Brotherhood of Man' or Bellamy's twenty-first-century Boston. By emphasising the ever-present threat of ideological collapse and ecological ruin (owing to Anarres' arid climate), Le Guin's world more closely resembles what Wells calls a 'kinetic utopia'—a flexible vision of 'hopeful' change that recognises the 'forces of unrest and disorder that inhere in things' (Wells, 2017: 207).

Le Guin's novel thus forms part of the emerging mode of American SF in the 1960s and 1970s that sought, as Fitting remarks, to '[break] through the apathy, complacency, and ideological self-deception of US society', one of a number of 'works in which the original recognition of the role of science and reason in human emancipation are reaffirmed' (1979: 72). The precise role of science and reason in human society is described by Le Guin herself in her 1982 essay, 'A Non-Euclidean View of California as a Cold Place to Be'. In this essay, Le Guin draws a distinction between 'yang' and 'yin' variants of utopia. Yang utopias are described as '[bright], dry, clear, strong, firm, active, aggressive, lineal, progressive, creative, expanding, advancing and hot' (1989: 90). Such worlds, Le Guin argues, stem from a 'euclidean', 'European', and 'masculinist' mindset (188) and encompass utopias from Plato through Bellamy's socialist Boston all the way up to Asimov's Foundation. Yin utopias, conversely, 'would be dark, wet, obscure, weak, yielding, passive, participatory, circular, cyclical, peaceful, nurturant, retreating, contracting, and cold'—in other words, 'non-euclidean, non-European, non-masculinist' utopias that move the utopian project beyond both technocratic imperialism and technological determinism (90). This type of utopia, Le Guin suggests, departs altogether from the notion of progress, adhering instead to a temporal structure of 'rhythmic recurrence'—a cyclical movement between past and future that returns always to the basic fact of existence in the present moment—in contrast to the relentless futurist outlook of yang utopias (90). Progress within yin utopias, in other words, is framed not as constant forward motion but as eternal return, encapsulated in the flow of 'biological rhythm' (91–2).

Given this preoccupation with seeking alternatives to traditional western narratives of rational progress, we might expect *The Dispossessed* to explicitly repudiate the exploitative principles of rationality and chauvinist humanism that have marked post-Enlightenment thought. For some critics, however, the question of how to categorise *The Dispossessed*—whether as a yang or yin utopia—remains unclear. Jim Jose, for example, notes that, despite Le Guin's criticisms of 'yang' technocratic utopias, the narrative of *The Dispossessed* 'is dominated by Shevek, a man imbued with euclidean reason and a European bias towards the promise of technology and science' (1991: 190). Far from diverging from the dominant narrative of rational humanism, Jose argues, '*The Dispossessed* is very much in the euclidean, European, and masculine mould' (190).

Moylan, meanwhile, argues that Shevek's development of the 'unified theory of Time' that underpins the workings of the ansible cannot be idealistically abstracted from the political complexities of the novel, and particularly from the capitalist economic relations that dominate A-Io. The ansible, Moylan argues, represents simply 'a useful new product to benefit the hierarchy, the bureaucratic leadership of all the known worlds who can now set up a meta-bureaucracy of centralized power for all the universe' (2014: 112). Far from repudiating the technoscientific Empires common to SF in the mid-century, then, Moylan's analysis suggests that *The Dispossessed* is committed to generating the very tool required by capitalism for their development.

This view of the League as a meta-bureaucracy, however, does not do justice to the complexity of Le Guin's Hainish works. Le Guin is concerned not with depicting the formation of a universal techno-imperialist complex (as in Asimov's *Foundation*, for example) but with describing, and exploring the interactions between, a host of cultures, peoples, and individuals from often highly contrasting worlds. One Hainish work, *Planet of Exile* (1966), for example, focuses on a League expedition to the planet 'Werel', where a group of Terran anthropologists are making a study of the local culture. The novel explores questions of cultural relativism: although the two main factions, the native 'Tevarans' and foreign Terrans, are both humanoid, descended from the same Hainish settlers, each faction adheres rigidly to a chauvinistic view of their own culture as more fundamentally or truly 'human' than the other. Hence, for the Terrans, the Tevarans are not humans but merely 'hilfs'—'highly intelligent life-forms'—while, to the Tevarans, the Terrans are not 'men' but alien 'farborns'. 'Human' (or 'man', in the terminology often used by Le Guin in her early works)[2] in this novel thus implies a qualitative as well as descriptive value: as in *The Word for World Is Forest*, to be thought of as 'human' or 'non-human' does not necessarily indicate anything regarding the biological status of the organism under consideration, but rather reveals the cultural biases and preconceptions of the individual doing the thinking.

The Tevarans and the Terrans eventually find themselves forced to band together to survive an invasion by the 'Gaal', a marauding and migratory people. The imperative of co-operation quickly breaks down both the scientific detachment of the Terrans and the xenophobia of the Tevarans as each comes increasingly to recognise themselves in the other. The novel finally ends on a note of ambiguous optimism: Agat, the Terran protagonist, stands amid the ruin wrought on Tevaran society by the defeated marauders, and realises that 'This was his fort, his city, his world; these were his people. He was no exile here' (1978: 212). Le Guin thus demonstrates a 'yin' resolution to her narrative: the relationship between Terrans and Tevarans moves from inner-directed self-preservation towards outer-directed communion, an embrace of the unknown or alien Other that seeks common ground without flattening cultural differences.

This yin pattern is repeated throughout Le Guin's works. The planet Gethen, for example, depicted in *The Left Hand of Darkness* (1969) and 'Winter's King' (1969), features an androgynous humanoid race that exhibits some distinctly non-'human' qualities: they undergo *kemmer*—periodic cycles of sexual fertility during which they temporarily develop either male or female sexual organs—while their social interactions are underpinned by *shifgrethor*, a subtle and ambiguous set of social

---

[2] Le Guin has at times been criticised for her use of such terminology, as well as her adherence to what some writers have described as a traditional masculine viewpoint in her novels. Joanna Russ, for example, in the afterword to her feminist story, 'When It Changed' (1972), remarks that she was partially inspired to write the story after reading Le Guin's *The Left Hand of Darkness*, which, although it features sexually androgynous characters, uses exclusively male pronouns. Le Guin's response to these criticisms has developed over time: in a 1976 essay, she remarks that 'He is the generic pronoun, damn it, in English' and expresses her dislike for invented pronouns—yet, in her 1989 response to that same essay, she acknowledges that her use of the male pronoun had indeed 'shaped, directed, controlled [her] own thinking' while writing the novel (Le Guin, 1989: 15). Le Guin's lack of explicit feminist engagement is perhaps partially counterbalanced by her rejection of 'masculine' narratives and linguistic forms as outlined in this discussion, as well as her later exploration of explicit feminist themes in works such as *Always Coming Home* (1985) and *Four Ways to Forgiveness* (1995).

protocols unknown, and perhaps unknowable, to non-Gethenians. Despite these alien qualities, however, League ambassador Genly Ai nevertheless establishes a deep bond with Estraven, a native of Gethen. The extent of their relationship is symbolised by their developing capacity for 'mindspeech', a form of telepathy. Even this telepathic connection, however, cannot fully bridge the cultural distance between Ai and Estraven: the bond produced by mindspeech is an 'austere and obscure one, not so much admitting further light ... as showing the extent of the darkness' (1979: 172).

Le Guin's formulation of telepathy thus figures not as the universal communicative medium depicted in *Skylark* or *The City and the Stars*, but conversely as a mode of indexing the cultural distance that inevitably arises between humans from radically different worlds. Mindspeech is first introduced in another novel, *Rocannon's World* (1966), in which Le Guin explicitly emphasises the role of cultural conditioning in identity formation. In this novel, Rocannon, an anthropologist dispatched by the League to study the culture of the planet 'Fomelhaut II', uncovers a planned attack on the League by a rogue faction. To prevent this attack, Rocannon immerses himself within the culture of Fomelhaut II, thus gaining the local power of mindspeech. Yet such knowledge comes at a cost: in the process of gaining a new set of cultural coordinates, Rocannon necessarily sacrifices his old ones, and with them his former cultural identity: 'Who are my people? I am not who I was. I am changed' (1978: 111).

Le Guin's narratives are thus multifaceted and morally complex: the League does not represent any straightforward *telos* of human progress, while her works stress ambiguous and open-ended yin—as opposed to straightforward yang—resolutions to narrative conflict. *The Dispossessed* can be regarded as an attempt to portray a yin utopia, although one in which, as Le Guin herself writes, the 'excess yang shows' (1989: 93). Le Guin's notion of technology attempts to puncture the widespread SF view of technological development as the dominant shaping force in human society. In contrast to the earlier works of Golden Age SF—in which, as discussed in the last chapter, technology replaces politics, economics, or any other phenomenon as the fundamental driver of social change in society—Le Guin insists that 'to count on technological advance for *anything but* technological advance is a mistake' (1989: 96, emphasis in original). Any concept of progress, she argues, that views the evolution of societies as an 'invasive, self-replicating, mechanical forward drive' can only result in disaster as, within such a view, humanity itself is transformed into a 'virus' that consumes both itself and the environment around it (96).

Yet Le Guin's depiction of Anarresti society is by no means *anti*-technological, since 'technology is an essential element of all cultures' (96). The original settlers of Anarres, Le Guin writes, 'knew that their anarchism was the product of a very high civilisation, of a complex diversified culture, of a stable economy and a highly industrialized technology' (1976: 85). Hence, they refused to 'regress to a pre-urban, pre-technological tribalism', instead concentrating on building roads and exchanging local resources (85). In this, as Laurence Davis argues, Le Guin displays 'an unusually nuanced attitude toward technology', offering a 'realistic utopian vision of a low technology, organically evolving society at peace with itself and its environment' (Davis and Stillman, 2005: 17, 18). Even the most prominent technological concern of the novel—Shevek's unified theory of time—is framed in terms as much metaphysical as mathematical. After many frustrated attempts to prove the validity of his temporal hypotheses, Shevek realises that the mathematical 'certainty' for which he has been striving is an enigma: the hypotheses lay in 'the region of the unprovable' (Le Guin, 1976: 233). Since its truth can never be demonstrated, Shevek is instead forced to begin 'simply assuming the validity' of his hypothesis, after which his research begins suddenly to produce results (233). His scientific breakthrough in this way becomes a matter of faith as much as reason, reflecting the limits of human epistemological penetration into the nature of the material world.

In a broader sense, Shevek realises that the objective and abstract quality of scientific investigation encourages a false separation of rational abstractions *about* the world from material and ethical practice *within* the world. To demonstrate the absurdity of this divide, Shevek refers repeatedly to an analogy concerning a rock thrown at a tree. In theoretical terms, the thrown rock can never reach the tree since, at any given moment, 'there's always half of the way left to go' before the distance between the two objects is traversed (31). In material terms, however, this statement is clearly nonsensical: 'After all, the rock does hit the tree' (190). Theory and reality are, in this case, clearly at odds with one another. Similarly, although 'a scientist can pretend that his work isn't himself, it's merely the impersonal Truth', in reality this distinction is contrived since an individual's understanding of the world—their understanding of 'Truth'—necessarily shapes that individual's interactions with the world (274). Hence, for example, Shevek insists that the study of time is not only a scientific but also an ethical matter, enabling us to see 'the difference between *now* and *not now*'—that is, the distinction between our present actions and their future consequences—and, having seen this difference, to 'try to make the best of it' (190, emphasis in original). Theoretical physics is thus in accord with ethical philosophy in entreating the individual to 'act responsibly' (190).

Not merely scientific discourse but all language is understood by Le Guin as involving ethical consideration. In an address delivered in 1986, she discusses the power of language to shape worlds and worldviews. As in her delineation of yang and yin utopias, Le Guin divides language into two opposing types: 'father tongue' and 'mother tongue' (1989: 147–60). Father tongue is the language of 'the expository, and particularly the scientific discourse': that form of discourse which separates the world into 'subject/object, self/other, mind/body, dominant/submissive, active/passive, Man/Nature, man/woman, and so on' (148–9). Mother tongue, conversely, is 'language not as mere communication but as relation, relationship. It connects' (149). In other words, whereas father tongue consists of language that separates, systematises, and rationalises, mother tongue instead relates, permeates, and interconnects.

Predictably enough, within Le Guin's works the emphasis is placed on mother over father tongues, with language conceived as an expression of localised and partial, rather than universal and totalising, subject positions. Her series of fantasy works set in the land of 'Earthsea', for example, depict a form of magic centred on 'Naming'—literally, the power to call a thing by its 'true name' (as distinct from its everyday 'use-name') so as to control it. The true name of a thing corresponds to its being, and hence the gap between signifier and signified, in the 'Old Speech' of magic, is closed: in Earthsea, to know the true name of a thing is to grasp the thing in and of itself. Yet magic does not thereby constitute a master discourse in the *Earthsea* texts. Names in Earthsea are so numerous that 'no man could learn them all'—a wizard 'can control only what is near him, what he can name exactly and wholly' (1993: 51). Furthermore, the power to control a thing by using its true name is dependent on place: 'the fish of the Open Sea', for example, 'do not know their own names and pay no heed to magic', while the ability to name things also diminishes the further a wizard moves from the central lands of Earthsea (166). Magic—here a form of language—is thus conceived in the *Earthsea* texts in local, rather than universal, terms: its potency is rooted to place, and so the possibility of a universal code by which to name and control the world is therefore precluded. Magic in the *Earthsea* series functions as the inverse to universalising scientific discourse: where the latter strives to be universal and totalising, the former is necessarily localised and partial.

Such distinctions are also of pivotal importance in *The Dispossessed*. Shevek's temporal theories represent a form of linguistic power: since the theory underpins the development of the ansible, the political body that gains access to the theory also gains absolute control of interstellar communications. The theory is thus highly sought after by numerous political bodies in the novel, including the governments of A-Io, Thu, and even 'Terra' (the name given to Earth, by this time an ecologically devastated planet). Shevek's reluctance to gift such a powerful political tool to any one nation leads him to disperse the theory among all the known worlds, thus removing the possibility of it being used as a political weapon by any one ideological faction. By undermining the possibility of the autocratic regulation of communication by whatever nation wields the theory, Shevek instead creates the possibility for 'relation'—a form of communication which 'goes two ways, many ways, an exchange' (1989: 149).

Hence, as Lewis Call notes, the ansible creates the possibility of 'a community of worlds linked together in radically egalitarian, non-hierarchical fashion' (2007: 103). Of course, this democratising move raises difficulties of its own. With the creation of the ansible, and the subsequent formation of the 'League' of planets, the idiosyncratic 'mother tongues' of each world come under threat by the necessary adoption of a universal language required for true interstellar communication. This threat is minimised in *The Dispossessed*, however, by the conditioning qualities of language itself that preclude the possibility of a truly 'universal' human mind to complement a universal dialect. The role of language in determining the thoughts—and, indeed, the extent of possible thoughts—of the individual mind is demonstrated, for example, by the syntactical structures of Pravic, the Anarresti language. In Pravic, possession is minimised: in place of 'my hand hurts', individuals say 'the hand hurts me', while 'This one is mine and that's yours' becomes 'I use this one and you use that' (1976: 55). Hence, for example, Shevek experiences discomfort in referring to 'his' rooms on Urras, having no prior experience with personal pronouns. As in the *Earthsea* texts, then, language in *The Dispossessed* is rooted always in place.

It follows that language itself disallows the possibility of a 'universal' human figure. Le Guin's fiction refuses abstractions in favour of localised 'embedded' identities and thus anticipates the posthumanist rejection of universal notions of humanity in favour of 'embedded' subject positions. As Braidotti remarks, 'universalism ... claims to a subject position that allegedly transcends spatio-temporal and geo-political specificities' and stresses 'dis-embodied' and 'dis-embedded, i.e., abstract' identities (2012: 22). Le Guin's repeated insistence on the conditioning effects of culture and language, together with her depiction of mother tongues and yin utopias, comprise 'a break from both universalism and dualism' (Braidotti, 2012: 22). Identity is contingent on *'social and cultural embeddedness'* (33)—the material conditions and local cultures or communities to which individuals belong. It is, in effect, a more sophisticated expression of the idea that mind is not separate from but *is* matter—that 'ideas are embedded in practice', as Haraway puts it, while material practice is shaped by ideas and preconceptions (2008: 282).

So, to what extent can Le Guin's novel be regarded as representing a real break with conventional notions of 'true' human selfhood—in other words, post-humans? It is true that her fiction focuses overwhelmingly on humans at the expense of radically non-human beings—nearly every race in the League of All Worlds, for example, is humanoid (with some notable exceptions, such as the sentient plant network depicted in her 1971 short story, 'Vaster Than Empires and More Slow'). Furthermore, the 'community of worlds' identified by Call is more accurately described as a community of *linguistic* worlds since the ansible tacitly separates those beings that have language from those that do not. This is significant in a novel so concerned with the relevance of ethics to technological endeavour: language has often been conceived as a fundamentally 'human' quality, the most historically durable precondition for ethical and political consideration. Yet Le Guin's emphasis on non-dualistic thinking, anti-imperialism, the ethical implications of scientific activity, and denunciation of universalist narratives in favour of embedded and localised identities clearly indicates a rejection of chauvinist or technocratic humanism. Her idea of the human recalls the reformed humanism of Huxley, insisting on a balance between the abstractions of the mind and the sensual world—yet Le Guin goes further in thinking about non-human nature as ethically equivalent with human life.

Le Guin's notions of human–nature relations were in part informed by the growing environmental awareness that marked the post-war period in the US. David Pepper highlights two dominant ideological trends in the history of western environmentalist thought: 'technocentrism', which argues for the capacity of contemporary science and technology to overcome human environmental degradation, and 'ecocentrism', which prioritises respect for the natural world over human activity and therefore calls for (often radical) social and economic restructuring (see Pepper, 1999: 10–46). Ecocentrism, Pepper remarks, takes at least partial inspiration from the *Tao Te Ching*, an ancient work of Chinese philosophy. Taoism stresses 'ultimate wholeness ... the reality underlying surface appearances' (23) and had an important influence on Le Guin's thought and writing.³ From Taoism, deep ecological ideologies derived a notion of the natural world as founded on the holistic interconnectivity of all things, including humanity. Deep ecology thereby stresses the need to treat humanity as simply another part of the ecosphere—of no greater intrinsic value than other natural elements. Given the noted Taoist influence on Le Guin's works, and her own description of Anarres as a 'yin' utopia contrasting the 'yang' of technocentric capitalism, it is useful to view Anarres as a depiction of a 'deep ecological' society in which human interactions with nature have evolved past utilitarian resource models.

Certainly, the novel emphasises the need for a more holistic dimension to human–nature relations. It does so, however, not by means of ecological apocalypse nor naïve visions of pastoral Arcadias—instead, Anarres is characterised by natural scarcity, which offers an effective means to demonstrate humanity's profound dependence on its natural–material environment. This dependence can be best seen in Le Guin's contrasting depictions of human–nature relations on Urras and Anarres. On his arrival to the Urrasti nation of A-Io, Shevek is immediately struck by the natural beauty and splendour of the planet: looking out the window of a high-rise apartment, he gazes with awe on the 'tenderness and vitality of the colours, the mixture of rectilinear human design and powerful, proliferate natural contours, the variety and harmony of the elements' (1976: 60). To Shevek, his window offers a view onto the very 'magnificence of life, rich in the sense of history and of seasons to come, inexhaustible' (61). It is not merely the splendour of the landscape but also its harmonious integration with human activity that impresses Shevek: 'the dark lines of lanes' and 'the graceful square tower' that overlook 'innumerable patches of green' countryside convey a sense of intricate interconnection between the natural and human realms (60). Contrasting the frequent visions of industrial eco-apocalypse found throughout the SF works of the 1960s and 1970s, the capitalist A-Io remains an environmental beauty spot, with hunting bans, restrictions on consumption, and sustainable fishing.

Yet Shevek's own position in this tableau—'looking down ... detached from the ground, dominant, uninvolved' (60)—undermines the impression of human–nature intimacy generated by this view.

---

³ The influence of Taoism on Le Guin's fiction has been well-noted: George Edgar Slusser, for example, highlights Taoism as 'the strongest single force behind her work' (Slusser, 2006: 3), while Le Guin herself has written that 'Taoism got to [her] earlier than modern feminism did' (Bernardo and Murphy, 2006: 4).

His elevated position implies both a remove from *and* dominance over nature: Shevek is not 'at one' with his natural environment but dominates it through his commanding view of the landscape, which becomes simply another commodity to be consumed by those with the leisure and wealth to attain the 'proper' perspective. For Cary Wolfe, such an act of 'looking' suggests a mode of shaping and controlling the visual world. Drawing on Derrida, Wolfe argues that the visual field is contingent on the *différance* of the 'invisible': certain elements of this field must be both present *and* unseen if the remaining elements of the field are to be made meaningful to the viewer, forming a 'semiotically organized visual field of meaning' (2010: 132). Consequentially, 'perceptual space'—such as Shevek's commanding view of the landscape around him—becomes 'organised around and for the looking subject' (132). Both the elements rendered invisible and the semiotic relationships between visible elements of the field depend on the preconceptions of the viewing subject.

In this way, the act of looking commands space by rendering 'invisible' certain features and semiotic relations within the visual field. In the case of Shevek's view of the landscapes of A-Io, this invisibility is two-fold. On one level, the natural world is recast as an aesthetic scene: Shevek's act of looking—and looking down—renders 'invisible' the existence of nature outside Shevek's apprehension of it, becoming 'enframed' as a visible tableau to be consumed. Furthermore, this act of observation is itself maintained by the 'invisible' structure of hegemonic capitalist hierarchies that make possible Shevek's very elevation above the world around him—an elevation available to him only by virtue of its being unavailable to others. And, furthermore, it is only on Urras that this impression of nature as privileged spectacle can be maintained—only in the resource-rich nation of A-Io in particular that nature and culture can be respectively formulated, to borrow a phrase from Haraway, as 'mirror and eye' (2004: 34).

Compare this with the depictions of nature on Anarres. Here, the natural environment, far from providing the gentle paradise that its early settlers expected, instead confronts its human inhabitants with constant challenge and hardship:

> [The] Eden of Anarres proved to be dry, cold, and windy, and the rest of the planet was worse. Life there had not evolved higher than fish and flowerless plants. The air was thin, like the air of Urras at a very high altitude. The sun burned, the wind froze, the dust choked (1976: 84).

For Shevek, the Anarresti environment is 'like a crude sketch in yellow chalk', 'barren, arid, and inchoate', containing 'vast beauty' yet at the same time 'hostile' (61). Given the scarcity of natural resources, the original settlers were forced to take seriously their intrusion into the ecosystem of Anarres, fitting themselves 'with care and risk into this narrow ecology' (158–9). Hence farmed animals are absent, fishing occurs only in small quantities, and fruiting trees are 'hand fertilized' to compensate for the lack of insects (159). Nature, in other words, is conceived as something *within*, rather than *against*, which humanity is situated—Le Guin's novel recreates a situation in which, as John Berger puts it, nature 'constitute[s] the first great circle of what surround[s] man' (2009: 3).

This intricate co-evolution is illustrated in the character of Takver, Shevek's lifelong lover. Takver, a marine biologist, speaks with longing of the ecological diversity of Urras—a world in which 'everywhere you looked animals, other creatures, [shared] the earth and air with you' (1976: 159). Yet Takver nevertheless achieves a more profound connection with the natural world than the inhabitants of A-Io. Her concern for Anarresti nature is 'much broader than love'—when she interacts with an element of nature, be it a 'leaf' or a 'rock', '[she] became an extension of it: it of her' (158). Her role as a scientist is thus informed by her understanding of her own place in that world—she is one of those 'souls', Shevek states, 'whose umbilicus has never been cut. They never got weaned from the universe' (158). Indeed, even Shevek himself is forced to check 'his physicist's arrogance' when confronted by the 'small, strange lives' of the marine life of Anarres (159).

Takver's alignment towards nature is thus founded on a basis of radical egalitarianism with the non-human Other—a recognition, as Le Guin puts it, of 'the mystery, the unreasonableness, the beauty, the stubborn wildness of the non-human world' (Bernardo and Murphy, 2006: 7). The marine life of Anarres, she insists, 'do not explain themselves and need not ever justify their ways to man' (Le Guin, 1976: 159). Shevek himself experiences such a moment of ontological parity while playing with an otter kept as a pet by an Urrasti acquaintance. Looking into the animal's 'gold, intelligent, curious, innocent' eyes, Shevek is 'caught by [the otter's] gaze across the gulf of being' (131). The intimate look here exchanged between Shevek and the otter contrasts strongly with his earlier detached contemplation of the countryside of A-Io—in this moment, Shevek realises that the otter is his '*Ammar* ... brother' (131). Shevek's sudden recognition of his commonality with this non-human being forces him to overcome his 'arrogance' and admit the otter's ethical parity—an instance of equivalence between the human and non-human informed by egalitarian rather than chauvinist principles.

The Dispossessed thus offers a vision of critical posthumanism at work. In keeping with our other works, this is a posthumanism with humanity very much at its core—as noted above, Le Guin's works are dominated by human figures or their 'fictional surrogates' (Latham, 2007: 118), and indeed by predominantly male human figures. Yet *The Dispossessed* recognises the fundamental integration of humanity *within*, and its fundamental parity *with*, the natural world. Her explicit repudiation of the chauvinist humanism of much earlier SF, her rejection of universals in favour of embedded identities and partial knowledges, and her recognition of the ontological equivalence of humanity with the non-human world—these features of Le Guin's works mark them, if not as radically post-*human*, then as strikingly and compellingly post-*humanist*.

Conclusion

Two vastly different forms of the post-human thus emerge from these two works. Each work responds to the social, cultural, and political conditions of the late twentieth century and the changes wrought upon the figure of the human by rapid and far-reaching developments in western society. Whereas *The Crystal World* retreats into the inner landscapes of the human psyche, ultimately cutting the human off from meaningful engagement with the external world, *The Dispossessed* re-examines the ethical foundations on which this entity called the 'human' has been constructed—whereas Ballard moves inward into the private world of the individual, Le Guin moves out, pressing and poking at the ethical limits of personhood and communality.

Nor is *The Dispossessed* alone in this re-examination. The emergence of several significant critical utopian works in the 1970s heralded a long overdue reappraisal of the humanist frameworks of much SF, particularly regarding gender. *The Dispossessed* is only one such work, part of a long effort on Le Guin's part to rethink the ethical dimensions of human society. The deconstruction of gender in Russ's *The Female Man*, or of sexuality and sexual identity in Delany's *Triton*, offer variations of the post-human as these authors critically engage with—rather than merely attack or eliminate—the figure of 'universal Man'. At the same time, of course, it is important not to be overly dismissive in appraising the posthumanist functions of *The Crystal World*: Ballard's work, as mentioned above, is a far cry from the chauvinist technocratic texts of Golden Age

SF, for example, or the earlier pulps, or even the mystical humanism of Clarke. Indeed, the disaster trilogy offers one avenue of escape from the very instrumental rationality lauded in those earlier works—even if this escape takes the form of a literal escape from all human life and sentiment.

In either case, the result is the re-evaluation of 'Man', the rational, masculine figure of western thought that had hitherto dominated SF. In my conclusion, I will return finally to the questions with which I began this study and resituate the analyses offered here within a wider commentary on the critical overlap between posthumanism and SF. I will then go on to suggest some of the ways in which this critical history of the human might usefully enrich our understanding of the posthuman in SF more generally.

Conclusion
Bio/Techno/Homo:
The future of the human in SF

'Why does it take three Jinxians to paint a skyscraper? ...
It takes one to hold the paint sprayer, and two to shake the skyscraper up and down.'

Early in Larry Niven's *Ringworld* (1970), Louis Wu, an earthly human, shares this joke with his companion, a 'Pierson's puppeteer' from the planet 'Hearth'. What exactly a 'Jinxian' might be is left unexplained, but we can assume that it is a form of alien life whose relationship with humanity is of sufficient vintage to render such a joke, as Louis intimates, stale and unoriginal—mere 'dead wood' (Niven, 2005: 11). At any rate, the puppeteer—a two-headed, three-legged being noted for its extreme caution in all areas of life—does not appreciate the humour.

Ringworld offers a good example of the tension between conventional humanist and radical posthumanist understandings of the subject in Anglophone SF on which I have focussed throughout this study. On the one hand, *Ringworld* features a host of non-human beings—Jinxians, puppeteers, 'kzins' (warmongering, feline beings)—that undermine human-centred biological essentialism. On the other, however, it is much less clear whether such beings are in fact as *subjectively* alien as their biological manifestations would imply: the easy communication and co-operation established between human and non-human beings suggest that there is significant psychological overlap between these radically different biological organisms. There is no recognisably non-human worldview here, a fact registered in the joke quoted above. This is a readily familiar kind of jibe, deployed to ridicule members of certain nationalities, cultures, or creeds as being of inferior intellectual 'stock'. Yet its utilisation in *Ringworld* indicates the extent to which such pre-existing human frames of reference remain unchanged by the encounter with radically Other alien life forms: such beings are instead subsumed into a pre-existing, and human-oriented, cultural framework.

In this example, the population mocked by the joke comprises an entire biological species, while humanity itself, it is implied, may be viewed as the 'normal' standard against which such things as intelligence are to be measured. Cultural and personal encounters with the Jinxians have not, then, caused a paradigm shift in the psychological makeup of Niven's characters—instead, the Jinxians are enfolded within an unchanged frame of human cultural reference.

Compare this to Frederik Pohl's use of a similar trope in 'The Day After the Day After the Martians Came' (1967). In this story, a group of journalists is assembled at a motel near Cape Kennedy, waiting for news regarding a recent probe that has arrived back from Mars bearing native Martian life forms. To pass the time, the journalists begin to tell jokes about the Martians. As in *Ringworld*, these jokes merely recycle tired digs at scorned populations, with the Martians in the place of the usual human 'out' groups, and with the result that, very soon, everyone 'was beginning to get tired of them' (1987: 23). The pessimistic owner of the motel eventually concludes that, in the long run, the unexpected discovery of the Martians will not impact on human affairs: 'I don't believe their coming here is going to make a nickel's worth of difference to anybody' (28). His bellhop Ernest, however, who is black, disagrees: he asserts that the encounter is going 'to make a difference to some people. Going to make a *damn* big difference to me' (28, emphasis in original).

The story ends on this ambiguous note and is open to several interpretations. On the one hand, Ernest's social position in American society—excluded from the dominant narratives of social and cultural discourse, and often the butt of those jokes now aimed at the Martians—may allow him to more readily identify with the liminal position of the Martians, and renders him more receptive to the potentially transformative social and cultural impacts that the Martians might generate. Rather than seeing them as merely another element in a familiar and unchanging narrative of white chauvinism, Ernest may instead view the Martians as a way of challenging and transforming those frameworks. On the other, Ernest may view the Martians as his replacement, so to speak, the ostracised inverse to the dominant white human, thus establishing a place for himself within an expanded human narrative that now views the Martians as the biological 'Other' to the Earthly species *homo sapiens*. In either case, the coming of the Martians will force a revision of some of the basic tenets of the western humanist framework.

These stories encapsulate two different modes of approaching the non-human that have informed the narrative frameworks of SF throughout its long history. The first is assimilative, in which the non-human is enfolded within existing human-centred cognitive and cultural frameworks. The second, conversely, is transformative, challenging those frameworks and motivating human characters to rethink their orthodox views regarding the supremacy of the default human figure: the white, rational, heterosexual male, endowed with the capacities for 'self-development and self-perfection' (Williams, 1986: 150). I have traced these two modes in the history of SF from the early nineteenth century to the 1970s. The human as it has been imagined in these works is balanced unsteadily between these opposing assimilative and transformative interpretations. These works gesture continuously towards the *possibility* for radical new modes of human and posthuman existence. At the same time, however, they also persistently retreat from the full consequences of this possibility, resulting in a liminal human figure caught between opposing ontological modes.

These modes, as I have shown, take numerous forms. The works of Verne, Conan Doyle, Smith, Asimov, and Ballard retain key aspects of the traditional western narrative of the human. Hence Verne's *Voyages extraordinaires* lay down a much-borrowed framework in which natural history is recast as a teleological narrative of human ascendancy; Conan Doyle borrows this framework in order to naturalise a set of European moral principles as 'essentially' human and thus hierarchise the human and 'pre-human' as respectively more and less deserving of moral consideration; Smith abstracts the human being from its material–biological basis altogether, projecting the rational 'human' as a set of intellectual qualities and painting *Skylark*'s Seaton as the *telos* of human technological achievement; Asimov conversely rejects the significance of the human individual, transferring the qualities of progressive development and self-perfection to the human species as a whole and interpreting human progress as a mechanistic process overseen by paternal institutions; and, finally, Ballard depicts the complete breakdown of human society as each individual achieves a mode of 'crystal' perfection, relegating the natural world to a subordinate position within a narrative of human utopian transcendence.

Conversely, the works of Shelley, Wells, London, Huxley, Clarke, and Le Guin offer more vivid and anxious accounts of the human relationships to technology and the natural world. Hence Shelley's *Frankenstein* offers a moral allegory regarding the dangers of transgressing natural 'law' in the service of 'perfecting' the human figure; Wells's *The War of the Worlds* imagines the inversion of European colonial practices by casting the English themselves as the victims of technological exploitation; London condemns the brutality of *fin-de-siècle* industrial capitalism, instead depicting a masculinist view of the ideal human as a 'perfected' mix of pragmatic rationalism and muscular development; Huxley laments the subversion of human agency by scientific management and consumerism and argues the need to holistically blend the animal and spiritual aspects of human life; Clarke infuses technological advancement with a sense of moral responsibility and imagines the human evolving, under the guidance of benevolent super-beings, towards a state of organic transcendence; and Le Guin rejects chauvinist humanism altogether by demonstrating the relativism of the humanist narrative, instead emphasising the need for ontological and ethical parity between the human and non-human worlds.

This division of these writers into assimilative and transformative strands is, of course, not unproblematic—London and Clarke, for example, sit uneasily in the transformative category, given that both ultimately deploy teleological notions of human self-development and self-perfection, while Ballard clearly differs in key respects from the earlier tradition of hard SF into which I have placed him here. A more nuanced understanding of these two modes, in which each work is viewed as a heterogeneous bundle of assimilative humanist and transformative posthumanist functions, is more constructive. Hence while *The Crystal World*, for example, reproduces a familiar narrative of the subordination of nature to the human desire for utopian transcendence, its images of natural catastrophe index the extent to which such humanist narratives had become untenable within the sociocultural conditions of the late twentieth century. In this way, *The Crystal World* undermines the social institutions and structures of the late twentieth century, only to then fall back on a familiar, if dramatically solipsistic, narrative of human transcendence.

The clearest posthumanist functions (to invoke the Blochean terms outlined in the introduction) to arise from the works examined here, I argue, are to be found in Le Guin's *The Dispossessed*, in which Shevek's encounter with the otter, for example, or Takver's interactions with the animal life of Anarres illustrate a radical degree of moral equivalence between the human and the non-human. Huxley, too, gestures towards such a possibility in his deconstruction of western 'Man', although his works lack a sustained ecological critique to supplement this deconstruction—his concerns remain fixated on that 'Man', however much Huxley disavows him. In Clarke, humanist and posthumanist functions come into conflict in the figures of the Star Child, the Great Ones, and the Overmind: beings clearly superior to humanity (which appears juvenile and insignificant in comparison) yet also possessing a level of transcendent consciousness that, it is implied, is wholly attainable by humanity itself, given sufficient time.

Other works—Shelley's *The Last Man*, Wells's *The Time Machine*, Asimov's *Foundation*, and Ballard's *The Crystal World*—exhibit what might be better described as '*anti*-humanist functions': these works, as I have shown, undermine entirely certain core tenets of humanism or, in some cases, the human itself, yet without offering the positive or constructive reconceptualisation of the human figure that is one of the distinguishing facets of posthumanist thought (see Ferrando, 2013: 26–32). Hence in Asimov's *Foundation*, for example, the very concept of an autonomous human individual is rendered untenable by the social and political atrocities of the mid-century period, suppressed in favour of a mechanistic model of human psychology and a broader framework of historical determinism. London's *The Iron Heel*, too, subverts human agency through a notion of historical determinism, although London subsequently attempts to recoup this agency by deploying an 'ideal' human figure derived from nineteenth-century humanist thought. And, finally, it is the works of Verne, Conan Doyle, and Smith that most readily exhibit humanist functions: the aggrandisement of human morality and rationality, the glorification of scientific thought and technological enterprise, and (in Smith) the complete abstraction of the human from its biological basis result in a transcendent human figure with complete command over the natural domain.

I would like to conclude by bringing my chronology of the human in SF up to date by considering more recent depictions of the human within the genre. One of the most significant developments in this regard was the advent of cyberpunk, the subgenre of SF which has drawn the bulk of posthumanist critical attention. Veronica Hollinger has undertaken a comprehensive examination of the humanist themes of cyberpunk, arguing that this subgenre 'can be situated among a growing (although still relatively small) number of science-fiction projects which can be identified as "anti-humanist"' (1990: 30).

Such anti-humanist SF, Hollinger goes on, derives partly from the feminist SF works of the 1970s, of which Joanna Russ's *The Female Man* (1975) offers perhaps the best-known example. Like the later works of cyberpunk, Russ's novel undertakes an explicit deconstruction of the human subject—in Russ's case, the default male at the centre of western culture and society—and instead offers a complex and highly experimental exploration of a number of female characters (including a fictionalised version of Russ herself). Russ sharply criticises the cultural tendency to view women as simply lesser versions of men: 'I didn't and don't want to be a "feminine" version or a diluted version or a special version or a subsidiary version or an ancillary version, or an adapted version of the heroes I admire. I want to be the heroes themselves' (1985: 206). At the same time, she criticises the construction of women's identities as centred around sacrificial acts: the expectation that women will be 'timid, incapable, dependant, nurturing, passive, intuitive, emotional, unintelligent, obedient, ... beautiful' and above all 'selfless', which Russ amends as *'self-less'* (205, emphasis in original). Like Le Guin's *The Dispossessed*, then, *The Female Man* explicitly repudiates the patriarchal humanist tradition in its shift away from self-identical characters towards ambiguous and shifting focalisations centred on several fluid character subjectivities.

This shift away from chauvinistic humanism in SF may be attributed, Hollinger argues, to the rise of cultural postmodernism, with its sceptical stance on the classical human subject, towards the end of the twentieth century (see Hollinger, 2005: 232–47). Such attitudes were most clear in the subgenre of cyberpunk. Michael Swanwick, in 'A User's Guide to the Postmoderns' (1986), divided the SF writers of the early to mid-1980s into the 'cyberpunks' and the 'humanists'. Whereas the latter category focusses on 'human characters who are generally seen as frail and fallible', the former is defined by a 'hot tech ambiance' and dense prose style that invokes the earlier experimentations of the New Wave writers (1986: 24, 48). Bruce Sterling has explicitly cited cyberpunk SF as heralding the arrival of the post-human: the 'technological destruction of the human condition leads not to futureshocked zombies but to hopeful monsters'—that is, to the possibility for radically new subjective orientations in a transformed world (quoted in Hollinger, 1990: 33). Cyberpunk literature centres on the recurring image of the human dissolution within technological frameworks: does this moment of bodily disintegration and subjective transformation symbolise a utopian release from the entrapments of embodiment or a catastrophic subversion of the human condition?

The answer, as ever, lies somewhere between these two poles. Consider, for example, the quintessential cyberpunk work, William Gibson's *Neuromancer* (1984). On the one hand, *Neuromancer* offers the paradigmatic depiction of virtuality, featuring sentient artificial intelligences, disembodied personalities, 'simstims' (devices that allow individuals to cast their consciousness into the bodies of others), virtual realities, and a host of other technologies that project the human beyond the margins of the body. 'The body is meat', remarks protagonist Case, a 'prison of his own flesh' (1993: 69), while he later sheds literal 'tears of release' when, after being excluded from the space of the 'matrix'—a virtual cybernetic space—for many years, he is once again able to experience the 'bodiless exultation of cyberspace' (12). On the other, however, the novel by no means affirms a *total* escape from the body. Indeed, Case's exclusion from the matrix is rooted in his very biology: he was injected with mycotoxins by a disgruntled former employer, resulting in a 'crippled' nervous system that prevents him from plugging in to cyberspace. Later, projecting his consciousness into the body of the assassin Molly, Case obtains a view of the corporeal that is far from Cartesian:

> The abrupt jolt into another flesh ... She was moving through a crowded street ... For a few frightened seconds he fought helplessly to control her body. Then he willed himself into passivity, became the passenger behind her eyes.
> ... Her body language was disorienting, her style foreign. She seemed continually on the verge of colliding with someone, but people melted out of her way, stepped sideways, made room (72).

This description of embodiment is marked by idiosyncrasies peculiar to the individual. Hence, although *Neuromancer* is open to the new possibilities of emerging technologies, it is also aware of the inescapable material reality of the body that underpins any 'virtual' experience.

In terms of the human archetypes described throughout this study, the human characters of *Neuromancer* are thus situated between the trans-human and the post-human. Indeed, the human archetypes outlined in this study continue to proliferate past the 1970s. The figure of the pre-human, for example, may be seen in the large number of zombie works to appear in the 2000s: films such as *28 Days Later* (2002), *Dawn of the Dead* (2004), and *Shaun of the Dead* (2004), the popular television show *The Walking Dead* (2010–present), and novels such as Max Brooks's *World War Z* (2006) and Stephen King's *Cell* (2006). Like its counterpart in the earlier works of Conan Doyle and London, the pre-human zombie is a figure of intellectual and moral regression: a degenerate human reduced to base 'animal' instincts. One common interpretation of this surge in zombie literature links it to post-9/11 fears concerning terrorism and migration: the recurring image of a 'horde' of debased humans invading the familiar spaces—the homes, shops, and city streets—of western society reflects wider cultural anxieties concerning the need to 'preserve' western civilisation from ostensible threats emerging from both religious extremism and mass east–west migration.[1]

The trans-human, meanwhile, is most clearly seen in the works of cyberpunk, although in a critical register far removed from the earlier

---

[1] See Muntean and Payne (2009) and Stratton (2011).

utopianism of Smith's *Skylark* series or, indeed, of the literature of the various transhumanist movements that appeared concurrently in the 1980s. The figure of the supra-human is evident in Greg Bear's highly regarded 1985 novel, *Blood Music*, in which a scientist develops a form of sentient bacteria that first infects and then assimilates human individuals into a massive, communal biomass formation, thus transforming the nature of human subjective experience. Other works—Kim Stanley Robinson's *Mars* trilogy (1992–1996), for instance, or Iain M. Banks' *Culture* series (1987–2012)—are also arguably informed by supra-humanist concerns, insofar as these works shift the narrative perspective (to varying degrees) from individual characters to the fate of the species as a whole. Robinson's works in particular are explicitly informed by debates about the environment, which forms part of a supra-humanist discourse: as Robinson states, environmental change 'play[s] out at planetary scales of space and time', demanding alternative narrative modes capable of addressing such mass social and natural trends (Canavan and Robinson, 2014: 243). Andrew Milner argues that one of the biggest issues facing the environmentalist movement is precisely that of narrativisation: how to tell the story of climate change—the defining 'grand narrative' of the twenty-first century—in such a way as to be accessible to the individual (see Milner et al., 2015: 12–27).

Finally, the key figure of the post-human can be readily detected throughout recent SF. It is evident, for example, in the increasing popularity of Afrofuturist SF by writers such as Octavia Butler and Samuel R. Delany in the 1980s and 1990s up to Nnedi Okorafor, Nalo Hopkinson, and N.K. Jemisin in recent years. Like the feminist SF that emerged in the 1970s, Afrofuturist SF attacks the presumptions of a humanist narrative that has historically situated whiteness as a default characteristic of the human subject, while also countering the relative dominance enjoyed by white authors throughout the history of the genre. A harder strain of posthumanist SF, meanwhile, may be seen in such works as Ted Chiang's 'Story of Your Life' (1998, filmed as *Arrival* in 2016), with its depiction of highly advanced, octopus-like alien beings and its elaborate explorations of the nature of subjectivity and temporality, and (in a quite different register) in Jeff VanderMeer's highly acclaimed *Southern Reach* trilogy (2014), which—like many of the 'New Weird' works that have appeared in the last number of years—features a range of bizarre inhuman beings and human–animal hybrids, deployed within an unsettling Lovecraftian narrative in which the boundaries between the human, non-human, and landscape are called continuously into question.

I would like to finish by emphasising two key points in relation to contemporary SF. Firstly, although postmodern SF, and cyberpunk in particular, has been widely noted for its explorations of the nature of human experience, these explorations do not constitute a radical break from earlier modes of SF. Thomas Foster has argued that cyberpunk must be read 'not as the vanguard of a posthumanism assumed to be revolutionary in itself, but instead as an attempt to intervene in and diversify what posthumanism can mean' (2005: xiii). In other words, the posthuman did not emerge within SF with the advent of cyberpunk or postmodern SF, but had in fact always been present—Foster uses the term 'pre-post-human' to describe the various instantiations of posthuman subjectivities and embodiments before the 'arrival' of the posthuman in the 1980s. Even this notion of the pre-post-human, however, is too crude to account for the diversity of human forms in the history of the genre: I have here attempted to offer a more complex genealogy of the human as a collection of fluid archetypes used in complex and contrasting ways, of which cyberpunk offers an intensified—but not radically *new*—inflection. Even this account, however, is necessarily limited in its scope. Nor do we necessarily need to identify instances of the radically *in*human—virtual consciousnesses, but also androids, robots, 'Creatures', and so on—to deconstruct the boundaries of the human: such beings highlight, rather than instigate, the blurring of the boundaries separating the human from the non-human.

Secondly, and more significantly, the human can be said *never* to have existed in SF. The diverse denotative and connotative significations linked to the term 'human' cannot be easily, or perhaps at all, summarised: although I have here outlined several tentative historical lineages of the human—the 'technophilic' and 'technophobic' tendencies traced out in chapters one to three, or what I have termed the assimilative and the transformative modes of (post)humanist engagement—it is evident that these cannot be readily understood in isolation from one another. Certainly, it is now clear that 'human' does not refer solely or consistently to the biological animal, *homo sapiens*, nor to Tom Shippey's tool-wielding animal, *homo faber*, nor to a transcendent and 'universal' consciousness, nor to Barthes's 'Family of Man' encompassing the whole of humanity, nor to a heterogeneous assemblage of embedded and embodied instantiations. At times, it may refer to one or several of these definitions—but, much like the rational 'Man' of the classical humanist narrative, when we begin to examine these human figures of SF in more detail we find that they lose their clear outlines, becoming blurred, inconsistent, or unstable.

In place of a definition of the human, I will instead conclude with some tentative answers to the questions with which I began this study. Processes of technological advancement have played a crucial role in defining the diverse meanings of the 'human' in SF works, whose orientations towards the non-human natural world also reveal a host of unconscious attitudes and values. Whether each writer construes the human as separate from or part of the technological and natural systems that surround it—or somewhere in between—is determined in large measure by their understanding of these basic conditions. For some, technology is a mere tool to facilitate human action within a natural world from which the human is wholly separate—for others, humanity is transformed through its contact with technology, compelled to recognise, to varying degrees, its fundamental rootedness in and equivalence with the non-human world. The 'human' thus comprises not a coherent figure in the history of SF, nor even a number of coherent figures, but rather a discursive site upon which may be projected any number of hopes and fears regarding the nature of human society and the human individual, the merits of instrumental rationalism, the ramifications of technological progress, the sanctity (or otherwise) of the body, the significance of the natural–material world, and the future of embodied subjectivity in all its various guises.

If it seems something of an evasion to conclude a critical history of the human in SF by concluding that the 'human' as such does not exist, this outcome derives from the very mechanisms of the genre itself. SF is a vehicle for imagining radical possibilities, and offers a complex and conflicting picture of the anxieties and anticipations concerning the present and the future of the human—'a vast being', to appropriate Jameson's description of SF itself, 'in perpetual change and transformation' (quoted in Franklin, 2009: 24).

The project of posthumanism, too, is the investigation of possibilities. The aim of any critical posthumanist undertaking is, firstly, to counter humanist narratives by demonstrating the extent to which they are bound up with hegemonic structures of oppression, exclusion, and control; and secondly, to offer alternative modes of theorising about the human that offer more inclusive, and less destructive, understandings of our relationship with the world around us and the beings that populate it. It is my hope that this study, by viewing these SF works from a variety of different angles, has raised some important questions concerning the possibility for both oppressive *and* productive ways of viewing the human relationship to technology and nature. To return to the liminal figure with which I began this study, if there is anything to be learned from the terrible example of the OncoMouse™—a 'dangerous vision' (to borrow a famous SF phrase) if ever there was one—it is that alternative visions of how we could do things may come from the most unexpected places, and it is never too late to begin the search.

Works Cited

Adorno, Theodor W., and Max Horkheimer, *Dialectic of Enlightenment: philosophical fragments* (Stanford University Press, 2002 [1944]).
Aldiss, Brian, (ed.), *Space Opera: science fiction from the Golden Age* (Futura Publications, 1973).
—, *Billion Year Spree: the history of science fiction* (Corgi Books, 1975 [1973]).
—, *Hothouse* (Panther Books, 1985 [1962]).
Althusser, Louis, *For Marx*, translated by Ben Brewster (Verso, 2005 [1965]).
Anderson, Poul, *Brain Wave*, in *Poul Anderson: SF Gateway Omnibus* (Gollancz, 2013 [1954]).
Arendt, Hannah, *The Human Condition*, second edition (University of Chicago Press, 1998 [1958]).
Armstrong, Tim, *Modernism, Technology, and the Body: a cultural study* (Cambridge University Press, 1998).
Asimov, Isaac, 'Social Science Fiction', in *Science Fiction: the future*, edited by Dick Allen (Harcourt Brace Jovanovich Inc., 1971), pp. 263–90.
—, *Foundation* (Panther Books, 1977 [1951]).
—, *Second Foundation* (Panther Books, 1979 [1953]).
—, *Asimov's New Guide to Science* (Penguin Books, 1987a).
—, *Foundation and Empire* (Grafton Books, 1987b [1952]).
—, *Before the Golden Age Trilogy* (Black Cat, 1988 [1974]).
—, *The Complete Robot* (HarperCollins, 1995a [1982]).
—, *I, Asimov: a memoir* (Bantam Books, 1995b [1994]).
—, *Gold: the final science fiction collection* (HarperCollins, 1996 [1995]).
—, *Foundation's Edge* (Harper Voyager, 2016 [1982]).
Bacon, Francis, *The New Atlantis* (Project Gutenberg, 2008 [1627]), gutenberg.org/files/2434/2434-h/2434-h.htm (accessed January 2020).
Badmington, Neil, *Posthumanism* (Palgrave, 2000).
—, *Alien Chic: posthumanism and the other within* (Routledge, 2004).
Bailer, Everett F., 'Review: Lost Worlds and Lost Opportunities: *The Annotated Lost World. The classic adventure novel* by Arthur Conan Doyle', *Science Fiction Studies* 23.3 (1996), pp. 335–62.
Ballard, J.G., 'Which Way to Inner Space?', *New Worlds* (May 1962), pp. 2–3, 116–18, luminist.org/archives/SF/NW.htm (accessed January 2020).

—, 'Time, Memory and Inner Space' (n.d., 1963), jgballard.ca/non_fiction/jgb_time_memory_innerspace.html (accessed January 2020).
—, *The Wind from Nowhere* (Penguin Books, 1967 [1961]).
—, *The Crystal World* (Triad Panther, 1978 [1966]).
—, *The Atrocity Exhibition* (Fourth Estate, 2006 [1970]).
—, *Miracles of Life: an autobiography* (Harper Perennial, 2008).
—, *The Drowned World* (Fourth Estate, 2012 [1962]).
—, *The Complete Short Stories, Vol. 2* (Fourth Estate, 2014a [2001]).
—, *High-Rise*, Kindle edition (Fourth Estate, 2014b [1975]).
Ballard, J.G., and Jeremy Lewis, 'An Interview with J.G. Ballard', *Mississippi Review* 20.1/2 (1991), pp. 27–40.
Barthes, Roland, *Mythologies*, translated by Jonathan Cape (Noonday Press, 1991 [1957]).
Bauman, Zygmunt, *Liquid Modernity* (Polity Press, 2000).
Bayley, Barrington J., 'The Four-Colour Problem', in Michael Moorcock (ed.), *New Worlds: an anthology* (Flamingo, 1983), pp. 42–71.
Bear, Greg, *Blood Music*, Kindle edition (Gollancz, 2011 [1985]).
Beauchamp, Gorman, '*The Iron Heel* and *Looking Backward*: two paths to utopia', *American Literary Realism, 1870–1910* 9.4 (1976), pp. 307–14.
—, 'Technology in the Dystopian Novel', *Modern Fiction Studies* 32.1 (1986), pp. 53–63.
Beaud, Michel, *A History of Capitalism, 1500–2000*, translated by Tom Dickman and Anny Lefebvre (Monthly Review Press, 2001 [1981]).
Bedford, Sybille, *Aldous Huxley: a biography* (Macmillan Papermac, 1993 [1973]).
Bell, Daniel, 'The Cultural Contradictions of Capitalism', *Journal of Aesthetic Education* 6.1/2 (1972), pp. 11–38.
Bellamy, Edward, *Looking Backward: 2000–1887* (Penguin Books, 1986 [1888]).
Berger, Albert I., 'Nuclear Energy: Science Fiction's Metaphor of Power', *Science Fiction Studies* 6.2 (1979), p. 121–8.
Berger, John, 'Why Look at Animals?', in *About Looking* (Bloomsbury, 2009), pp. 3–28.
Berkove, Lawrence, 'Jack London and Evolution: from Spencer to Huxley', *American Literary Realism* 36.3 (2004), pp. 243–55.
Berliner, Jonathan, 'Jack London's Socialistic Social Darwinism', *American Literary Realism* 41.1 (2008), pp. 52–78.
Berman, Marshall, *All That Is Solid Melts into Air: the experience of modernity* (Penguin Books, 1988 [1982]).
Bernardo, Susan M., and Graham J. Murphy, *Ursula K. Le Guin: a critical companion* (Greenwood Press, 2006).
Blish, James, *Cities in Flight* (Legend, 1991 [1981]).
—, *A Case of Conscience* (Gollancz, 2014 [1958]).
Bloch, Ernst, *The Principle of Hope*, translated by Neville Plaice, Stephen Plaice, and Paul Knight (MIT Press, 1995 [1959]).

Bloom, Harold, (ed.), *Modern Critical Interpretations: Ursula K. Le Guin's* The Left Hand of Darkness (Chelsea House Publishers, 1987).
Bode, Christoph, 'Aldous Huxley (1894–1963)', in *Classics in Cultural Criticism, Vol. I: Britain*, edited by Bernd-Peter Lange (Peter Lang, 1990), pp. 343–73.
Booker, M. Keith, *Monsters, Mushroom Clouds, and the Cold War: American science fiction and the roots of postmodernism, 1946–1964* (Greenwood Press, 2001).
Bould, Mark, and China Miéville (eds.), *Red Planets: Marxism and science fiction* (Wesleyan University Press, 2009).
Boyer, Paul, *By the Bomb's Early Light: American thought and culture at the dawn of the atomic age* (University of North Carolina Press, 1994 [1985]).
Brackett, Leigh, *The Long Tomorrow* (Gollancz, 2013 [1955]).
Bradbury, Ray, *The Martian Chronicles* (Simon and Schuster, 2012 [1950]).
Braidotti, Rosi, 'Interview with Rosi Braidotti', in *New Materialism: interviews and cartographies*, edited by Rick Dolphijn and Iris van der Tuin (Open Humanities Press, 2012).
—, *The Posthuman* (Polity Press, 2013).
Brigg, Peter, *J.G. Ballard* (Borgo Press/Wildside Press, 1985).
Broderick, Damien, *Reading by Starlight: postmodern science fiction* (Routledge, 2005 [1995]).
Brunner, John, *Stand on Zanzibar* (Arrow Books, 1984 [1969]).
Bullock, Alan, *The Humanist Tradition in the West* (W.W. Norton & Company, 1985).
Burling, William J., 'Marxism', in *The Routledge Companion to Science Fiction*, edited by Mark Bould, Andrew M. Butler, Adam Roberts, and Sherryl Vint (Routledge, 2009), pp. 237–45.
Burroughs, Edgar Rice, *Tarzan of the Apes* (Modern Library, 2003 [1914])
—, *John Carter of Mars: the collection* (Purple Rose Books, 2010 [1912]).
—, *The Land That Time Forgot* (Gollancz, 2014 [1918]).
Call, Lewis, 'Postmodern Anarchism in the Novels of Ursula K. Le Guin', *SubStance* 36.2 (2007), pp. 87–105.
Callenbach, Ernest, *Ecotopia*, Kindle edition (Bantam, 2009 [1975]).
Campbell Jr., John W., *Islands of Space*, in *Amazing Stories Quarterly* 4.2 (Spring 1931), pp. 146–230, archive.org/details/Amazing_Stories_Quarterly_v04n02_1931-Spring_frankenscan (accessed January 2020).
—, 'Atomic Age', in *Astounding Science Fiction* 36.3 (November 1945), pp. 5–6, 98, luminist.org/archives/SF/AST.htm (accessed January 2020).
—, 'Twilight', in *The Science Fiction Hall of Fame, Vol. 1*, edited by Robert Silverberg, (Sphere Books, 1972 [1970]), pp. 39–61.
—, 'The Battery of Hate', in *Science Fiction of the 30's*, edited by Damon Knight (Bobbs-Merrill Company, 1975).
Canavan, Gerry, and Kim Stanley Robinson, *Green Planets: ecology and science fiction* (Wesleyan University Press, 2014).
Čapek, Karel, *R.U.R. & War with the Newts* (Gollancz, 2011 [1920]).

Cheng, John, *Astounding Wonder: imagining science and science fiction in interwar America* (University of Pennsylvania Press, 2012).
Childs, Peter, *Modernism* (Routledge, 2000).
Clarke, Arthur C., *Childhood's End* (London, 1970 [1953]).
—, *The Lion of Comarre and Against the Fall of Night* (Corgi Books, 1975 [1968]).
—, *Imperial Earth* (Pan Books, 1977 [1975]).
—, 'On Moylan on *The City and the Stars*', *Science Fiction Studies* 5.1 (1978), pp. 88–90.
—, *The Fountains of Paradise* (Pan Books, 1980 [1979]).
—, *The Songs of Distant Earth* (Grafton Books, 1986).
—, *2001: A Space Odyssey* (Arrow Books, 1988 [1968]).
—, *Astounding Days: the science fictional autobiography* (Gollancz, 1989).
—, *Rendezvous with Rama* (Orbit, 1998 [1974]).
—, *The Collected Stories* (Gollancz, 2000).
—, *The City and the Stars* (Gollancz, 2001a [1956]).
—, *The Space Trilogy* (Gollancz, 2001b).
Clarke, Bruce, *Posthuman Metamorphoses: narrative and systems* (Fordham University Press, 2008).
Clarke, Bruce, and Manuela Rossini (eds.), *The Cambridge Companion to Literature and the Posthuman* (Cambridge University Press, 2017).
Clarke, I.F., *Voices Prophesying War 1763–1984* (Panther Arts, 1970 [1966]).
Clute, John, 'Isaac Asimov', in *A Companion to Science Fiction*, edited by David Seed (Blackwell Publishing, 2005), pp. 264–74.
—, 'Huxley, Aldous', in *The Encyclopedia of Science Fiction*, edited by John Clute, David Langford, Peter Nicholls, and Graham Sleight (Gollancz, 2019), sf-encyclopedia.com/entry/huxley_aldous (accessed January 2020).
Connolly, Thomas, 'Utopia and the Countryside in H.G. Wells's Scientific Romances', *Foundation: the international review of science fiction* 127 (2017), pp. 20–32.
Csicsery-Ronay Jr., Istvan, 'Science Fiction and Empire', *Science Fiction Studies* 30.2 (2003), pp. 231–45.
—, *The Seven Beauties of Science Fiction* (Wesleyan University Press, 2008).
Cummings, Ray, 'Brigands of the Moon: Part 1', in *Astounding Stories of Super Science* 1.3 (March 1930), pp. 306–58, luminist.org/archives/SF/AST.htm (accessed January 2020).
Darwin, Charles, *On the Origin of Species* (Oxford University Press, 2008 [1859]).
Davies, Tony, *Humanism* (Routledge, 1997).
Davis, Laurence, and Peter Stillman (eds.), *The New Utopian Politics of Ursula K. Le Guin's* The Dispossessed (Lexington Books, 2005).
Deane, Bradley, 'Imperial Barbarians: primitive masculinity in lost-world fiction', *Victorian Literature and Culture* 36.1 (2008), pp. 205–25.
Delany, Samuel R., *Triton* (Corgi, 1977 [1976]).
Delany, Samuel R., and R.M.P., 'On *Triton* and Other Matters: an interview with Samuel R. Delany', *Science Fiction Studies* 17.3 (1990), pp. 295–324.

Derrida, Jacques, 'The Animal that Therefore I Am (More to Follow)', translated by David Wills, *Critical Enquiry* 28.1 (2002), pp. 369–418.
Dick, Philip K., *Ubik* (Panther Books, 1984 [1969]).
—, *Do Androids Dream of Electric Sheep?* (HarperCollins, 1993 [1968]).
Dirda, Michael, *On Conan Doyle: Or, The Whole Art of Storytelling* (Princeton University Press, 2011).
Disch, Thomas, *The Dreams Our Stuff Is Made From: how science fiction conquered the world* (Free Press, 1998).
Douglas, Gordon, (dir.), *Them!* Warner Bros. Studios, 1954.
Doyle, Arthur Conan, *Tales of Unease*, edited by David Stuart Davies (Wordsworth Editions, 2000).
—, *The Lost World and Other Thrilling Tales* (Penguin Books, 2001).
—, *Sherlock Holmes: the complete stories* (Wordsworth Editions, 2006).
—, *A Life in Letters*, edited by Jon Lellenberg, Daniel Stashower, and Charles Foley (Harper Perennial, 2008).
—, *The Lost World and Other Stories* (Wordsworth Classics, 2010).
—, *Memories and Adventures* (Cambridge University Press, 2012 [1924]).
—, *The White Company*, Kindle edition (Vintage, 2015).
—, *Sir Nigel* (2018a [1906]), gutenberg.org/files/2845/2845-h/2845-h.htm (accessed January 2020).
—, *The Crime of the Congo* (2018b [1909]), arthur-conan-doyle.com/index.php?title=The_Crime_of_ the_Congo (accessed January 2020).
—, 'The Vital Message' (2018c [1919]), arthur-conan-doyle.com/index.php?title=The_Vital_Message (accessed January 2012).
—, *The History of Spiritualism* (2019 [1926]) arthur-conan-doyle.com/index.php?title=The_History_of_Spiritualism (accessed January 2020).
Eliot, T.S., 'The Waste Land', in *The Waste Land and Other Poems* (Faber and Faber, 1999 [1972]).
Elkins, Charles, 'Isaac Asimov's "Foundation" series: historical materialism distorted into cyclical psycho-history', *Science Fiction Studies* 3.1 (1976), pp. 26–36.
Ellul, Jacques, *The Technological Society*, translated by John Wilkinson (Vintage Books, 1964 [1954]).
Ferrando, Francesca, 'Posthumanism, Transhumanism, Antihumanism, Metahumanism, and New Materialisms: differences and relations', *Existenz* 8.2 (2013), pp. 26–32.
Finney, Jack, *The Body Snatchers* (Gollancz, 2010 [1954]).
Firsching, Lorenz J., and R.M.P., 'J.G. Ballard's Ambiguous Apocalypse', *Science Fiction Studies* 12.3 (1985), pp. 297–310.
Fisher, Mark, *Capitalist Realism: is there no alternative?* (Zero Books, 2009).
Fitting, Peter, 'The Modern Anglo-American SF Novel: utopian longing and capitalist cooptation', *Science Fiction Studies* 6.1 (1979), pp. 59–76.
—, 'Positioning and Closure: on the "reading effect" of contemporary utopian fiction', *Utopian Studies* 1 (1987), pp. 23–36.
Forster, E.M., 'The Machine Stops', in *The Science Fiction Hall of Fame, Volume IIB*, edited by Robert Silverberg (Avon Books, 1974 [1973], pp. 248–79).

Foster, John Bellamy, *Marx's Ecology: materialism and nature* (Monthly Review Press, 2000).
Foster, Thomas, *The Souls of Cyberfolk: posthumanism as vernacular theory* (University of Minnesota Press, 2005).
Foucault, Michel, *The History of Sexuality, Vol. 1*, translated by Robert Hurley (Pantheon Books, 1978).
—, *Society Must Be Defended: lectures at the Collège de France 1975–76*, translated by David Macey (Picador, 2003 [1997]).
Franklin, H. Bruce, 'What Are We to Make of J.G. Ballard's Apocalypse?' (n.d. [1979]), jgballard.ca/criticism/ballard_apocalypse_1979.html (accessed January 2020).
—, 'What Is Science Fiction—and How It Grew', in *Reading Science Fiction*, edited by James Gunn, Marleen Barr, and Matthew Candelaria (Palgrave Macmillan, 2009), pp. 23–32.
Freedman, Carl, 'Science Fiction and Utopia: a historico-philosophical overview', in *Learning from Other Worlds: estrangement, cognition and the politics of science fiction and utopia*, edited by Patrick Parrinder (Liverpool University Press, 2000), pp. 72–97.
—, (ed.), *Conversations with Isaac Asimov* (University Press of Mississippi, 2005).
Frost, Laura, 'Huxley's Feelies: the cinema of sensation in *Brave New World*', *Twentieth Century Literature* 52.4 (2006), pp. 443–73.
Fukuyama, Francis, *Our Posthuman Future: consequences of the biotechnology revolution* (Farrar, Straus, and Giroux, 2002).
Gernsback, Hugo, 'A New Sort of Magazine', in *Amazing Stories* 1.1 (April 1926), p. 3, https://archive.org/stream/Amazing_Stories_v01n01_1926-04_Team-DPP#mode/2up (accessed January 2020).
Gibson, William, *Neuromancer* (HarperCollins, 1993 [1984]).
Gilman, Charlotte Perkins, *Herland* (Hesperus, 2015 [1915]).
Glotfelty, Cheryll, and Harold Fromm (eds.), *The Ecocriticism Reader: landmarks in literary ecology* (University of Georgia Press, 1996).
Glover, Jonathan, *Humanity: a moral history of the twentieth century* (Yale University Press, 2001 [1999]).
Godwin, Tom, 'The Cold Equations', in *Astounding Science Fiction* 53.6 (August 1954), pp. 62–84, luminist.org/archives/SF/AST.htm (accessed January 2020).
Gomel, Elana, *Science Fiction, Alien Encounters, and the Ethics of Posthumanism: beyond the Golden Rule* (Palgrave Macmillan, 2014).
Gomel, Elana, and Stephen A. Weninger, 'Romancing the Crystal: Utopias of Transparency and Dreams of Pain', *Utopian Studies* 15.2 (2004), pp. 65–91.
Goody, Alex, *Technology, Literature and Culture* (Polity Press, 2011).
Graham, Elaine, *Representations of the Post/Human: monsters, aliens, and others in popular culture* (Manchester University Press, 2002).
Greenland, Colin, *The Entropy Exhibition: Michael Moorcock and the British New Wave in Science Fiction*, Kindle edition (Gollancz, 2013 [1983]).

Gunn, James, *The Road to Science Fiction: from Heinlein to here* (Borealis, 1979).
—, *Isaac Asimov: the foundations of science fiction* (Oxford University Press, 1982).
Haggard, H. Rider, *She* (Penguin Popular Classics, 1994 [1887]).
Halberstam, Judith, and Ira Livingstone (eds.), *Posthuman Bodies* (Indiana University Press, 1995).
Haldeman, Joe, *The Forever War* (Gollancz, 2006 [1974]).
Halliday, R.J., 'Social Darwinism: a definition', *Victorian Studies* 14.4 (1971), pp. 389–405.
Hamilton, Edmond, *Crashing Suns* (Ace Books, 1965).
Hanahan, Douglas, et al., 'The origins of oncomice: a history of the first transgenic mice genetically engineered to develop cancer', *Genes and Development* 21.18 (2007), pp. 2,258–70, genesdev.cshlp.org/content/21/18/2258.full (accessed January 2020).
Haraway, Donna, *Modest_Witness@Second_Millenium.FemaleMan©_Meets_Onco-Mouse™: feminism and technoscience* (Routledge, 1997).
—, *The Haraway Reader* (Routledge, 2004).
—, *When Species Meet* (University of Minnesota Press, 2008).
Hardt, Michael, and Antonio Negri, *Empire* (Harvard University Press, 2000).
Harrison, Harry, *Make Room! Make Room!* (Penguin Books, 2013 [1966]).
Harrison, M. John, 'Sweet Analytics', in *New Worlds: an anthology*, edited by Michael Moorcock (Flamingo, 1983), pp. 332–7.
Harvey, David, *The Conditions of Postmodernity: an enquiry into the origins of cultural change* (Blackwell, 1992 [1990]).
Hassler, Donald M., 'Some Asimov Resonances from the Enlightenment', *Science Fiction Studies* 15.1 (1988), pp. 36–47.
Hayles, N. Katherine, *How We Became Posthuman* (University of Chicago Press, 1999).
Hayman, Randy, 'Review: Tips for Lost Students: *The Lost World* by Arthur Conan Doyle', *Science Fiction Studies* 32.3 (2005), pp. 516–18.
Healy, Raymond J., and J. Francis McComas, *Adventures in Time and Space* (Ballantine Books, 1974 [1946]).
Heidegger, Martin, *The Question Concerning Technology and Other Essays*, translated by William Lovitt (Garland, 1977).
—, *Being and Time*, translated by John Macquarrie and Edward Robinson (Blackwell, 2001 [1927]).
Heinlein, Robert, *The Past Through Tomorrow* (Gollancz, 2014 [1967]).
Herbert, Frank, *Dune* (NEL Books, 1984 [1965]).
Herbrechter, Stefan, *Posthumanism: a critical analysis*, eBook version (Bloomsbury, 2013 [2009]).
Hidgon, David Leon, *Wandering into Brave New World* (Rodopi, 2013).
Hobsbawm, Eric, *The Age of Extremes: 1914–1991* (Abacus, 2006 [1994]).
Hollinger, Veronica, 'Cybernetic Deconstructions: cyberpunk and postmodernism', *Mosaic* 23.2 (1990), pp. 29–44.

—, 'Science Fiction and Postmodernism', in *A Companion to Science Fiction*, edited by David Seed (Blackwell Publishing, 2005), pp. 232–47.

—, 'Posthumanism and Cyborg Theory', in *The Routledge Companion to Science Fiction*, edited by Mark Bould, Andrew M. Butler, Adam Roberts, and Sherryl Vint (Routledge, 2009), pp. 267–78.

Hull, Keith N., 'What Is Human? Ursula LeGuin [sic] and Science Fiction's Great Theme', *Modern Fiction Studies* 32.1 (1986), pp. 65–74.

Huxley, Aldous, *Jesting Pilate* (George H. Doran Company, 1926).

—, *Do What You Will* (Watts & Co., 1937 [1936]).

—, *Ends and Means* (Chatto & Windus, 1938 [1937]).

—, *Point Counter Point* (Chatto & Windus, 1974 [1928]).

—, *After Many a Summer* (Granada Publishing, 1980 [1939]).

—, *The Hidden Huxley*, edited by David Bradshaw (Faber and Faber, 1994).

—, *Brave New World & Brave New World Revisited* (Harper Perennial, 2004 [1958]).

—, *Brave New World & Brave New World Revisited* (Harper Perennial Modern Classics, 2005b [1946]).

—, *Island* (Vintage Books, 2005c [1962]).

Huxley, Julian, 'Transhumanism', in *New Bottles for New Wine* (Chatto & Windus, 1957), pp. 13–17.

Huyssen, Andreas, *After the Great Divide: modernism, mass culture, postmodernism* (Indiana University Press, 1986).

Ingersoll, Earl G., et al., 'A Conversation with Isaac Asimov', *Science Fiction Studies* 14.1 (1987), pp. 68–77.

James, Edward, *Science Fiction in the Twentieth Century* (Oxford University Press, 1994).

Jameson, Fredric, 'Postmodernism and Consumer Society', in *The Anti-Aesthetic: essays on postmodern culture*, edited by Hal Foster (Bay Press, 1983), pp. 111–25.

—, *Archaeologies of the Future* (Verso, 2005).

Jose, Jim, 'Reflections on the Politics of Le Guin's Narrative Shifts', *Science Fiction Studies* 18.2 (1991), pp. 180–97.

Joyce, James, 'An Encounter', in *Dubliners* (Penguin Books, 2000 [1914]), pp. 11–20.

Kafka, Franz, *The Trial*, Kindle edition (Wisehouse Classics, 2016 [1925]).

Kant, Immanuel, 'An Answer to the Question: What Is "Enlightening"?', in *The Age of Enlightenment, Vol. 2*, edited by Simon Eliot and Beverley Stern (Open University Press, 1979 [1784]).

Kemp, Peter, *H.G. Wells and the Culminating Ape* (Macmillan, 1982).

Kern, Stephen, *The Culture of Time and Space, 1880–1918* (Harvard University Press, 2003 [1983]).

Kerslake, Patricia, *Science Fiction and Empire* (Liverpool University Press, 2010 [2007]).

Khouri, Nadia, 'Utopia and Epic: ideological confrontation in Jack London's *The Iron Heel*', *Science Fiction Studies* 3.2 (1976), pp. 174–81.

Kincaid, Paul, *What It Is We Do When We Read Science Fiction* (Beccon Publications, 2008).
Kipling, Rudyard, *The Man Who Would Be King and Other Stories*, edited by Louis L. Cornell, e-book edition (Oxford World Classics, 1999 [1888]).
Kubrick, Stanley (dir.), *Dr. Strangelove* (Columbia Pictures, 1964).
—, (dir.), *2001: a space odyssey* (MGM, 1968).
Labor, Earle, *Jack London: an American life*, Kindle edition (Macmillan, 2013).
Lang, Fritz (dir.), *Metropolis* (UFA, 1927).
Latham, Rob, 'Biotic Invasions: ecological imperialism in New Wave science fiction', *Yearbook of English Studies* 37.2 (2007), pp. 103–19.
—, (ed.), *The Oxford Handbook of Science Fiction* (Oxford University Press, 2014).
Latour, Bruno, *We Have Never Been Modern* (Harvester Wheatsheaf, 1993 [1991]).
Le Guin, Ursula K., *The Dispossessed* (Panther Books, 1976 [1974]).
—, *Three Hainish Novels* (Nelson Doubleday, 1978).
—, *The Left Hand of Darkness* (Panther Books, 1979 [1969]).
—, *The Word for World Is Forest* (Panther Books, 1980 [1972]).
—, *Always Coming Home* (Bantam Books, 1987 [1985]).
—, *The Lathe of Heaven* (Grafton Books, 1988 [1971]).
—, *Dancing at the Edge of the World* (Grove Press, 1989).
—, *A Wizard of Earthsea*, in *The Earthsea Quartet* (Penguin Books, 1993 [1968]).
—, 'The Carrier Bag Theory of Fiction', in *The Ecocriticism Reader: landmarks in literary ecology*, edited by Cheryll Glotfelty and Harold Fromm (University of Georgia Press, 1996), pp. 149–54.
—, *Four Ways to Forgiveness* (Vista, 1997 [1995]).
—, *The Wind's Twelve Quarters & The Compass Rose* (Gollancz, 2015).
Lem, Stanislaw, *Solaris*, translated by Joanna Kilmartin and Steve Cox (Faber and Faber, 2003 [1961]).
Lemke, Thomas, *Biopolitics*, translated by Eric Frederick Trump (New York University Press, 2011).
Lewis, C.S., *Voyage to Venus* (Pan Books, 1972 [1943]).
—, *Out of the Silent Planet* (Pan Books, 1978 [1938]).
—, *That Hideous Strength* (HarperCollins, 2005 [1945]).
Lindsay, David, *A Voyage to Arcturus* (Gollancz, 2003 [1920]).
London, Jack, *The Social Writings of Jack London*, edited by Philip S. Foner (Citadel Press, 1964 [1947]).
—, *The Call of the Wild, White Fang, and Other Stories* (Penguin Books, 1993 [1981]).
—, *The Collected Science Fiction and Fantasy of Jack London, Vol. 1: Before Adam & Other Stories* (Leonaur, 2005a).
—, *The Collected Science Fiction and Fantasy of Jack London, Vol. 2: The Iron Heel & Other Stories* (Leonaur, 2005b).

—, *The Collected Science Fiction and Fantasy of Jack London, Vol. 3: The Star Rover & Other Stories* (Leonaur, 2005c).

—, *The People of the Abyss* (Hesperus Press, 2013 [1903]).

—, *The Sea Wolf* (Wordsworth Classics, 2015 [1904]).

London, Jack, and Charles Warren Stoddard, 'The Letters of Jack London to Charles Warren Stoddard', *Missouri Review* 23.2 (2000), pp. 97–118.

Luckhurst, Roger, 'The Many Deaths of Science Fiction: a polemic', *Science Fiction Studies* 21.1 (1994), pp. 35–50.

Lycett, Andrew, *Arthur Conan Doyle: the man who created Sherlock Holmes*, Kindle edition (Phoenix, 2008).

Macherey, Pierre, 'Jules Verne: the faulty narrative', in *A Theory of Literary Production*, translated by Geoffrey Wall (Routledge & Kegan Paul, 1978 [1966]), pp. 159–240.

Mandelbaum, Maurice, *History, Man, & Reason: a study in nineteenth-century thought* (Johns Hopkins Press, 1974 [1971]).

Marcuse, Herbert, *One-Dimensional Man* (Routledge, 2007 [1964]).

Marx, Karl, *Essential Writings of Karl Marx*, edited by David Caute (Panther Books, 1967).

Matheson, Richard, 'Born of Man and Woman', in *Magazine of Fantasy and Science Fiction* 1.3 (Summer 1950), pp. 108–11, luminist.org/archives/SF/FSF.htm (accessed January 2020).

—, *I Am Legend* (Gollancz, 2001 [1954]).

McAleer, Neil, *Odyssey: the authorised biography of Arthur C. Clarke* (Gollancz, 1993).

McKee Charnas, Suzy, *Walk to the End of the World and Motherlines* (Women's Press, 1989 [1974]).

McNeill, Ian, *An Encyclopedia of the History of Technology* (Routledge, 2002 [1990]).

Mellor, Anne K., 'Making a "monster": an introduction to *Frankenstein*', in *The Cambridge Companion to Mary Shelley*, edited by Esther Schor (Cambridge University Press, 2006).

Merrill, Judith, 'That Only a Mother', in *Astounding Science Fiction* 41.4 (June 1948), pp. 88–95, luminist.org/archives/SF/AST.htm (accessed January 2020).

Merritt, A., *The Moon Pool* (Overlook Press, 2009 [1919]).

Miller, Ryder W., *From Narnia to Space Odyssey: the war of ideas between Arthur C. Clarke and C.S. Lewis* (ibooks, inc., 2003).

Miller, Walter J., 'Way of a Rebel' (2010 [1954]), gutenberg.org/files/32416/32416-h/32416-h.htm (accessed January 2020).

Milner, Andrew, et al., 'Ice, Fire and Flood: science fiction and the Anthropocene', *Thesis Eleven* 131.1 (2015), pp. 12–27.

Mingers, John, *Self-Producing Systems: implications and applications of autopoiesis* (Springer, 1995).

Moore, C.L., 'No Woman Born', in *Astounding Science Fiction* 34.4 (December 1944), pp. 134–77, luminist.org/archives/SF/AST.htm (accessed January 2020).
More, Max, 'Transhumanism: towards a futurist philosophy', *Extropy* 6 (1990), pp. 6–12, hpluspedia.org/wiki/Extropy_Magazines (accessed January 2020).
Moskowitz, Sam, *Seekers of Tomorrow* (Ballantine Books, 1967 [1961]).
Moylan, Tom, 'Ideological Contradiction in Clarke's *The City and the Stars*', *Science Fiction Studies* 4.2 (1977), pp. 150–7.
—, *Demand the Impossible*, edited by Raffaella Baccolini (Peter Lang, 2014 [1986]).
Mullen, R.D., 'Review: The Garland Library of Science Fiction', *Science Fiction Studies* 2.3 (1975), pp. 280–8.
Mumford, Lewis, *Technics and Civilisation* (Harbringer Books, 1963 [1934]).
Muntean, Nick, and Matthew Thomas Payne, 'Attack of the Living Dead: Recalibrating in the Post-September 11 Zombie Film', in *The War on Terror and American Popular Culture: September 11 and beyond*, edited by Andrew Schopp and Matthew B. Hill (Fairleigh Dickinson University Press, 2009), pp. 239–58.
Nayar, Pramod K., *Posthumanism* (Polity Press, 2014).
Nicholls, Peter, and Cornel Robu, 'Sense of Wonder', in *The Encyclopedia of Science Fiction*, edited by John Clute, David Langford, Peter Nicholls, and Graham Sleight (Gollancz, 2019), sf-encyclopedia.com/entry/sense_of_wonder (accessed January 2020).
Nietzsche, Friedrich, *The Will to Power*, translated by Walter Kaufmann and R.J. Hollingdale, edited by Walter Kaufmann (Vintage Books, 1968 [1901]).
Niven, Larry, *Ringworld* (Gollancz, 2005 [1970]).
O'Brien, Fitz-James, *The Diamond Lens and Other Stories* (Hesperus Press, 2012).
Odle, E.V., *The Clockwork Man* (HiLoBooks, 2013 [1923]).
Page, Michael, *The Literary Imagination from Erasmus Darwin to H.G. Wells: science, evolution, and ecology* (Ashgate Publishing Company, 2012).
Pak, Chris, *Terraforming: ecopolitical transformations and environmentalism in science fiction* (Liverpool University Press, 2016).
Pal, George (dir.), *The War of the Worlds* (Paramount Pictures, 1953).
Pepper, David, *Modern Environmentalism: an introduction* (Routledge, 1999).
Pepperell, Robert, *The Posthuman Condition: consciousness beyond the brain* (Intellect Books, 2003 [1995]).
Piercy, Marge, *Woman on the Edge of Time*, Kindle edition (Del Rey, 2016 [1976]).
Poe, Edgar Allen, *Tales of Mystery and Imagination*, edited by Graham Clarke (Everyman, 1994 [1908]).
Pohl, Frederik, 'The Day After the Day After the Martians Came', in *Dangerous Visions*, edited by Harlan Ellison (Gollancz, 1987 [1967]), pp. 21–9.

Polidori, John William, 'The Vampyre' (2009 [1819]), gutenberg.org/files/6087/6087-h/6087-h.htm (accessed January 2020).
Portelli, Alessandro, 'Jack London's Missing Revolution: Notes on *The Iron Heel*', *Science Fiction Studies* 9.2 (1982), pp. 180–94.
Priestley, J.B., 'They Come from Inner Space', in *Thoughts from the Wilderness* (Heinemann, 1957 [1953]), pp. 20–6.
Pringle, David, 'What Is This Thing Called Space Opera?', in *Space and Beyond: the frontier theme in science fiction*, edited by Gary Westfahl (Greenwood Press, 2000), pp. 35–47.
Pursell, Carroll, *The Machine in America: a social history of technology*, second edition (Johns Hopkins University Press, 2007 [1995]).
Ranisch, Robert, and Stefan Lorenz Sorgner (eds.), *Post- and Transhumanism: an introduction* (Peter Lang, 2014).
Reid, Conor, 'The Heretofore Lost World of (Irish) Science Fiction', *Science Fiction Studies* 43.1 (2016), pp. 154–7.
Rieder, John, *Colonialism and the Emergence of Science Fiction* (Wesleyan University Press, 2008).
Roberts, Adam, *Science Fiction* (Routledge, 2000).
Romero, George A. (dir.), *Night of the Living Dead* (Walter Reade Organization, 1968).
Ross, Andrew, 'Getting out of the Gernsback Continuum', *Critical Inquiry* 17.2 (1991), pp. 411–33.
Russ, Joanna, *The Female Man* (Women's Press, 1985 [1975]).
Russell, Bertrand, 'Bertrand Russell, review in *New Leader*, March 1932', in *Aldous Huxley: the critical heritage*, edited by Donald Watt (Routledge, 1997 [1975]), pp. 210–12.
Sagan, Carl, and L.S. Shklovskii, *Intelligent Life in the Universe* (Holden-Day Inc., 1966).
Said, Edward, *Culture and Imperialism* (Vintage Books, 1994).
Sanders, Scott, 'Invisible men and women: the disappearance of character in science fiction', *Science Fiction Studies* 4.1 (1977), pp. 14–24.
Schaffner, Franklin J. (dir.), *Planet of the Apes* (20th Century Fox, 1968).
Seed, David, 'The Course of Empire: a survey of the imperial theme in early Anglophone science fiction', *Science Fiction Studies* 37.2 (2010), pp. 230–52.
Shelley, Mary, *Frankenstein, or The Modern Prometheus* (Great Writers Library, 1987 [1818]).
—, *The Last Man* (Wordsworth Classics, 2004 [1826]).
Shelley, Percy Bysshe, 'A Vindication of Natural Diet', in *The Prose Works of Percy Bysshe Shelley: volume 1* (Clarendon Press, 1993 [1813]).
Sherard, R.H., 'Jules Verne at Home', in *McClure's Magazine* (January 1894), web.archive.org/web/20000829031954/https://jv.gilead.org.il/sherard.html (accessed December 2020).
Shippey, Tom, 'Literary Gatekeepers and the Fabril Tradition', in *Hard Reading: learning from science fiction* (Liverpool University Press, 2016 [1994]).

Shute, Neville, *On the Beach* (Vintage, 2009 [1957]).
Simak, Clifford, *City* (Gollancz, 2011 [1952]).
Slusser, George Edgar, *The Farthest Shores of Ursula K. Le Guin* (Wildside Press, 2006).
Smith, Cordwainer, *The Instrumentality of Mankind* (Gollancz, 2009 [1975]).
Smith, E.E., 'Skylark Three: Part 1', in *Amazing Stories* 5.5 (August 1930a), pp. 388–414, archive.org/details/Amazing_Stories_v05n05_1930-08_-_Teck (accessed January 2020).
—, 'Skylark Three: Part 2', in *Amazing Stories* 5.6 (September 1930b), pp. 540–64, archive.org/details/Amazing_Stories_v05n06_1930-09_Qshadow-cape1736 (accessed January 2020).
—, 'Skylark Three: Part 3', in *Amazing Stories* 5.7 (October 1930c), pp. 606–33, 657–8, archive.org/details/Amazing_Stories_v05n07_1930–10 (accessed January 2020).
—, 'The Skylark of Valeron: Part 4', in *Astounding Stories*, 14.3 (November 1934a), pp. 120–42, luminist.org/archives/SF/AST.htm (accessed January 2020).
—, 'Triplanetary: Part 1', in *Amazing Stories* 8.9 (January 1934b), pp. 10–36, archive.org/details/Amazing_Stories_v08n09_1934-01_bogof39-El_PM (accessed January 2020).
—, 'Triplanetary: Part 2', in *Amazing Stories* 8.10 (February 1934c), pp. 73–99, archive.org/details/Amazing_Stories_v08n10_1934-02 (accessed January 2020).
—, 'The Skylark of Valeron: Part 6', in *Astounding Stories* 14.5 (January 1935a), pp. 62–78, luminist.org/archives/SF/AST.htm (accessed January 2020).
—, 'The Skylark of Valeron: Part 7', in *Astounding Stories* 14.6 (February 1935b), pp. 136–54, luminist.org/archives/SF/AST.htm (accessed January 2020).
—, *The Skylark of Space* (Panthers Books, 1974 [1928]).
—, *First Lensman* (Panther Science Fiction, 1979 [1950]).
Smith, E.E., and Lee Hawkins Garby, 'The Skylark of Space: Part 1', in *Amazing Stories* 3.5 (August 1928a), pp. 390–417, archive.org/details/Amazing_Stories_v03n05_1928-08_ATLPM-Urf (accessed January 2020).
—, 'The Skylark of Space: Part 2', in *Amazing Stories* 3.6 (September 1928b), pp. 528–59, archive.org/details/Amazing_Stories_v03n06_1928-09 (accessed January 2020).
—, 'The Skylark of Space: Part 3', in *Amazing Stories* 3.7 (October 1928c), pp. 610–36, 641, archive.org/details/Amazing_Stories_v03n07_1928–10_missing_ifc_ibc_bc (accessed January 2020).
Soper, Kate, *What Is Nature?* (Wiley, 1995).
Spencer, Herbert, *Social Statics, Together with Man Versus the State* (D. Appleton and Company, 1913 [1892]).

Spinrad, Norman, 'No Direction Home', in *No Direction Home: an anthology of science fiction stories by Norman Spinrad* (Fontana/Collins, 1977 [1971]), pp. 9–24.

—, *Bug Jack Barron* (Toxic, 1999 [1969]).

Stapledon, Olaf, 'Interplanetary Man', in *Journal of the British Interplanetary Society* 7.6 (1948), pp. 213–33, archive.org/details/OlafStapledonInterplanetaryMan (accessed January 2020).

—, *Last and First Men* (Magnum Books, 1978 [1930]).

—, *Star Maker* (Gollancz, 1999 [1937]).

Stephenson, Gregory, *Out of the Night and into the Dream: a thematic study of the fiction of J.G. Ballard* (Greenwood Press, 1991).

Sterling, Bruce, (ed.), *Mirrorshades* (Arbor House, 1986).

Stevenson, Robert Louis, *The Strange Case of Dr. Jekyll and Mr. Hyde, The Merry Men and Other Tales and Fables* (Wordsworth Classics, 1999 [1993]).

Stoker, Bram, *Dracula* (Penguin Books, 1994 [1897]).

Stratton, Jon, 'Zombie Trouble: zombie texts, bare life and displaced people', *European Journal of Cultural Studies* 14.3 (2011), pp. 265–81.

Sturgeon, Theodore, *More Than Human* (Ballantine Books, 1968 [1953]).

Suvin, Darko, 'Introduction: The Science Fiction of Ursula K. Le Guin', *Science Fiction Studies* 2.3 (1975), p. 203

—, *Metamorphoses of Science Fiction: on the poetics and history of a literary genre* (Yale University Press, 1979).

Swanwick, Michael, 'A User's Guide to the Postmoderns', *Isaac Asimov's Science Fiction* 10.8 (August 1986), p. 24–48, luminist.org/archives/SF/ASI.htm (accessed January 2020).

Taliaferro, John, 'Introduction', in Edgar Rice Burroughs, *Tarzan of the Apes* (Modern Library, 2003 [1914]), pp. xi–xviii.

Taylor, Jonathan S., 'Geographical Imaginings in the Work of J.G. Ballard', in *Lost in Space: geographies of science fiction*, edited by Rob Kitchin and James Kneale (Continuum, 2002), p. 90–103.

Toffler, Alvin, *Future Shock* (Bantam Books, 1971 [1970]).

Turner, Frederick Jackson, 'The Significance of the Frontier in American History' (2007 [1893]), gutenberg.org/files/22994/22994-h/22994-h.htm (accessed January 2020).

Van Vogt, A.E., *Slan* (Panther Books, 1985 [1940]).

Vandenberghe, Frederic, 'Posthumanism, or the cultural logic of global neo-capitalism', in *What's Critical About Critical Realism? Essays in reconstructive social theory* (Routledge, 2014).

Varricchio, Mario, 'Power of Images/Images of Power in *Brave New World* and *Nineteen Eighty-Four*', *Utopian Studies* 10.1 (1999), pp. 98–114.

Veblen, Thorstein, 'A Memorandum on a Practicable Soviet of Technicians' (Batoche Books, 2000 [1919]), pp. 86–104.

Verne, Jules, *Journey to the Centre of the Earth* (Penguin Books, 1994a [1864]).

—, *Around the World in Eighty Days* (Penguin Popular Classics, 1994b [1873]).

Vint, Sherryl, *Bodies of Tomorrow: technology, subjectivity, science fiction* (University of Toronto Press, 2007).

Vonnegut, Kurt, 'The Big Space Fuck', in *Again, Dangerous Visions*, edited by Harlan Ellison, Kindle edition (Gollancz, 2012 [1972]).

Wagar, W. Warren, 'J.G. Ballard and the Transvaluation of Utopia', *Science Fiction Studies* 18.1 (1991), p. 53–70.

Weber, Max, *The Protestant Ethic and the Spirit of Capitalism* (Routledge Classics, 2001 [1930]).

Wells, H.G., *The War of the Worlds* (Everyman, 1993a [1898]).

—, *The Shape of Things to Come* (Everyman, 1993b [1930]).

—, *Seven Famous Novels: The Time Machine / The Island of Doctor Moreau / The Invisible Man / The First Men in the Moon / The Food of the Gods / In the Days of the Comet / The War of the Worlds* (Heinemann/Octopus, 1977).

—, *Men Like Gods* (Dover Thrift Editions, 2016 [1923]).

—, *The First Men in the Moon & A Modern Utopia* (Wordsworth Classics, 2017 [1904]).

West, Rebecca, 'Rebecca West, review in *Daily Telegraph*, February 1932', in *Aldous Huxley: the critical heritage*, edited by Donald Watt (Routledge, 1997 [1975]), pp. 197–201.

Wilcox, Fred M. (dir.), *Forbidden Planet* (MGM, 1956).

Wilhelm, Kate, *Where Late the Sweet Birds Sang* (Gollancz, 2006 [1976]).

Williams, Raymond, *The Country and the City* (Oxford University Press, 1975).

—, *Keywords: a vocabulary of culture and society* (Oxford University Press, 1986 [1976]).

—, *Tenses of Imagination: Raymond Williams on Science Fiction, Utopia and Dystopia*, edited by Andrew Milner (Peter Lang, 2011).

Williamson, Jack, 'The Legion of Space: Part 3', in *Astounding Stories* 13.4 (June 1934), pp. 113–32, luminist.org/archives/SF/AST.htm (accessed January 2020).

—, *The Legion of Space / The Humanoids / Terraforming Earth / Wonder's Child* (Gollancz, 2014).

Wilson, Kenneth, 'Fiction and Empire: the case of Sir Arthur Conan Doyle', *Victorian Review* 19.1 (1993), pp. 22–42.

Winters, Jerome K., *Science Fiction, New Space Opera and Neoliberal Globalism: Nostalgia for Vision* (University of Wales Press, 2016).

Wolfe, Cary, *What Is Posthumanism?* (University of Minnesota Press, 2010).

Wong, Amy R., 'Arthur Conan Doyle's "Great New Adventure Story": journalism in *The Lost World*', *Studies in the Novel* 47.1 (2015), pp. 60–79.

World Intellectual Property Organization (WIPO), 'Bioethics and Patent Law: The Case of the Oncomouse', *WIPO Magazine* 3 (2006), pp. 16–17, wipo.int/wipo_magazine/en/2006/03/article_0006.html (accessed January 2020).

Wyndham, John, *The Chrysalids* (Penguin Books, 2008 [1955]).

Wynne, Catherine, *The Colonial Conan Doyle: British imperialism, Irish nationalism, and the gothic* (Greenwood Press, 2002).

Zamyatin, Yevgeny, *We* (Penguin Modern Classics, 1977 [1924]).

Zoline, Pamela, 'The Heat Death of the Universe', in *New Worlds: an anthology*, edited by Michael Moorcock (Flamingo, 1983), pp. 145–56.

Index

28 Days Later, 197
334, 152
2001: a space odyssey, 142, 143, 146, 149

Adventures in Time and Space, 113–114
After Many a Summer, 87–88
Against the Fall of Night, 137
Age of Catastrophe, 72, 74
Aldiss, Brian, 32, 49, 95, 156–157
alienation, 81–82, 112, 119, 130, 133, 137, 146, 155–156, 161–168, 171
All-Story, 95
Amazing Stories, 76, 93, 134
Amazing Stories Quarterly, 96, 103
Anderson, Poul, 119
animalism, 24, 28, 43–44, 60–64, 66, 79, 88–89, 92–93, 194, 197
animals, 1–3, 7, 11, 32, 36, 39, 160, 172, 187–188, 194, 198
anthropocentrism, 9, 97
anthropology, 174, 178, 180
anti-humanism, 60, 143, 195
anti-humanist functions, 195
'Arena', 125
Argosy, 95
Around the World in Eighty Days, 34–35
Arrival, 198
art, 16

Asimov, Isaac, 17, 24–25, 96, 112–113, 114, 116, 118, 121–133, 147, 151, 176, 177, 178, 193, 195
assimilative narratives, 20–21, 67, 110, 147, 193–194, 199
  see also transformative narratives
Astounding Stories of Super Stories, 76, 81, 93
atomisation, 24, 144
  see also mass society
The Atrocity Exhibition, 155, 159, 162
autopoiesis, 10, 12, 13, 19
  see also Heidegger, Martin

Bacon, Francis, 30, 31, 94
Ballard, J.G., 25, 149, 150, 155, 159–173, 188–189, 193, 194, 195
Banks, Iain M., 198
'The Battery of Hate', 98
Bayley, Barrington J., 155
Bear, Greg, 18, 198
Becoming, 14, 49, 58, 59
Before Adam, 53–54, 58, 62
Being, 12, 13–14, 49, 58
Bellamy, Edward, 50–51, 57, 171, 177
'The Big Space Fuck', 151
biopolitics, 82, 84, 102, 112, 121, 122–123, 129–130, 131–132, 133, 147
biopower, 15, 130

219

'Black Destroyer', 125
Blish, James, 125, 129
Blood Music, 198
'Blowups Happen', 116
the body, 7, 8, 10, 16, 18, 21, 25, 60–62, 70, 82, 87, 105–109, 113, 116, 119, 130, 131, 138, 141–142, 144–146, 147, 156, 160, 170–172, 182, 183, 196–197, 200
The Body Snatchers, 119
'Born of Man and Woman', 117
Brackett, Leigh, 117
Bradbury, Ray, 6, 117
Brain Wave, 119
Brand, Stewart, 156
Brave New World, 24, 70, 78–93, 94, 98, 102, 129, 137
Brave New World Revisited, 81
Brigands of the Moon, 103
'The Brooklyn Project', 119
Brunner, John, 152, 157
Bug Jack Barron, 151, 154
Bulwer-Lytton, Edward, 38
Burroughs, Edgar Rice, 38, 47, 60–61, 62, 71–72, 95, 154
Burroughs, William, 154
Butler, Octavia, 18, 198
Butler, Samuel, 38

The Call of the Wild, 58, 62
Callenbach, Ernest, 158
Campbell, John W., 97, 98, 103, 104, 114, 116, 123, 126, 127–128, 132
Čapek, Karel, 76, 116, 120
capitalism, 2, 5, 15, 23, 25, 27, 28, 50–51, 52, 53, 54–55, 57–58, 59, 60, 63–64, 66, 70, 73, 77, 79, 83, 84, 91, 94, 98, 101, 102, 136–137, 151, 152, 160, 161, 173, 176, 178, 185, 186, 193
Carson, Rachel, 156
A Case of Conscience, 125
The Caves of Steel, 124
Cell, 197

Chiang, Ted, 198
'Child's Play', 119
Childhood's End, 135, 142–143, 146
The Chrysalids, 119
Cities in Flight, 125, 129
City, 117, 129
The City and the Stars, 24–25, 112, 125, 134–146, 147, 180
Clarke, Arthur C., 24–25, 81, 112–113, 118, 121, 125, 134–146, 147, 151, 173, 189, 193–194
The Clockwork Man, 77
'The Cold Equations', 125
'The Comet', 73
Conan Doyle, Arthur, 23, 28, 37–50, 52, 60, 64, 65, 66, 71, 72, 73–74, 79, 95, 104–105, 109, 120, 126, 175, 193, 195, 197
'Crashing Suns', 106
creative destruction, 28, 47
'Creatures of the Light', 97–98
Crichton, Michael, 18
The Crystal World, 25, 149, 150, 159–173, 188, 194, 195
Culture series, 198
'A Curious Fragment', 54
cybernetics, 10, 17–18, 197
cyberpunk, 17, 18–19, 195, 196, 197–198, 199
cyborg, 6, 7–8, 9, 10, 11, 19
  see also 'Manifesto for Cyborgs'
Cyrano de Bergerac, 30

Dangerous Visions, 153
Darwin, Charles, 32, 45, 54
Darwinism, 39
  see also evolution, social Darwinism
Dawn of the Dead, 197
'The Day After the Day the Martians Came', 192
degeneracy, 23, 63–66, 84, 97–98, 197
dehumanisation, 53, 59, 63, 64–66, 67, 77, 79, 81, 86, 138

Del Rey, Lester, 114, 116
Delany, Samuel, 138–139, 158, 188, 198
'Devolution', 97
Dick, Philip K., 17, 18, 119, 153, 154–155, 173
disability, 117
Disch, Thomas, 116, 152, 167
disembodiment, 10, 17, 20, 97, 108, 143–144, 196–197
see also the body, telepathy
The Dispossessed, 25, 149, 150, 158, 173–189, 194, 196
Do Androids Dream of Electric Sheep? 17, 153
Dr. Strangelove, 153
Dracula, 29, 44
The Drought, 159, 163
The Drowned World, 159, 163
Du Bois, W.E., 73
dualism, 2, 8, 109, 172, 184
Dune, 152, 157
dystopia, 5, 24, 58, 75, 77, 78, 120, 150, 158, 164, 166, 168, 171

Earthsea series, 182
ecology, 33, 150, 153, 156–158, 175, 177, 185, 187, 194
Ecotopia, 158
Egan, Greg, 18
Eliot, T.S., 76, 163
Ellis, Sophie W., 97–98
Ellison, Harlan, 153
embeddedness, 6, 9–10, 144, 150, 183–184, 188, 199
embodiment, 6, 8, 9, 10, 17, 18–19, 22, 61, 107, 137, 144, 153, 170–171, 196–197, 199, 200
see also the body
'Empire', 112, 113, 119–121, 126, 146
Empire series, 125
empiricism, 30, 36, 62, 99–100, 102, 141–142
'An Encounter', 95

Ends and Means, 80–81
enframing, 12–13, 14, 16, 94, 166
England, George Allen, 135
Enlightenment, 15, 28, 30–31, 36, 37, 96, 103, 107, 109, 113, 141, 178
environmentalism, 33, 156, 184–185, 198
eugenics, 38, 76, 117, 132
evolution, 2, 4, 9, 11, 17, 19, 23, 27, 28, 32–33, 34, 37, 38–40, 42, 45, 46, 47–50, 52–55, 56–57, 60, 62, 63, 65, 66–67, 69, 71, 73, 96, 97, 105, 107, 108, 112, 117, 121, 126, 129, 137, 138, 142–143, 144, 146, 157, 158, 161, 170, 187
see also natural history, social Darwinism
'The Eye of the Lens', 155

Factor X, 2–3
'The Facts in the Case of M. Valdemar', 31
family resemblances, 17, 22
Farmer, Philip José, 156
'The Father Thing', 119
The Female Man, 158, 188, 195–196
feminism, 9, 73, 158, 179n, 195, 198
fin-de-siècle, 27, 50, 53, 57, 67, 193
Finney, Jack, 119
The First Men in the Moon, 53
First World War, 24, 69, 70, 71, 72–73, 76, 119, 132
Flammarion, Camille, 33, 95
Forbidden Planet, 125
Ford, Henry, 57, 74, 78, 81, 91, 111
Fordism, 24, 57, 70, 81, 85, 86, 100
The Forever War, 153
Forster, E.M., 77, 171
Foundation series, 24–25, 112–113, 121–133, 147, 176, 177, 178, 195
The Fountains of Paradise, 135

'The Four-Colour Problem', 155
Frankenstein, 17, 29–32, 37, 50, 78, 193
French Revolution, 30
'Friend Island', 73
'The Funeral', 158
future history, 73, 116, 129
Future Shock, 152

geology, 36, 41–42, 47, 160
  see also natural history
Gernsback, Hugo, 17, 76, 93, 95, 96–97, 99, 134
Gibson, William, 17, 18, 196–197
Gilman, Charlotte Perkins, 38, 50, 73
Godwin, Tom, 125
'Golden Age of SF', 17, 24, 93, 112–121, 123, 126, 128, 132, 134, 137, 138, 180, 188–189

Haggard, H. Rider, 38
Haldeman, Joe, 153
Hamilton, Edmond, 74, 97, 106, 126
Harrison, Harry, 152
Harrison, M. John, 150–151, 152, 156
Hasse, Henry, 98
'He Who Shrank', 98
Healy, Raymond J., 113–114
'The Heat Death of the Universe', 155
Heidegger, Martin, 12–13, 14, 16, 166
Heinlein, Robert, 100, 114, 116, 120, 129, 151
Herbert, Frank, 157
Herland, 73
High-Rise, 161–163
historical determinism, 55, 57, 59–60, 66–67, 129, 195
historical materialism, 9, 59
The History of Spiritualism, 73
Hoffman, E.T.A., 31
homo faber, 11, 102, 199

homo gestalt, 111–112
homo sapiens, 70, 105, 106, 108, 121, 130, 192, 199
Hopkinson, Nalo, 198
Hothouse, 156–157
'How I Became a Socialist', 57
Hudson, W.H., 50
human agency, 6, 24–25, 52, 55, 57–58, 59–60, 67, 69, 70, 75–76, 77, 82, 83–84, 85, 91–92, 93, 94, 98, 102, 110, 112, 113, 116, 118–119, 131–132, 133, 147, 149, 162, 194, 195
human archetypes, 22–23, 197–199
human exceptionalism, 9–10
humanism, 2–3, 5, 6–7, 8–9, 15–16, 20–22, 32, 36, 42, 45, 51, 52, 54, 60, 65–67, 69–70, 73, 77–78, 94–95, 96–97, 102, 105, 107, 110, 112, 120–121, 123, 129, 132, 142–143, 146–147, 150, 152, 153, 156, 162, 173, 175, 178, 184, 188–189, 191, 192, 194–196, 198–200
humanist functions, 195
Huxley, Aldous, 24, 70, 77, 78–93, 94, 98, 102, 103, 109–110, 116, 120, 137, 143, 171, 184, 193–194
Huxley, Julian, 69, 96
Huxley, T.H., 45, 53, 54

I Am Legend, 119
I, Robot, 17
'The Illuminated Man', 160
Imperial Earth, 140
imperialism, 4, 38–40, 42, 44–46, 47, 48–50, 66–67, 72, 73, 95, 103–105, 109, 114, 115, 119–120, 125–127, 139, 140, 141, 161, 163–166, 173, 177, 178, 184
individualism, 6, 12, 24–25, 52, 55–58, 59–60, 61, 65–66,

70–71, 77, 79, 80–83, 85, 86, 91–92, 94–95, 98, 101–102, 107–108, 109, 110, 111–113, 118–119, 120–121, 122–123, 128–132, 133, 143–147, 149, 153, 156, 161–162, 163–164, 167–168, 172–173, 179, 181–182, 188, 193, 195, 198, 200
industrialisation, 5, 7, 23, 27–28, 50–51, 52–53, 54, 58, 59, 61, 63–64, 66, 67, 75, 76–77, 79, 81–82, 83, 85, 90, 94, 98, 100–101, 118, 120, 152, 158, 181, 185, 193
inhuman in nineteenth-century literature, 31, 33–34
instrumental rationalism, 75, 98, 110, 156, 161, 168, 189, 200
The Instrumentality of Mankind, 129
intellectualism, 9, 23, 28, 31, 60–62, 65, 70, 71–72, 79, 80–81, 84, 85, 92–93, 95, 97, 105–109, 110, 130, 138, 143, 193, 197
Intelligent Life in the Universe, 140
Invasion of the Body Snatchers, 119
The Iron Heel, 18, 23, 28, 50–66, 67, 112, 177, 195
Island, 80, 88
The Island of Doctor Moreau, 4, 16, 53
Islands in the Sky, 134
Islands of Space, 103, 104

Jemisin, N.K., 198
jolly journey, 49, 72, 104
Jones, Langdon, 155
Jones, Raymond F., 116, 119
Joshua discourse, 79
Journey to the Centre of the Earth, 35–36
Joyce, James, 95, 96

Kafka, Franz, 77
King, Stephen, 197
Kipling, Richard, 43, 50, 104

Kubrick, Stanley, 149, 153

The Land of Mist, 73–74
The Land That Time Forgot, 71–72
Lang, Fritz, 77
language, 8, 48, 107, 182–184
Last and First Men, 73, 81, 135
The Last Man, 32–33, 37, 195
'The Last Men', 97
Lathe of Heaven, 152
Le Guin, Ursula, 25, 149, 150, 152, 157, 173–189, 193–194, 196
The Left Hand of Darkness, 17, 173, 179
The Legion of Space, 103
Lem, Stanislaw, 153
Lensman series, 94, 105–106, 107, 125
Lewis, C.S., 134, 135
'life-worshipper', 24, 70, 79, 89–93, 109
Lindsay, David, 74
London, Jack, 23, 28, 50–66, 66–67, 79, 95, 109, 112, 120, 177, 193–194, 195, 197
Long Jr., Frank Belnap, 97
The Long Tomorrow, 117
Looking Backward, 50, 57, 177
Lord Dunsany, 173
The Lord of the Rings, 122
The Lost World, 23, 28, 37–50, 52, 55, 64, 66–67, 71–72, 104–105, 126, 140, 175
lost-world literature, 28, 37–38, 39, 47–49, 61, 71, 73, 95, 104
Lovecraft, H.P., 74
Lumen, 95

'The Machine Stops', 77
Make Room! Make Room! 152
'The Man that Evolved', 97
'Manifesto for Cyborgs', 7–8, 18
Mars trilogy, 198
The Martian Chronicles, 6
Marx, Karl, 9, 51, 56, 62, 65
Marxism, 59, 64

masculinity, 28, 42–43, 60, 61–62, 66, 79, 135, 158, 177–178, 179n, 189, 193
  see also primitive masculinity
mass society, 24–25, 70, 81–83, 98, 101–102, 111–113, 118–121, 131–133, 146, 147, 198
  see also, alienation, atomisation
materialism, 9–10, 20
  see also autopoiesis, mind versus matter
Matheson, Richard, 117, 119
McComas, J. Francis, 113–114
McKay Charnas, Susan, 168
Meek, S.P., 98
Men Like Gods, 72–73, 76
Merrill, Judith, 117
Merritt, A., 38, 47
Metropolis, 77
Micromégas, 95
Miller, Walter J., 116
mind versus matter, 9–10, 16, 19–20, 107–110, 143–145, 184
  see also materialism
A Modern Utopia, 59
modernism, 47, 118, 126, 170
modernity, 15, 27–28, 52, 54, 57–58, 60, 70, 77, 91–92, 94, 101–102, 120, 126, 170, 171
The Moon Pool, 47
Moorcock, Michael, 151–152, 153
Moore, C.L., 119
More, Max, 69
More than Human, 111–112
Morris, William, 50, 111

The Naked Sun, 124
National Socialism, 132–133
natural history, 39, 40, 41–42, 44, 48, 55, 121, 170, 193
  see also evolution
nature, 2–18, 20, 28, 29–33, 35–36, 38–42, 44–50, 52–58, 60–66, 71–72, 75, 79, 86–87, 89, 94–95, 96–99, 102, 107, 109–110, 118, 121, 124, 126, 130, 137–138, 141–143, 150, 156–157, 158, 160–163, 166–167, 170, 172–173, 174, 184–188, 193–195, 198, 200
'Nerves', 116
Neuromancer, 17, 196–197
The New Atlantis, 30, 94
New Guide to Science, 124
New Wave SF, 150, 153–157, 196
New Worlds, 153
Nietzsche, Friedrich, 13–14, 53, 55–56, 65, 67
Night of the Living Dead, 149
Niven, Larry, 152, 191–192
'No Woman Born', 119

O'Brien, Fitz-James, 31
O'Conor Sloane, T., 93
Odle, E.V., 77, 135
Okorafor, Nnedi, 198
On the Beach, 117
On the Origin of Species, 48
OncoMouseTM, 1–3, 5–6, 11–12, 16, 18, 200
ontological hygiene, 3, 32
overpopulation, 152

Pal, George, 116–117
The Past Through Tomorrow, 116, 129
pastoralism, 25, 136–137, 138–139, 141, 153, 185
patriarchy, 73, 114, 153, 158, 196
The People of the Abyss, 63–65
'The Person from Porlock', 119
Piercy, Marge, 18, 158
Planet of the Apes, 149
Planet of Exile, 178–179
Poe, Edgar Allen, 31, 34, 38
poiesis, 12, 16
Point Counter Point, 79, 80
Pohl, Frederick, 192
Polidori, John William, 31
positivism, 30, 33–34, 96–97, 136–137

posthumanism, 2–3, 5–22, 29, 32–33, 37, 67, 72, 109–110, 112, 117, 120, 123, 147, 149–150, 183–184, 188–189, 191, 193, 194–195, 198
see also humanism
posthumanist functions, 21–22, 37, 188, 194–195
postmodernism, 18, 196
pre-human, 23, 28, 39, 47, 52, 64, 65, 66–67, 161, 193, 197
Prelude to Space, 134
Priestley, J.B., 154
primitive masculinity, 28, 42–43, 60–61, 66
A Princess of Mars, 47
progress, 23, 27, 30, 35–36, 46, 48, 61, 63, 67, 69, 72–73, 76, 78, 94, 96, 97–98, 101, 103, 106–109, 111, 112, 114–116, 121, 123, 124, 129–130, 133, 135, 139–141, 156, 168, 177–178, 180, 193, 200
pulp SF, 17, 24, 69, 76, 78, 81, 93–110, 113, 114, 127, 128, 133, 134–135, 138, 142, 143, 189

rationalisation, 13–16, 31, 33, 34, 37, 76–77, 81, 94, 113, 171–172, 182
reason, 8–9, 14, 37, 46, 60, 61, 72, 107, 123, 131, 132–133, 177–178, 181
Rendezvous with Rama, 142
'Rescue Party', 135
Ringworld, 152, 191–192
Robinson, Kim Stanley, 198
Robot series, 124, 131
Rocannon's World, 180
Romero, George A., 149
Rupert, M.F., 73, 98
R.U.R., 76
rurality, 62–63, 86–87, 137–139, 185
Russ, Joanna, 158, 179n, 188, 195–196

Sagan, Carl, 140
'The Sandman', 31
The Sands of Mars, 134
'Scanners Live in Vain', 119
The Scarlet Plague, 58, 62, 63, 65
Schaffner, Franklin J., 149
scientific knowledge, 35–36, 41–42
scientific romance, 3, 52, 63, 76, 135
The Sea Wolf, 58, 62
Second World War, 24, 100, 113, 115, 116, 118–119, 120, 127, 133, 141, 147, 152, 164
'The Sentinel', 135
The Shape of Things to Come, 76
Shaun of the Dead, 197
She, 45
Shelley, Mary, 17, 19, 23, 28–33, 37, 50, 66, 193, 195
Sherlock Holmes, 37
Shklovskii, L.S., 140
Shute, Neville, 117
'The Significance of the Frontier in American History', 61
Silent Spring, 156
Simak, Clifford, 114, 117, 129
Sir Nigel, 43
Skylark series, 24, 70, 93–109, 125, 127, 130, 138, 175, 180, 195, 198
Slan, 119
Smith, Cordwainer, 119, 129
Smith, E.E. 'Doc', 24, 70, 93–110, 120, 125, 126, 127, 143, 175, 193, 195, 198
social Darwinism, 38, 45, 54, 132
see also evolution
socialism, 23, 27, 28, 50–53, 54, 55–57, 58, 59–60, 62, 65, 66, 158, 177
Solaris, 153
The Songs of Distant Earth, 135
Southern Reach trilogy, 198
Spencer, Herbert, 27, 45, 54, 66, 143
Spinrad, Norman, 151–152, 154

Stand on Zanzibar, 152
Stapledon, Olaf, 17, 33, 73, 74, 81, 103, 134, 135, 143–144, 146–147
Star Maker, 17, 74, 143
The Star Rover, 58
Star Trek, 152
Sterling, Bruce, 18, 196
Stevens, Francis, 73
Stoker, Bram, 29, 44
'Story of Your Life', 198
Strange Case of Dr. Jekyll and Mr. Hyde, 44
'The Strength of the Strong', 54
A Study in Scarlet, 45
Sturgeon, Theodore, 111–112, 114
'Submicroscopic', 98
supra-human, 24–25, 112, 121, 123, 131, 146–147, 198
Swift, Jonathan, 30, 94, 171

Tarzan, 60–61, 62
Taylor, Frederick, 74
Taylorism, 57, 81, 83, 91, 101–102
technique, 14
technocracy, 24–25, 75, 76, 77, 78, 79, 82, 83, 85, 95, 96, 97, 109, 110, 112, 113, 115, 120, 130, 138, 142, 146, 147, 151, 157, 177, 178, 184, 188
technological advancement, 5, 7, 56, 70, 74, 78, 80, 84, 101, 124, 151–152, 194, 200
technological determinism, 76–77, 109, 156, 177
technology as principle or system, 12–16
technophilia, 24, 75–78, 93, 110, 113, 120, 164, 199
technophobia, 24, 70, 75–78, 80, 93, 113, 120, 164, 199
teleology, 10, 36, 49, 72, 97, 108–109, 193, 194
telepathy, 107, 119, 130–131, 137–138, 180
Tenn, William, 119

'The Terminal Beach', 160
'The Terror of John Blue Gap', 41
'That Only a Mother', 117
Them! 117
'There Will Come Soft Rains', 117
The Time Machine, 3, 53, 157, 195
Toffler, Alvin, 152
Tolkien, J.R.R., 122, 152
transcendence, 6, 8–10, 18, 25, 33, 34, 69, 70, 85, 89, 105, 107, 109, 112–113, 138, 139, 142–144, 147, 149, 150, 162, 168, 171–173, 193–195, 199
transformative narratives, 20–21, 109, 147, 193–194, 199
see also assimilative narratives
trans-human, 24, 69, 71, 77–78, 85, 93, 94, 102, 109, 197
transhumanism, 10, 69, 107, 198
The Trial, 77
Triton, 158, 188
Turner, Frederick, 61
Twenty Thousand Leagues Under the Sea, 17, 35–36, 125
'Twilight', 97

Ubik, 154–155
universalism, 9, 25, 102, 108, 110, 167, 182–184
urbanisation, 40, 44, 54, 62–63, 67, 76, 83, 86–87, 116–117, 137–138, 163–164, 166, 181
utopia, 21, 23, 25, 27, 28, 30, 50–52, 55, 56n, 58–60, 63, 66, 69, 73, 76, 79, 80, 85, 88, 93, 94, 96, 97, 98, 101, 102, 109, 116, 120, 136, 138, 150, 153, 157–158, 162, 168, 170–173, 176–178, 180, 181, 182, 184, 185, 188, 193, 194, 196, 198
utopia, critical, 21–22, 158, 176–177, 188
utopian functions, 21

'The Vampyre', 31
Van Vogt, A.E., 114, 116, 119, 125

VanderMeer, Jeff, 198
'Vaster than Empires and More Slow', 184
Veblen, Thorstein, 75
Verne, Jules, 17, 23, 28–29, 30, 34–37, 38, 39–40, 42, 46, 47, 48, 49, 52, 53, 66, 120, 125, 134, 140, 193, 195
'Via the Hewitt Ray', 73, 98
'A Vindication of Natural Diet', 32
violence, 42–46, 66
Voltaire, 30, 95
Vonnegut, Kurt, 151
A Voyage to Arcturus, 74
Voyages extraordinaire, 34

Walk to the End of the World, 158
The Walking Dead, 197
The War of the Worlds, 3–5, 17, 19, 194
The War of the Worlds (1953 movie), 116–117
The Waste Land, 76
We, 77
'The Weapons Shop', 116
weird fiction, 74
Well, H.G., 1, 3–5, 6, 16, 17, 19, 20, 30, 33, 38, 50, 52–53, 54, 55–56, 59, 60, 66–67, 72–73, 76, 79–80, 116–117, 134, 135, 157, 177, 193, 195
'What Was It? A Mystery', 31
When the Sleeper Wakes, 53, 56n
Where Late the Sweet Birds Sing, 153
'Which Way to Inner Space?' 159
The White Company, 43
White Fang, 62
whiteness, 8, 18, 73, 97, 114, 127, 133, 140, 153, 192, 193, 198
Whole Earth Catalog, 156
Wilcox, Fred M., 125
Wilhelm, Kate, 153, 158
Williamson, Jack, 96–97, 103, 109, 119
'Winter's King', 179
'With Folded Hands...', 119
With Her in Ourland, 73
Woman on the Edge of Time, 158
Wonder Stories, 76, 97
The Word for World Is Forest, 175, 179
World War Z, 197
Wyndham, John, 49n, 119, 134, 166

Zamyatin, Yevgeny, 77, 80, 116
Zoline, Pamela, 155–156